Relating architecture to landscape

E & FN SPON

An imprint of Routledge

London and New York

Relating architecture to landscape

Edited by
Jan Birksted

First published 1999
by E & FN Spon, an imprint of Routledge
11 New Fetter Lane, London EC4P 4EE

Simultaneously published in the USA and Canada
by Routledge
29 West 35th Street, New York, NY 10001

Design by
Asuka Sawa
Typeset in Akzidenz Grotesk by
Stephen Cary
Printed and bound in Great Britain by
Biddles Ltd., Guildford and King's Lynn

British Library Cataloguing in Publication Data
A catalogue record for this book is available from the British Library

Library of Congress Cataloguing in Publication Data
Relating architecture to landscape / edited by Jan Birksted.
            p.   cm.
        Includes bibliographical references and index.
        ISBN 0-419-23150-1 (pbk.)
        1. Landscape architecture.   2. Gardens – Design.   3. Architecture.
        I. Birksted, Jan, 1946-
        SB472.R46   1998   98-18215
        712–dc21   CIP

ISBN 0 419 23150 1

Contents

Acknowledgements   vii

Introduction   1
Jan Birksted

Section One
The Modernist context   13

Introduction   15

Introduction to *Modern Gardens* (1953)
Sir Peter Shepheard   17

Section Two
Relating architecture to landscape
through elements and materials
                                         39

Introduction   41

Time and temporality in
Japanese gardens
Mara Miller   43

Detailing and materials of
outdoor space:
the Scandinavian example
Jan Woudstra   59

Playing with artifice:
Roberto Burle Marx's gardens
Jacques Leenhardt 77

Section Three
Relating architecture to landscape
through geometry, form and scale   103

Introduction   105

External interior/internal exterior spaces
at the Maeght Foundation
Jan Birksted   106

A landscape 'fit for a democracy':
Jože Plečnik at Prague Castle (1920–1935)
Caroline Constant   120

Tokyo as emblem of a postmodern paradigm
Augustin Berque   147

The re-invention of the site
Thomas Deckker   158

Section Four
Relating architecture to landscape
through collaborations   175

Introduction   177

Architect and landscape architect working
together: Scharoun and Mattern
Peter Blundell Jones   178

Dimitri Pikionis in situ
Dimitri Philippides and Agni Pikionis   194

Landscape architecture: ecology, community, art
John Hopkins   205

Section Five
Contemporary case studies   229

Introduction   231

The necessity of invention:
Bernard Lassus's garden landscapes
Stephen Bann   233

The prospect at Dungeness:
Derek Jarman's garden
Jan Birksted   244

Building in Nature
Peter Salter   261

Parc St. Pierre, Amiens
Sandra Morris   269

List of contributors   281

Index   285

Acknowledgements

Without the active support and interventions of Peter Salter and Nicholas Weaver, the conference 'Rethinking the architecture/landscape relationship', which took place in March 1996 and which formed the starting-point for this book, would never have taken place. I would like to thank the staff and students of the UEL School of Architecture who helped in many ways. Andrew Higgott provided continuous support, including general moral support. Thomas Deckker and his students mustered time and energy. So did Joan Tremble and her staff, and Czes Bany, and Albert and Terry, the technicians at UEL School of Architecture, who overcame innumerable technical problems. Three students – Troels Laerfeldt, Jonathan Dawes and Julian Ogiwara – worked tirelessly during the conference. I would also like to thank Professor Frank Gould, Vice-Chancellor of the University of East London, who helped overcome problems relating to copyright and to translation when it came to publishing this book.

I would like to thank Susan Mallone, librarian at the School of Architecture of the University of East London, who has dealt with hundreds of requests and never fails to find the book, the article or the reference that is needed. Sheila Harvey at the Landscape Institute also regularly answers queries. Without the help of Mary F. Daniels at the Special Collections in the Loeb Library at the Graduate School of Design, Harvard, my current research about the Maeght Foundation would not be possible.

This book would not be what it is without the contribution of Asuka Sawa, who has designed it while finishing her degree at the Royal College of Art. Caroline Mallinder, my Commissioning Editor, has facilitated and allowed, through her efforts and support, the unusual production methods of this book.

It has been a pleasure to work with the contributors to this book, both during the conference and in the preparation of the book. Many other people have helped. Nikos Papadakis helped to put me in contact with Agni Pikionis. Nicholas Weaver, Jan Woudstra and Mike O'Pray read my essay on Derek Jarman's garden and each brought to this task their particular skills and knowledge. So did James Heesom in reading my essay on the Maeght Foundation, and Andrew Stephenson in reading my introduction.

I would like to thank my daughter, Sasha, who drew the plans for the Maeght Foundation and for Prague Castle as well as drawings for several chapters including the ones on Roberto Burle Marx and on Dimitri Pikionis. The organisation of the conference and the work on the book was not made easier by the fact that our house was ruined by a flood at just that time. I would like to thank my parents for putting up with us living in their house during this period of rebuilding and of conference organisation – during which period we also lived through my father's illness and death. I owe a big debt to my wife Dana and my children, Noah and Sasha, who put up with my absences – physical and/or mental – during the long hours of preparation first of the conference and then of the book.

Jan Birksted

Introduction

> To write of the modern is to entertain the hope of the postmodern; to evoke that which is not yet built, transformed, laid waste, or irrevocably ruined; and to conjure up that ineffable 'other' world that lies beyond our present proliferation of useless objects.[1]

Such hopes and fears, voiced by Kenneth Frampton in the late 1980s, lie at the source of this collection of essays too. But now in the late 1990s the opportunity arises for showing what *has* been built that challenges this 'proliferation of useless objects'. Some things laid waste and irrevocably ruined have even provided the very opportunity to build on their wasteland precisely that 'ineffable other world' previously only conjured up in the imagination. In some exemplary cases, horrific ecological destruction has given place, as if through guilt and reparation, to ecological rebirth. Examples would be Peter Latz's *Landschaftspark* at Duisburg-Nord and Richard Haag's *Gasworks Park* in Seattle. Tschumi's *Parc de la Villette* in Paris would be a more controversial one since it has also been described as littered with precisely that 'proliferation of useless objects' which prevents the 'unique moment of beauty'.[2] So, this book sets out to present some contemporary examples in architecture, landscape architecture and garden design, that offer other models perhaps than the legacy of the Modern Movement and that lie at the borderline of what is normally accepted and at the cutting-edge of what is usually done. It is my hope that this book might stimulate both practising designers and students who are dealing with these issues live.

Indeed, garden designers, landscape architects and architects are urgently reconsidering the legacy of the Modern Movement, a legacy sometimes described in terms of a simple and radical separation between landscape and architecture, grounded in Le Corbusier's statement that

> One clear image will stand in my mind forever: the Parthenon. Stark, stripped, economical, violent; a clamorous outcry against a landscape of grace and terror. All strength and purity.[3]

1

It has been said that 'Le Corbusier regarded the landscape and plant materials almost as generic greenery'[4] whose contrasting forms and textures highlighted the architecture. The analysis of Le Corbusier's approach to the landscape in the context of his overall philosophy[5] reveals a powerful and complex emotional response to nature, the landscape and to garden design,[6] reminiscent of Ruskin and even of Viollet-le-Duc's fascination with mountains[7] – a response so powerful that it has even been described as the driving force of Modernist design,[8] both metaphorically[9] and literally.[10] It would seem that concepts of 'nature' and visions of 'landscape' are so powerful in Modernism because they are folded into other key Modernist concepts: nature as process and process as creativity,[11] nature as 'primitive' and the 'primitive' as authentic.[12] The paradoxical result is that 'nature' and landscape are simultaneously to be tapped as the authentic source of creativity and not to be touched because of this sanctified status. Hence the wide range of responses to landscape and to landscape design amongst architectural Modernists,[13] from the crafting of the materials of the land by someone like Neutra[14] to the direct confrontation with the elemental aspects of nature to be found at the Casa Malaparte.[15] Hence also the multiple and complex range of responses to landscape amongst Modernist landscape architects since Modernism 'both vitally influenced and deeply confused garden designers...'[16]

The point is therefore not so much to reverse the legacy of the Modern Movement as to document the multiple and complicated aspects of its relatively unknown history.[17] These essays form part of that ongoing process of documentation. These historical examples focus predominantly on the 1950s, the very recent historical background to the contemporary case studies. This historical research forms part of that on-going effort to document twentieth century landscape architecture through surveys and in-depth studies[18] that might suggest different possible histories, so far hidden and repressed. In line with this, the classic 1953 text – now out of print – by Peter Shepheard on *Modern Gardens* is reprinted here.[19]

Yet this is not a book about historical development over time, but about specific key moments in history, historical moments that have been overlooked or forgotten, emerging moments, potential moments of leverage. As Fredric Jameson has written, 'to say, in short, that synchronic systems cannot deal in any adequate conceptual way with temporal phenomena is not to say that we do not emerge from them with a heightened sense of the mystery of diachrony itself.'[20]

Another reason for the renewed interest in landscape and gardens is the understanding that they convey cultural meanings and intellectual ideas. Gardens and landscapes were, from the Renaissance through to the eighteenth century, powerful expressions of intellectual ideas and cultural perspectives. This historical involvement of landscapes and gardens with contemporary thought and culture is often regretted as a phenomenon which twentieth century Modernism brought to an end. Stephen Bann refers to this when he writes that 'our culture has evacuated all the serious and political and philosophical content which great gardens like Stowe and Ermenonville undoubtedly possessed at the time of their creation.'[21] Ian Hamilton Finlay's garden would be the exception.[22] This aspect of the meaning of landscapes and gardens is also being addressed in contemporary research and is leading to a particularly rich field of multidisciplinary studies.[23] Here again, this collection of essays forms part of that ongoing contemporary process of research, documentation and analysis.

A further reason for the renewed interest in the interaction between architecture and landscape design is the growing concern with post-industrial landscapes – disused factories, abandoned mines – as well as the new landscapes of motorways with their suburban shopping malls, business parks and office developments, located at the intersections and junctions of these major international and inter-state motorways. These post-industrial landscapes are also documented in several recent books[24] so that, again, this book forms part of the ongoing effort to document recent and contemporary landscape architecture.

But this collection of essays has another aim too. In both the historical and contemporary examples in these essays, we do not always find the same stark differences between the materials and the spatial qualities of architecture and of landscape architecture that we often observe around us. The intention behind this collection of essays is to raise the question of what, if anything, remains specific to architecture or to landscape architecture. Landscape architects and garden designers share with architects a range of design concerns and concepts: scale, geometry, space, texture, perspective, light, boundary, edge, solid and void, circulation, frame, transition, threshold, axis and cross-axis, hierarchy, levels and gradients, hard edge and soft edge, sustainability and ecology, social usefulness, and so on. But do they work with these concepts and notions in different ways? It is sometimes suggested that the essential dimension of the planted green landscape is the dimension of time[25] or that the rural landscape – as opposed to the urban landscape – can give rise to 'careful observation, one in which the eye grows restful and contemplative',[26] a quality of space perhaps reminiscent of Sven-Ingvar Andersson's concept of 'negative space'.[27] While Andersson has said that architecture and landscape architecture are identical because of their mutual and identical concern with space,[28] others have suggested that this concern for space is completely different because of the different material and spatial qualities. Fairbrother describes how trees in towns mediate between the scale of humans and of buildings since 'they are large enough to register on the large scale, and particularly because they have vertical mass'[29] while at the same time the tree 'in detail is in our own human scale of perfection – twigs and buds and leaves and flowers belong closely and intimately to our personal range'.[30] Baljon suggests that the urban park should provide a place 'slow and serious perhaps for the rhythm of this age, but because of the quality of intimacy and, at the same time, unemotionality, a unique moment of beauty'.[31] In such statements, we can begin to see a range of possible relationships, different and complementary. Here again, this collection of essays forms part of the ongoing process of analysis of the experience of landscape and architecture.[32] In the final analysis, a binary conception of architectural design as different from landscape architecture and from garden design must be replaced either by a graduated and gradual axis where one end represents architecture as landscape and the other end represents landscape as architecture with a range of continuous variations between the two, or by a Klein group[33] where the differences and similarities – criss-crossing and overlapping – are superimposed in complex ways so that any one binary opposition is denied. To explore these differences and similarities, this book is organised into thematic sections – however much the various themes may overlap from one section to the next – on materials and textures (Section Two), on geometry and form (Section Three) and on professional collaborations (Section Four).

And this brings me to the last purpose of this collection of essays. It is not just practising designers who observe, analyse and interpret. Historians do so too. It is my hope that this book might also provoke historians and theorists – within architectural history, landscape history and cultural geography – to think about what is specific to architecture and to landscape architecture since significant historical and theoretical analysis requires initial observation and description. Given the negligible role of landscape and gardens within art history, such preoccupations with methods are sorely needed.[34] With the founding of the discipline of art history in the nineteenth century, studies of architecture and art played equally important roles.[35] Today, the battery of analytic methods used in art history[36] are being redeployed in the analysis of architecture. There is even a sense of trying to write about architecture in a new way, in parallel to developments in art history[37] where there has been an exploration into the kinds of visual and spatial observations that can be used to describe and analyse works of art.[38] There have also been analyses of the phenomenon of vision itself, as in the seminal studies by Hubert Damisch,[39] Rosalind Krauss,[40] Alpers,[41] Crary[42] and others. Though conceptualisations of perspective – for example, Brunelleschi's perspectival experiment[43] or William Kent's study of the perspectival theories of Italian Renaissance theatre[44] or Scharoun's notion of 'aperspectival space'[45] – have been central to the development of architectural spaces and of landscape spaces in practice, conceptualisations of perspective – for example, Panofsky's *Perspective as Symbolic Form* (1927) and Foucault's *Les Mots et Les Choses* (1966) – have been less central to the development of architectural theory and history. Finally, art history has also involved both a critique of the very status of perspectival vision as opposed to other forms of experience such as touch,[46] and a refinement of theories of vision based in psychoanalytical theory. The latter have been imported from art history to analyse architectural spaces and landscape spaces, as in Beatriz Colomina's study of the work of Loos[47] or Anthony Vidler's analysis of 'uncanny' spaces[48] or Simon Pugh's study of Rousham.[49] Because empirical studies of perspectival vision were originally imported from art historical analyses of art objects,[50] they privilege the visual and often consider the mechanics of vision without movement. But the whole point of the experience of landscape and of architecture is movement. And when one considers movement through three-dimensional space involving several participants and several perspectives, vision becomes even more complex[51] and unstable.[52] Perspectival vision is reconceptualised not as graphic lines, but as 'shots' or 'takes' in a 'field' – and then film often becomes an operative metaphor.[53] It is at this point that psychoanalytical notions of perspective in architectural history and theory begin to lead to other concerns such as time,[54] which in turn tends to transform concepts of space[55] as well as actual built spaces,[56] and to other related subject areas such as landscape.[57] It was James Ackerman who commented that

4

'in reflecting on the ways in which villas respond to the landscape, one must remember to look not only *at* them, but out *from* them.'[58] The essays in this book will raise the themes of types of vision and perspective.

In art history, such enquiries into the very constitution of visual phenomena and spatial experiences have led to the investigation of meaning in works of art that appear to deny the very possibility of meaning, either because of their abstraction[59] or because of their enigmatic appearance.[60] While these analyses have barely touched architecture, the legacy of Kant has virtually prevented their development in the analysis of landscapes and gardens. Kant distinguished between the pleasures of sensuality and the pleasure of reflective judgement[61] in such a way that landscape design and garden design were firmly established – or should one say disestablished? – as sensual and therefore beyond the domain of art[62] since landscape architecture

> ... does, however, actually take its forms from nature (at least at the very outset: the trees, shrubs, grasses, and flowers from forest and field), and to this extent is not art.[63]

This fundamental Kantian expulsion of landscape design and garden design from art history results in placing them beyond the reach of the theories, methods and concepts of the analytical disciplines of art history and cultural studies. Garden and landscape history are excluded and marginalised.[64] Hence the importance of rethinking the materiality and the spatiality of landscape architecture and of garden design.

6

1 Kenneth Frampton, 'In search of the modern landscape', in S. Wrede and W.H. Adams (eds), *Denatured Visions, Landscape and Culture in the Twentieth Century* (New York: The Museum of Modern Art, 1991), pp. 42–61; p. 61.

2 Lodewijk Baljon, *Designing Parks, An examination of contemporary approaches to design in landscape architecture, based on a comparative design analysis of entries for the Concours International: Parc de la Villette, Paris, 1982–3* (Amsterdam: Architectura & Natura Press, 1992), p. 238.

3 Le Corbusier, Statement at CIAM, 1933.

4 Marc Treib, **'Introduction'**, in Marc Treib (ed.), *Modern Landscape Architecture: A Critical Review* (Cambridge, Mass.: The MIT Press, 1993), pp. viii–xi; p. ix.

5 See Paul V. Turner, *La Formation de Le Corbusier, Idéalisme & Mouvement Moderne* (Paris: Editions Macula, 1987) and Marc Perelman, *Urbs Ex Machina, Le Corbusier* (Paris: Les Editions de la Passion, 1986); Fondation Le Corbusier, *Le Corbusier et la Nature, Rencontres des 14–15 Juin 1991* (Paris: Fondation Le Corbusier, 1991).

6 See Mary Patricia May Sekler, 'Le Corbusier, Ruskin, the Tree, and the Open Hand', in Russell Walden (ed.), *The Open Hand, Essays on Le Corbusier* (Cambridge, Mass.: The MIT Press, 1977) pp. 42–95; Caroline Constant, 'From the Virgilian dream to Chandigarh', *Architectural Review,* Vol. CLXXXI, No. 1079, January 1987, pp. 66–72; Tim Benton, 'Nature and the sacred: sign and symbol', in Arts Council of Great Britain, *Le Corbusier, Architect of the Century* (London: Arts Council of Great Britain, 1987), p. 246; Christopher Pearson, 'Le Corbusier and the acoustical trope: an investigation of its origins', *Journal of the Society of Architectural Historians,* Volume 56, Number 2, June 1997, pp. 168–183; Romy Golan, *Modernity and Nostalgia, Art and Politics in France between the Wars* (New Haven and London: Yale University Press, 1995).

7 See Pierre A. Frey and Lise Grenier, *Viollet-le-Duc et la Montagne* (Paris: Glénat/CNMHS/ITHA, 1993).

8 David Matless traces a similar 'nature-mysticism' back to early twentieth-century geography. See D. Matless, 'Nature, the modern and the mystic: tales from early twentieth century geography', *Transactions of the Institute of British Geography,* N.S. (1991) , pp. 272–286.

9 See Caroline Constant, 'The Barcelona Pavilion as landscape garden, modernity and the picturesque', *AA Files 20,* pp. 46–54.

10 See Rosalind Krauss, 'The grid, the /cloud/, and the detail', in D. Mertins (ed.), *The Presence of Mies* (Princeton: Princeton University Press, 1994), pp. 133–155.

11 See Christopher Green, 'The architect as artist', in Arts Council of Great Britain, *op. cit.*, pp. 110–118.

12 See William Curtis, *Le Corbusier, Ideas and Forms* (London: Phaidon, 1986), and Joseph Rykwert, *On Adam's House in Paradise, The Idea of the Primitive Hut in Architectural History* (Cambridge, Mass.: The MIT Press, 1981).

13 See J. Birksted, 'From landscape to architecture, allegories, icons, metaphors and symbols', *Issues in Architecture, Art and Design*, Vol. 3, No. 2, 1994, pp.4–23.

14 See William Marlin (ed.), *Nature Near, Late Essays of Richard Neutra* (Santa Barbara: Capra Press, 1989).

15 Marida Talamona, *Casa Malaparte* (Princeton: Princeton Architectural Press, 1992). This approach is also to be found in the work of Sverre Fehn, who describes it as 'a dialogue between nature and architecture. A tree and a building become very beautiful because of this dialogue' (quoted in *Time*, 21 April 1997, p. 69).

16 Jane Brown, *The English Garden in Our Time; From Gertrude Jekyll to Geoffrey Jellicoe* (Woodbridge: Antique Collectors' Club, 1986), p. 111. I believe that this confusion arises because of Le Corbusier's dual, if not dialectical, attitude to the landscape: the landscape is to be revered to such an extent that it must remain untouched.

17 Kenneth Frampton was able to write that 'there is to date no decent account of the history of twentieth-century landscape design' (*op. cit.*, p. 42) though this statement has been criticised as being symptomatic of the twentieth-century devaluation of landscape architecture: '... this history is poorly served by the discourses of modern art and architectural history which have relegated the landscape and nature to a minor, repressed, or misrepresented other' (Elizabeth K. Meyer, 'Landscape architecture as modern other and postmodern ground', in Harriet Edquist and Vanessa Bird (eds), *The Culture of Landscape Architecture* (Melbourne: Edge Publishing, 1994; pp. 13–34; p. 13). And John Dixon Hunt has written: 'Now one of the most striking aspects of modern landscape architecture is its ignorance of history. [...] Maybe in this belated discovery of modernist zeal it was difficult not to confuse knowledge of history with historicist design which it rightly wished to reject. [...] Of all the modern arts none has displayed such a meager command of analytical, including rudimentary philosophical, language as landscape studies' (Dixon Hunt, 1993, 'The dialogue of modern landcape architecture with its past', in Marc Treib (ed.), *op. cit.*, pp. 134–143; pp. 134–5). More recently a new wave of histories are beginning to fill this void. See Peter Walker and Melanie Simo, *Invisible Gardens, The Search for Modernism in the American Landscape* (Cambridge, Mass.: The MIT Press, 1994); Malene Hauxner, *Fantasiens Have, Det moderne gennembrud I havekunsten og sporene I dens landskab* (Copenhagen: Arkitektens Forlag, 1993); M. Knuijt, H. Ophuis, P. Van Saane and D. Louwerse (eds), *Modern Park Design, Recent Trends* (Bussum: Thoth, 1993); M.J. Vroom, *Outdoor Space, Environments Designed by Dutch Landscape Architects since 1945* (Bussum: Thoth, 1992); M. Mosser and G. Teyssot (eds), *The History of Garden Design, The Western Tradition from the Renaissance to the Present Day* (London: Thames & Hudson, 1990); D. et J.-P. Dantec, *Le Roman des Jardins de France* (Paris: Plon, 1987); M. Treib and D. Imbert, *Garrett Eckbo, Modern Landscapes for Living* (Berkeley: University of California Press, 1997). Garden and landscape theory is documented in C.A. Wimmer, *Geschichte der Gartentheorie* (Darmstadt, 1987).

18 A recent in-depth study would be Caroline Constant, *The Woodland Cemetery: Toward a Spiritual Landscape, Erik Gunnar Asplund and Sigurd Lewerentz 1915–61* (Stockholm: Byggforlaget, 1994).

19 Peter Shepheard, *Modern Gardens* (London: The Architectural Press, 1953).

20 Fredric Jameson, *The Prison-House of Language, A Critical Account of Structuralism and Russian Formalism* (Princeton: Princeton Architectural Press,

1972), p. xi. In a sense, one is here relying on a Nietzschean view of history as discontinuity, or on a genealogical history as practised by Foucault, to bring to consciousness lost causes. In both cases, Alois Riegl's notion of evaluative equality of all historical periods is essential.

21 Stephen Bann,'The garden and the visual arts in the contemporary period: Arcadian, post-classicists and land artists', in Mosser and Teyssot (eds), *op. cit.*, pp. 495–506; p. 503.

22 See Yves Abrioux, *Ian Hamilton Finlay, A Visual Primer* (London: Reaktion Books, 1992).

23 See John Dixon Hunt, *Gardens and the Picturesque, Studies in the History of Landscape Architecture* (Cambridge, Mass.: The MIT Press, 1992); M. Francis and R.T. Hester (eds), *The Meaning of Gardens* (Cambridge, Mass.: The MIT Press, 1990); Robert Harrison, *Forets, Essai sur l'imaginaire occidental* (Paris: Flammarion, 1992); Max Oelschlaeger, *The Idea of Wilderness* (New Haven and London: Yale University Press, 1991); Augustin Berque, *Médiance de milieux en paysages* (Montpellier: Reclus, 1990); Dominique Bourg, *Les Sentiments de la nature* (Paris: Editions La Découverte, 1993); Salim Kemal and Ivan Gaskell (eds), *Landscape, Natural Beauty and the Arts* (Cambridge: Cambridge University Press, 1993); Eric Hirsch and Michael O'Hanlon (eds), *The Anthropology of Landscape, Perspectives on Place and Space* (Oxford: The Clarendon Press, 1995); Simon Schama, *Landscape and Memory* (London: HarperCollins, 1995); E.H. Zube, *Landscapes, Selected Writings of J.B. Jackson* (Amherst: The University of Massachusetts Press, 1970); J.B. Jackson, *A Sense of Place, a Sense of Time* (New Haven and London: Yale University Press, 1994); V. Fumagalli, *Landscapes of Fear; Perceptions of Nature and the City in the Middle Ages* (Oxford: Polity Press, 1993); M.M. Bell, *Childerley* (Chicago: Chicago University Press, 1994); J.G. Turner, 'The sexual politics of landscape: images of Venus in eighteenth-century English poetry and landscape gardening', *Studies in Eighteenth-Century Culture*, Vol. II, 1982, pp. 343–366; D. Cosgrove, *The Palladian Landscape, Geographical Change and its Cultural Representations in Sixteenth-Century Italy* (Leicester: Leicester University Press, 1993); J. Murdoch, 'A villa in Arcadia', in S. Pugh (ed.), *Reading Landscape, Country-City-Capital* (Manchester: Manchester University Press, 1988), pp. 121–144; C. Clunas, *Fruitful Sites, Garden Culture in Ming Dynasty China* (London: Reaktion Books, 1996). One here begins to enter an area where *real* nature and landscapes merge with represented images of landscapes: see N. Green, *The Spectacle of Nature: Landscape and Bourgeois Culture in Nineteenth-century France* (Manchester: Manchester University Press, 1990); C.S. Wood, *Albrecht Altdorfer and the Origins of Landscape* (London: Reaktion Books: 1993); J. Taylor, *A Dream of England, Landscape, Photography and the Tourist's Imagination* (Manchester: Manchester University Press, 1994). The problem of meaning is discussed in M. Treib, 'Must landscapes mean?: Approaches to significance in recent landscape architecture', *Landscape Journal*, Vol. 14, No. 1, Spring 1995, pp.46–62.

24 See J.B. Jackson, *op. cit.*; Udo Weilacher, *Between Landscape Architecture and Land Art* (Basel: Birkhauser, 1996); Michael Spens, *Landscape Transformed* (London: Academy Editions, 1996); Sutherland Lyall, *Designing the New Landscape* (London: Thames & Hudson, 1991); Michael Lancaster, *The New European Landscape* (London: Butterworth, 1995).

25 'Gardens articulate space in the interests of articulating time' (Mara Miller, *The Garden as an Art* (Albany: State University of New York, 1993), p. 39).

26 Lodewijk Baljon, *op. cit.*, p. 238.

27 See Sten Dunér, 'Besok hos en Topiarius I Sodra Sandby', in S. Hoyer, A. Lund and S. Moldrup, *Tilegnet Sven-Ingvar Andersson* (Copenhagen: Arkitektens Forlag, 1994), pp. 118–129.

28 Sven-Ingvar Andersson, unpublished lecture given at the conference *Rethinking the*

architecture/landscape relationship, School of Architecture, University of East London, 29–31 March 1996.

29 N. Fairbrother, *The Nature of Landscape Design* (London: Architectural Press, 1974), p. 155.

30 N. Fairbrother, *op. cit.*, p. 91.

31 Lodewijk Baljon, *op. cit.*, p. 238.

32 See C. Steenbergen and W. Reh, *Architecture and Landscape, The Design Experiment of the Great European Gardens and Landscapes* (Amsterdam: Thoth, 1996); Van der Ree, Smienk and Steenbergen, *Italian Villas and Gardens* (Amsterdam: Thoth, 1992); T. Higuchi, *The Visual and Spatial Structure of Landscapes* (Cambridge, Mass.: The MIT Press, 1983); H. Moggridge, 'Notes on Kent's garden at Rousham', *Journal of Garden History*, Vol. 6, No. 3, July–September 1986, pp. 187–226; C.W. Moore, W. J. Mitchell, W. Turnbull, *The Poetics of Gardens* (Cambridge, Mass: The MIT Press, 1988).

33 See Rosalind Krauss, 'Sculpture in the expanded field', in Rosalind Krauss, *The Originality of the Avant-Garde and Other Modernist Myths* (Cambridge, Mass.: The MIT Press, 1985), pp. 276–290.

34 It is interesting to note how the leading courses in cultural geography include discussion of data collection (participant observation, field work, etc.) but exclude analysis of the very nature of the visual, spatial and other qualities of those very landscapes to be investigated. It is in this area of phenomenology and 'poetics' (as described by the Russian Formalists) that the analysis of the built environment lags behind art history. Indeed, in art history and theory, there is a long-standing tradition of such methodological discussion traceable back to Lessing's classical Enlightenment study (see G.E. Lessing, *Laocoon, An Essay on the Limits of Painting and Poetry*, reprint, Indianapolis: Bobbs-Merrill, 1962) and through modern linguistics (see T. Hawkes, *Structuralism and Semiotics*, London: Methuen & Co., 1977) and phenomenology (see G.A. Johnson, *The Merleau-Ponty Aesthetics Reader*, Evanston, Illinois: Northwestern University Press, 1993). A recent art historical discussion would include Jonathan Crary, *Techniques of the Observer, On Vision and Modernity in the Nineteenth Century* (Cambridge, Mass.: The MIT Press, 1990). A recent study within architectural design is T. Porter, *The Architect's Eye: Visualization and depiction of space in architecture* (London: E. & F.N. Spon, 1997).

35 See Michael Podro, *The Critical Historians of Art* (New Haven and London: Yale University Press, 1982).

36 See R. S. Nelson and R. Shiff (eds), *Critical Terms for Art History* (Chicago: Chicago University Press, 1996).

37 See the parallel between Rosalind Krauss, *The Optical Unconscious* (Cambridge, Mass.: The MIT Press, 1993) and Jennifer Bloomer, *Architecture and the Text: The (S)crypts of Joyce and Piranesi* (New Haven and London: Yale University Press, 1993). See also Robert Harbison, *Thirteen Ways, Theoretical Investigations in Architecture* (Cambridge, Mass.: The MIT Press, 1997).

38 See C. Harrison, F. Frascina and G. Perry, *Primitivism, Cubism, Abstraction* (New Haven and London: Yale University Press with the Open University, 1993).

39 Hubert Damisch, *L'Origine de la Perspective* (Paris: Flammarion, 1993).

40 Rosalind Krauss, *The Optical Unconscious* (Cambridge, Mass.: The MIT Press, 1993).

41 Svetlana Alpers, *The Art of Describing, Dutch Art in the Seventeenth Century* (London: Penguin Books, 1989).

42 Jonathan Crary, *Techniques of the Observer, On Vision and Modernity in the Nineteenth Century* (Cambridge, Mass.: The MIT Press, 1990).

43 See J. Elkins, *The Poetics of Perspective* (Ithaca and London: Cornell University Press, 1994).

44 See Elisabetta Cereghini, 'The Italian origins of Rousham', in M. Mosser and G. Tyessot (eds), *The History of Garden Design, The Western Tradition from the Renaissance to the Present Day* (London: Thames & Hudson, 1991), pp. 320–322.

45 See P. Blundell Jones, *Hans Scharoun* (London: Phaidon, 1995).

46 See Richard Shiff, *Cézanne and the End of Impressionism* (Chicago: Chicago University Press, 1984); David Levin (ed.), *Modernity and the Hegemony of Vision* (Berkeley: University of California Press, 1993); Martin Jay, *Downcast Eyes, The Denigration of Vision in Twentieth-Century French Thought* (Berkeley and Los Angeles: University of California Press, 1993).

47 Beatriz Colomina, 'The split wall: domestic voyeurism', in Beatriz Colomina (ed.), *Sexuality and Space* (Princeton: Princeton Architectural Press, 1992), pp. 73–128.

48 Anthony Vidler, *The Architectural Uncanny* (Cambridge, Mass.: The MIT Press, 1992).

49 Simon Pugh, *Garden–Nature–Language* (Manchester: Manchester University Press, 1988).

50 See the classic studies by G. Pollock, *Vision and Difference, Femininity, Feminism and Histories of Art* (London: Routledge, 1988), L. Mulvey, *Visual and Other Pleasures* (London: Macmillan, 1989) and N. Bryson, *Vision and Painting, The Logic of the Gaze* (London: Macmillan, 1983).

51 Allen S. Weiss, *Mirrors of Infinity, The French Formal Garden and 17th Century Metaphysics* (Princeton: Princeton Architectural Press, 1995).

52 See Louis Marin, *Le Portrait du Roi* (Paris: Les Editions de Minuit, 1981).

53 See Giuliana Bruno, 'Bodily architectures', *Assemblage*, December 1992, pp. 106–111; D. Agrest, *Architecture from Without* (Cambridge, Mass: The MIT Press, 1991). See also M. O'Pray and A.L. Rees (eds), *Undercut*, No. 7/8 (London: London Film-Makers' Co-op., Spring 1983), which discusses landscape and the garden in film studies.

54 See Fredric Jameson, *The Seeds of Time* (New York: Columbia University Press, 1994), and Peter Carl, 'Architecture and time: a prolegomena', in *AA Files 22*, pp. 48–59.

55 See Caroline Constant's analysis of 'scenographic space' in *The Palladio Guide* (London: The Architectural Press, 1985). See also M.R. Michel, 'Scenography and perspective in eighteenth-century French gardens', in M. Moser and G. Teyssot, *op. cit.*, pp. 243–250.

56 See Eisenman Architects, *Unfolding Frankfurt* (Berlin: Ernst & Sohn, 1991).

57 See S. Wrede and H.A. Adams (eds), *Denatured Visions, Landscape and Culture in the Twentieth Century* (New York: MOMA, 1991).

58 James Ackerman, 'Introduction', *Perspecta 22: Paradigms of Architecture, Journal of the Yale School of Architecture* (New York: Rizzoli, 1986), pp. 11–33; p. 25.

59 See M. Leja, *Reframing Abstract Expressionism, Subjectivity and Painting in the 1940s* (New Haven and London: Yale University Press, 1993); B. Fer, 'Metaphor and Modernity: Russian Constructivism,' *Oxford Art Journal*, 12:1, 1989, pp.14–29.

60 F. Orton, *Figuring Jasper Johns* (London: Reaktion Books, 1994); C. Dilnot and M.

Garcia-Padilla, 'The difference of allegory', *Journal of Philosophy and the Visual Arts*, 1989, pp. 41–53.

61 'Agreeable arts are those whose purpose is merely enjoyment. [...] Fine art, on the other hand, is a way of presenting that is purposive on its own and that furthers [...] the culture of our mental powers to facilitate social communication. The very concept of the univeral communicability of a pleasure carries with it the requirement that this pleasure must be a pleasure of reflection rather than one of enjoyment arising from mere sensation. Hence aesthetic art that is also fine art is one whose standard is the reflective power of judgment, rather than sensation proper' (Kant, *The Critique of Judgment*, para. 305–306).

62 Deleuze and Guattari point out how Kant, in *The Third Critique of Judgment*, goes beyond all notions of reason and rationality, but this is clearly at the cost of associating 'nature' with this position. See G. Deleuze and F. Guattari, *Qu'est-ce que la Philosophie?* (Paris: Les Editions de Minuit, 1991). See also J.-F. Lyotard, *Lecons sur l'Analytique du sublime* (Paris: Galilée, 1991).

63 Kant, *op. cit.*, para. 323.

64 And, vice versa, there is of course a long, complex and active tradition of art historical writing about representations of nature, landscape and gardens that lies beyond the scope of this first book.

12

Section One
The Modernist context

14

Introduction

In addition to issues of historical interest, Peter Shepheard's forward-looking text raises issues that remain topical or have become even more topical: issues about collaborations between architects and landscape architects, about the appropriate use, grouping and maintenance of plants both in aesthetic and in ecological terms, about different types of drawing in architecture and in landscape architecture, about factory-produced hard materials and surfaces, about post-industrial landscapes. He defines very precisely the role of the landscape architect with the result that 'the landscape architect needs to be not less but something more than an architect.' Because our global environment consists of processes and that the role of the landscape architect involves harmonizing and balancing these processes, and because architecture exists within that world of environmental and global processes, architecture too is a complex system of processes – of heating, of cooling, of condensation, and so on. In this respect, architecture is a kind of landscape architecture. Sir Peter Shepheard himself writes:

> My *Modern Gardens* was published by the Architectural Press in 1953. At the time, after World War II, England was full of optimism. Government, led by 'philosophical' politicians, had laid the foundations for the reconstruction of Britain with the new Ministry of Town and Country Planning and the Planning Act of 1947. But now the small band of landscape architects who had survived the war found themselves as key players in multifarious environmental tasks. They were already involved in the New Towns, in the rebuilding of the bombed towns, and in many rural problems. The Festival of Britain, with its South Bank Exhibition, had played a vital part in showing what could be done with a derelict urban site when all the environmental professions truly collaborate. The Architectural Press saw *Modern Gardens* as a sequel to F.R.S. Yorke's *The Modern House*, but I saw it as a chance to state some principles at a time when the future held such promise.

15

16

Clematis vitalba

Sir Peter Shepheard

Introduction to *Modern Gardens* (1953)

THE WORD MODERN APPLIED TO ARCHITECTURE, though useful, is already tarnished with suspicion, and one cannot apply it to gardens without at least a gesture of apology. Nevertheless, its strongest critics cannot deny that there exists a great deal of architecture which may be described as part of the modern movement in that it not only belongs to but is inspired by the age in which we live. This book attempts to illustrate examples of landscape architecture which belong to the same category.

Such examples are hard to find. Here and there excellent work is being done which shows not only that modern architecture can be given a worthy landscape setting, but also that it may soon be possible to find landscape architects who can deal imaginatively with the vast new opportunities created for them by modern town and country planning. But no large body of recognizably modern landscape architecture exists, and in only a few countries is there a strong school of designers.

The reasons for this are not clear. Is landscape architecture perhaps too little susceptible of design in the architectural sense – too dependent on the craftsman, the weather and posterity – to be brought within a system of education from which a school of designers might be expected to issue? My answer is no; but certainly no such educational system exists, and most modern schools of landscape are in an experimental stage. Perhaps, in England at least, with the private patron abolished and the public authorities not always alive to their responsibilities, the profession of landscape architecture offers too limited a reward to attract the best men; certainly the amount of work entrusted to professional landscape architects in England in the past few years has occupied very few people, and even for some of these it has been part-time work combined with architecture or town planning.

But there may be more fundamental reasons. For example, it should be remembered that in architecture the two great motive forces of the modern movement were on the one hand the new opportunities being created by technical and social progress and on the other the new structural techniques. In landscape architecture new opportunities are certainly being created, but the technique of garden construction is still fundamentally the same as it was in the eighteenth century. Even the invention of modern earth-moving machinery, which may seem revolutionary, has in fact merely accelerated and cheapened processes which were used by Capability Brown. In horticulture also, in spite of the advance of science and the discovery of new plants, there has been no change in technique which could have influenced landscape architecture in the way in which frame construction, for example, influenced architecture. If this lack of revolutionary technical changes is one of the reasons why landscape has failed to produce its own modern movement, the continuity

18

Cypripedium calceolus

of traditional technique has certainly not resulted in the preservation of the traditional principles of the English landscape movement of the eighteenth century. Indeed, the extreme decadence of late nineteenth- and twentieth-century landscape design is an example – if any is needed – of the uselessness of a tradition of technique without those traditions of thought and sensibility which create a style.

Lastly, modern architecture owes much to the aesthetic of functionalism. Very few architects, of course, were out-and-out functionalists, and few will now admit that they ever had anything to do with it, but it was a historical influence of some importance in architecture which was absent, in the nature of things, from garden design. The functionalists made peace with their consciences in the end by saying that beauty was itself one of the functions of architecture; but architecture has others, whereas a garden has not. Nor can the garden designer eschew ornament, for the garden is itself an ornament; and even the advocate of simplicity and restraint – both admirable qualities – cannot seek for plain surfaces and simple forms when his material is Nature's own complex and rampant vegetation.

The idea of landscape architecture as a separate profession from that of architecture is, of course, quite new. Up to the end of the eighteenth century, and later, few architects regarded themselves as incompetent to design the landscape settings of their buildings and even those who specialized in landscape design, like Capability Brown, practised architecture on a large scale as well. But with the gradual professionalization of architecture and the steadily increasing complexity of the architect's work, the design of landscape has largely passed to specialists, and become itself professionalized. Both trends did some harm, as well as much good. There are few people left today who still regret the establishment of the architect as an independent professional agent between the client and the building industry; and of these few, the serious ones, such as Walter Gropius, want the architect to participate in a modernized building industry in quite a different role from that he played in the eighteenth century. But the architect's independence as a professional agent is won at the cost of an increasing separation from the actual technique of building; some regard this as a disaster, others argue that the more highly organized the building industry becomes and the more diverse its techniques, the more valuable will be the independence of the architect. The latter are probably right; the pitfalls of dilettantism and technical ignorance can be avoided by the architect who is awake to what is happening in building and who methodically informs himself about it. In landscape, however, there is a difference: the technique of landscape construction, and with it the organization of the industry, have remained simple and traditional; it is therefore theoretically possible for the landscape architect to play something very like his eighteenth-century role as artist-entrepreneur. Given the thorough apprenticeship training which the traditional system demands, this would theoretically produce good designers, expert in the craft as well as the theory of their job. But in fact the tradition of design is dead and the vocation and apprenticeship do not exist; some good works by the heads or chief designers of contracting firms prove the exceptions to a vast output of mediocrity, or worse, which goes by the name of landscape gardening. To remedy such a situation one needs to found an educational system for landscape architects, and to reinstate landscape architecture as a vocation and as a service to the community. The British Institute of Landscape Architects, which was founded for such ends, is, I think, right to assume that the modern landscape architect should be an independent professional agent, brought up to collaborate with the architect and the engineer on equal terms and with a similar background, thoroughly trained in both practice and theory and with strong convictions about the first principles of his profession.

First principles have played little part in the design of landscape in England since the flowering of the English landscape garden some two hundred years ago. One of the few English aesthetic achievements which won international fame, the *jardin anglais* was

19

reproduced in various forms and with varying degrees of misunderstanding all over Europe and America. Its principles owed as much to philosophy as to aesthetics; or, at least, its aesthetic principles fitted closely the permanent liberal and anti-authoritarian trends of English thought. It was anti-formal and gladly accepted nature and the native climate and flora which the Italian-French renaissance formal tradition could not do, and was influenced – especially in its later stages – by Oriental ideas from China and Japan. These influences, however vaguely comprehended, strengthened its philosophic and spiritual side. It is probably true to say that at the end of the eighteenth century the English landscape movement was nearer to an integral concept of landscape and building – something distantly like the Chinese *feng shui* – than the West has ever been.

The nineteenth century provided no opportunity for such a concept to flourish; industrialization and the chaotic development of towns, industries and communications took place without benefit of landscape architecture, except, perhaps, in the great urban parks of the mid-century period by Paxton and others, which still owe much to the great tradition.

In general, the nineteenth century was one of rampant eclecticism. Along with the collapse of the tradition and the abandonment of its principles went a vast increase in the plant material available for gardens. The very richness of this material, and the abundant supply of labour for maintaining gardens, led to enormous elaboration not only of design but of the cumbersome and expensive techniques of cultivating all kinds of tender tropical plants. In spite of the care lavished on their cultivation, few could be made to look at home in England; and the fashion, in any case, called rather for grotesquerie than appropriateness. It is, indeed, difficult now to imagine the full ugliness of the great Victorian gardens in their heyday; one sees them with their blowsy architecture softened and crumbled by time, their conservatories empty or in ruins. The armies of gardeners whose warfare with nature was so one-sided, and who would almost have been capable of painting the roses as they did in Alice's dream, have gone, and nature's ivy and moss and weeds have shrouded their work in the most pleasing kind of decay.

Towards the end of the century two contemporary voices were raised in strong protest against the prevailing fashions, and both were prophets of a new style of gardening. William Robinson, the professional gardener, hated above all 'architects' gardens', and conducted a ferocious controversy with Blomfield in which neither saw the other's point of view, and in which the right, to modern eyes, lay on Robinson's side. Gertrude Jekyll, the amateur to whom Lutyens owed much, including wonderful gardens for some of his best houses, was particularly interested in colour in the flower garden, but she was a great lover of plants and the most practical and charming writer on gardening in the last century. Both Robinson and Jekyll disliked the grotesque and blatant use of exotic plants in bedding out, and advocated simpler forms of gardening based on plants which would flourish in the English climate; both admired cottage gardens, and both loved native and naturalized plants grown in what they called the 'wild' garden.

The revolutionary influence of these two writers was widespread, and many of the finest modern gardens in Europe show it still. For instance, almost all the plants grown in the Stockholm parks today were favourite plants of Jekyll and Robinson. But in England their influence, though strong, developed along lines of which neither of them would have approved. Thus Miss Jekyll was an enthusiast for wall and water gardens, and wrote an excellent book about them, full of imagination and sensibility, and with photographs which clearly illustrate the principles she had worked out. This book, admirable though it is, is nevertheless at least partly responsible for the miles of dreary dry-walling and crazy paving and the thousands of inappropriate lily pools which are one of the most persistent incongruities in today's gardens, both public and private. Perhaps in one respect this misinterpretation was inevitable. For even Jekyll herself had no conscious theory of garden

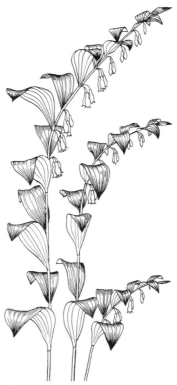

Polygonatum multiflorum

22

Scilla nutans

design to compare with that of any of the great eighteenth-century landscapists; she had great sensibility and impeccable taste but, like all the Victorians, she tended to see garden design as a series of separate items – the water garden, the rose garden, the border, and so on. Her great understanding of nature, and especially of plants, enabled her to weld these separate parts into a harmonious programme of design, especially for the large private garden which was her peculiar field. But her contemporaries, tired of the old tricks, welcomed her new ones, and the wall garden, the water garden and the wild garden, together with the rock garden, reformed more or less according to Reginald Farrer, took the place of carpet-bedding and conservatories as new turns in their bill of varieties.

Thus landscape architecture, which, since the days of the picturesque movement, had tended to turn a deaf ear to the aesthetic controversies of more than a hundred years, found itself in the early twentieth century untouched by the art-nouveau and the beginnings of the modern movement in architecture and town planning. Today modern architecture may fairly be said to have won its first battles all over the world, but in very few of them has it had any assistance from landscape architecture. Even now one sees many great modern buildings whose setting is an incongruous medley of dwarf walls, crazy-paving, and all the tricks of the Edwardian landscape gardener; and everywhere one can find housing, architecturally sound, but spoilt by a complete absence of any understanding of what can and what cannot be done with the space between buildings. This is the more unfortunate because modern architecture needs the landscape architect. One of the best qualities of the modern movement is its increasing awareness of the connection between the space within buildings and the space around them, and of the interdependence of building and site. Many architects are already designing housing which takes every advantage of its site, which is well planned and beautifully composed in three dimensions but which fails because of the designer's ignorance of the principles and technique of landscape design, and perhaps his inability to find a landscape architect who speaks the same aesthetic language as himself.

Moreover, not only have we an architecture with more than the beginnings of an aesthetic and a philosophy of its own, but in many countries, and especially in England, there is a political and administrative organization committed to physical planning not merely of towns but of whole regions which is creating vast opportunities for the development of an aesthetic and philosophy of town and country planning to which the planner, the architect and the landscape architect will each contribute. Behind many of the projects of the modern state – for example, the county development plans, the neighbourhood plans, new towns, national parks, and nature reserves – lie essentially philosophical ideas which have never before been applied to the common good on this scale. If the landscape architect is to play his full part in such projects, he must be more than a mere planner of gardens, just as the modern architect must be more than a designer of buildings. It is, for instance, becoming accepted that a modern community, whether new town or reconstruction, should have a properly organized plan in which dwellings, local shopping centres, schools and other buildings are related to one another in a convenient and orderly way, and in which there is a unified open space system in which playgrounds, walkways and gardens all have their place. In such a plan the work of the landscape architect should not be confined to the parks and gardens only; he should be available to collaborate with the architect on the preservation of existing natural features, such as streams and ponds and trees, on the linking of the parks and gardens with each other by walks and smaller open spaces, and on all the planting problems involved in the building layouts, the verges, street trees, house gardens and so on. He should also be involved, with the architect and the engineer, in the design of street lighting, and the placing of drains and other services, all of which can make planting difficult if not impossible unless they are considered soon enough.

The process of town and country planning through the development plans, and the

23

establishment of national parks and nature reserves, are beyond the scope of this book. Each contains many problems of the preservation and development of landscape in the widest sense. Some country authorities are beginning to be aware of this, and some industrialists have shown a welcome interest in using the landscape architect to fit such things as mines and cement works into the countryside. But these are merely pointers to the kind of work which waits to be done throughout the country. The most obvious field of all is the national parks and nature reserves; it is indeed disappointing to see that so little has yet been done to secure advice on architecture and landscape for these commissions, the whole object of which is to preserve the delicate balance between man and nature which exists in the areas under their control. And apart from these major tasks, it is worth remembering the great amount of work which could be done, at no great cost, throughout the country in healing the effects of bad development by judicious planting; there is hardly a town anywhere which has not some scar of industry or railway yard, gasworks or speculative building, which could be healed by the careful planting of the right trees in the right places.

My own attitude to the work of the landscape architect is, of course, coloured by the fact that I am myself an architect of buildings. Not that this needs any apology: our English tradition of landscape was nursed from the start by architects, and the design of landscape on every scale depends on that same faculty by which the architect works – a fully developed visual imagination and an understanding of form, colour and texture, of space and light and scale. No theory of architecture is adequate which does not embrace landscape also; no rules are valid which both cannot use. It is useless to think of the landscape architect as a gardener with a smattering of architectural knowledge. Rather he is an architect whose faculties have been further extended to include a wider perception of nature, and to enable him to work on the different scale and with the living materials of landscape.

First, the landscape architect is concerned with the existing site; with its character and the *genius loci*. Buildings also, and especially modern buildings, must, of course, fit the site and acknowledge its character; but landscape *is* the site, and the landscape architect's work is all alteration of what exists. His first rule must be to let well alone: to preserve the natural features in which the character of the place resides; these will be not only the shape of the ground and its vegetation, its trees, ponds and streams, but often old buildings, walls and pavings which, if they can be rescued from the municipal passion for tidiness, help more than anything else to prevent the flight of the *genius loci* from a scene of drastic change, such as the development of a housing scheme or the creation of a public park.

Second, the landscape architect's chief raw materials are on the one hand simple building constructions, and, on the other, vegetation. Simple constructions, that is, compared to the complexity of modern building; for although a landscape architect may occasionally be involved in retaining walls, dams and other fairly elaborate structures, he will normally be concerned with such things as garden walls, steps and pavings. Simple though these are, there is more to be learnt about them from experience than from books, and this should include, if possible, actual manual practice in laying and building. The technique of paving, for example, is much misunderstood both by architects and builders, and it is nowadays extremely difficult to get sound and beautiful paving laid. This is due partly to stinting first cost – almost always, with paving, a false economy – but mainly to ignorance of the craft itself; for example, to failing either to allow for settlement of the paving with the movement of the ground, or to make the expensive substructure which is needed to prevent it; or perhaps to the useless and unsightly cementing of joints in stone paving on a sand bed. It is a great pity that the traditional stone pavings, in slabs, setts and boulders, are giving way on grounds of, first, cost, to cheap concrete. Not only have the stone pavings an infinite variety of colour and texture, but as they will stand for centuries,

Tulipa sprengeri

Tulipa clusiana

25

Epilobium angustifolium

increasing constantly in beauty, it is probable that they are, in the long run at least, as cheap as concrete slabs and surfaces which break up rapidly under hard wear and exposure unless extremely well laid and finished.

It is, however, in his knowledge of his plant material that the landscape architect is most clearly distinguished. So complex is vegetation, and so different from the architect's inert media, that it will always be the chief difficulty in the training of those who approach landscape via an architectural course. For all the wider fields of the landscape architect's work, he will need to know the ecology of the various forms of natural vegetation; the study, that is, of the relation between plants, climate and soil, between one type of plant and another, and between plants and animals, including man. The delicate ecological balance on which the existing landscape depends is easily disturbed, and the landscape architect may be called upon to adjust or restore it. Secondly, he must have a general knowledge of the plants used in horticulture, and a detailed knowledge of those he intends to use himself; not merely, of course, to identify them, but to know their character of growth at all ages and in each season, and their cultural requirements. This is a formidable task: there are many tens of thousands of plants in cultivation, and the landscape architect's own vocabulary of plants may contain thousands of names. He will, of course, never expect to know as many plants as the systematic botanist, but his knowledge of the plants he uses must be extremely intimate, and it is not likely that such knowledge will be acquired in a lifetime by any but enthusiasts, who not only observe but also grow plants themselves. Horticulture, being one of those crafts in which theory must be reinforced by experience, is often regarded as a mystery; and it is true that those gardeners with enough intelligence to profit by experience do acquire that magical-seeming deftness in growing plants which people call 'green fingers'. It is, of course, wrong to think that this reduces the value of theory – in fact, theory enormously increases the value of 'green fingers' – but the landscape architect cannot easily instruct gardeners to carry out his designs if he has no first-hand experience of the practice of their craft.

But plants are not only objects of cultivation, they are the material in which the landscape architect designs; in doing so, he must not forget to regard himself as a kind of deputy for nature herself; he will depart from her principles at peril of absurdity. For although vegetation is a living material, it is still subject to aesthetic laws, and these can only be formulated by reference to the order found in nature. This, which is one of the main fascinations of the landscape architect's work, is universally misunderstood. Because plants are generally regarded – quite rightly – as intrinsically beautiful things, it is popularly supposed that it is enough to plant them, whether trees or flowers, anywhere, in the hope of a beautiful result. And so one finds some old garden where all was once greenness and shade, cut and defaced with beds of garish flowers; or a great traffic roundabout, where one would expect smoothness and simplicity, incongruously decked with garish suburban shrubs; or the great sweep of an arterial road, whose majestic verges should be part of the countryside, littered and vulgarized by puny pink trees. In all these, and a thousand more, it is not the plants which are ugly, but their incongruous use. One can safely assume that there is no natural plant – a species, that is, and not a garden variety or sport – which has not some natural place or habitat in which it grows in fitness and beauty. Taken out of this natural environment, it may refuse to grow; but even if it grows, it will often look strange or awkward and, in sufficiently unsuitable surroundings, will strike a jarring and ugly note in the scene. Some plants have a more universal character than others. Many climbing plants and many vigorous, independent weeds, have the habit of fitting in to almost any background; and native plants are generally, but not always, more likely to fit in than exotic ones. There are few English gardens in which the splendid native ivy could not make itself gracefully at home, and it is not easy to go wrong with climbers like jasmine or honeysuckle, clematis or the vines. Many strong-growing weeds, such as the native foxglove or the larger heracleums, have the same fitness, especially for those places in which they have sown themselves; and those aquatic plants which will grow in English ponds and rivers usually look well, whether native or not. At the other extreme are the cacti, aloes and agaves, which have such an air of the sunlit desert about them that they are pathetically incongruous in most other settings; or plants of striking form, such as the monkey-puzzle *araucaria* and other conifers, which have a dominating character that is often unwelcome; or plants with violently-coloured flowers, such as the universal geranium or *pelargonium*, *agrostemma*, *calendula* and a host of annual bedding plants, many of which are natives of arid countries, where they grow amid sparse vegetation and stones, and where their brilliance is dimmed by dazzling sunshine; in the soft northern light of England, which causes even the green of the grass and the red of the bracken to glow like fire, their colours become incandescent, and will scorch holes in any landscape when seen from a distance. Between these two extremes of adaptability and exclusiveness lie the vast mass of cultivated plants, all of which can, more or less easily, be made to look ugly in certain situations.

So far, I have referred to natural species only. As soon as one begins to contemplate the work of the plant breeder in hybridizing plants and creating new varieties, it is obvious that the assumption that no plant is intrinsically ugly is no longer valid. It is true, of course, that individual plants of a species vary in nature, and that by breeding from the better and stronger forms strains can be improved in beauty and vigour; and careful crossing of one species with another has produced thousands of worthy and beautiful plants in which gardens have been growing richer for centuries. But with the commercialization of plant breeding the competition between breeders to sell new and 'improved' varieties produces year by year, along with one or two good plants, dozens of worthless deformities which have nothing to commend them but their novelty. Fifty years ago Gertrude Jekyll was protesting vigorously against this insane competition; but there have been no signs of its decrease since then. Among its worst manifestations are the doubling of flowers that are prettier single; the variegation of the leaves of trees and shrubs that are better green; the striving for absurd unnatural colours, especially blue – the blue primrose, the blue tulip, the blue rose; the creation of fastigiate or upright-growing forms of normally graceful trees, such as 'ama-no-gawa', a hideously deformed cherry with branches raised like the ribs of an inside-out umbrella, which has actually been recommended as a street tree because its branches do not interfere with passing traffic! This worst of horrors has recently been surpassed by the production of a fox-glove which, instead of the lovely one-sided spire tapering from open flowers at the base to packed buds at the tip, thrusts up a stiff column of fat flowers which open all together and are packed all round the stem like corn on the cob – all the grace and wonder of the foxglove thrown away for a blowsy show. One could list hundreds of such enormities, and thousands of lesser 'improved' varieties in which the shape, size or colour of a plant has been altered for the worse; and their number may well be increased by the new understanding of the chromosome structure of plants. The production of these monsters is not only a waste of time; it has two further serious results: first, the vigour of the older types is often sacrificed in the process (and little enough said about this in the advertisements!); second, and more serious, the older types tend to be superseded by the new, and in some cases have gone out of cultivation altogether. Many nurserymen are fortunately aware of these dangers, and some even specialize in the old and tried varieties of plants.

It would, of course, also be absurd to imply, in protesting against novelty and monstrosity, that plant breeding and hybridization is in itself a bad thing; even those who, like myself, tend to prefer natural species, must admit the age-old debt of gardeners to the plant breeders for the wonders they have made of the rose, the carnation, the lily and hundreds of the other famous plant families, by an understanding of the character with

29

Digitalis purpurea

30

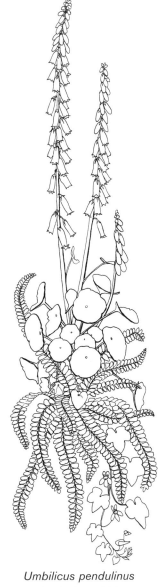

Umbilicus pendulinus
Asplenium viride

which nature originally endowed them. This ineffable character of a natural species of plant (or of any living thing) is beauty itself; the absolute unity of character which informs every diverse part of a plant is itself a more perfect demonstration of aesthetic unity than can be formulated in words. The oak tree's bark, its knotted twigs, its green leaf-stalks, its smooth leaves, and shiny acorns in their glaucous cups, are all diverse forms; and yet each is so pervaded by the unity of the oak tree's character that none of them can possibly be imagined as part of any other species of tree. It is when the plant breeder, by chromosome-polyploidy, or viruses, or by breeding from sports or giants, produces plants with parts which have not this unity with each other, that ugliness results. Plants of this kind are deformities; a foxglove with a taller and more graceful stature, with richer colouring, with a rosy stem or deeper spots inside its corolla may well be more beautiful, as a girl with smoother skin and larger eyes is beautiful; but a foxglove with flowers all round its stem is like a girl with eyes all round her head. The recognition of this character of plant form is the first requisite of a good plantsman, as of a good landscape architect; both must be capable of being described, in the words of Horace Walpole about Capability Brown, as 'Dame Nature's second husband'.

And so the landscape architect is faced with a vast array of cultivated plants, all of which, except some monstrosities, have something to commend them, and all some place in which he would find them useful. He will learn first the identification and then the habits of more and more of them, reinforcing his reading with observation and his observation with culture of the plants themselves; he will visit gardens and make notes of plants that appeal to him, of their habit and growth under various conditions, of their time of flowering, of variations in form and colour and vigour, and from a card-index of such notes he will soon find that he has a more intimate knowledge of his own favourite plants than can ever be got from books.

In addition to his feeling for the individual plant, he must acquire an understanding of the way in which plants grow in association with one another. There is in any landscape a series of natural associations in which plants grow; most of these are stages in the development of what the ecologist calls the climax vegetation of each climatic region, such as broad-leaved deciduous forest, or tropical jungle, or tundra; but at each stage the vegetation achieves a balance between dominant and other plants as they struggle for survival; and the study of how plants adjust themselves to each other, and how each finds its own place in the process, will reward the designer of gardens which are, after all, merely highly artificial associations in which the balance is maintained by human interference instead of natural selection. In this, again, man makes many mistakes, while nature makes none. In any tract of wild ground, whether woodland or seashore, marsh or mountain, roadside pond, or indeed almost any neglected corner of waste land, one finds a miraculously appropriate assortment of plants, each one holding its own fit place and growing as best it may to add its own contribution, whether mean or magnificent, to the living pattern. The pattern, at each stage, has the same kind of unity in its component plants as the oak tree has in its twigs and leaves and acorns; the kind of unity which one aims at but seldom achieves in a garden. The shingle bank behind the shore, for instance: white pebbles, and bleached tufts of marram, curly grey sea-kale, the glaucous horned poppy with huge yellow flowers, and the silver sea-holly, white-veined and bonelike, stained in flower and stem with the blue of the sea; an austere pattern, dry and sunlit, with no hint of luxuriance, and full of the pale bright colours of the sky. Quite different is the heather moorland: a thick mantle of vegetation growing in the acid peat formed of its own decay, windshorn and full of deep and brilliant colour; the heather and the gorse cushioned against the wind, the green of the short turf starred with tiny flowers of milkwort and tormentil, the springs and streams glowing with red and green mosses; wherever a rock or clough gives shelter, a tiny luxuriance breaks out of fern and pennywort, ivy and rowan. Different, again, is the woodland: looking up at the canopy of trees against the sky, one can see how each tree grows out towards the others, forming an intricate polygon which never quite touches its neighbour, the outermost twigs almost meeting but never crossing those of the next tree; below, the floor of the wood has its own vegetation according to the density of the canopy; the fir wood, black and bare, with saprophytes and fungi standing up whitely in the darkness; the beech wood, after its spring bluebells, which use the light before the leaves come on the trees, a smooth red floor with orchids and brambles in the clearings; the mixed wood full of every kind of shade-loving shrub and herb and moss, and, when enough light comes in, one of the most favourable situations for tall and splendid plants such as the foxglove, the rosebay willow-herb, the monkshood and the columbine.

Each of these patterns, in which the balance is preserved by ecological conditions, could be violated more or less easily by the introduction of alien plants. The seashore and moorland less easily perhaps, if only because those plants which would stand the austere conditions would already have some of the qualities of those making up the pattern; one could, nevertheless, imagine calendulas growing hideously among the sea-holly, and I have actually seen *Hydrangea hortensis* flaunting its papery, sophisticated blues on a sheltered moorland bank. While for woodland desecration one has only to look at the actual destruction of whole woodland paradises by *Rhododendron ponicum* to see that a plant can be both luxuriant and ugly; in its pontic home, with plants of its own size to fight, it may be magnificent. And yet the deciduous woodland is an ideal setting for naturalizing alien plants, as many gardens show: one of the most perfect accessible examples being certain parts of the wild garden at the British Royal Horticultural Society's gardens at Wisley, in Surrey, in which, with superb gardening technique, plants from all over the world have been grown to make a perfectly beautiful undergrowth in a typical English oak wood.

The lessons to be learnt from a study of these natural patterns of growth are not, of course, confined to the naturalization of plants or to dealing with natural landscape. They will suggest principles, which I have neither space nor ability to formulate, and which may not even be capable of verbal formulation, for placing all plants in surroundings other than their natural ones. For example, the English landscape, man-made though it is, has acquired an acceptable and beautiful pattern which is as easily violated by unsuitable alien trees as any natural one; it is not the foreignness of the trees but their incongruity that is at fault. Again, the use of flowers in gardens and elsewhere should be governed by the rule that flowers, especially those with bright colours which tend to dazzle the eye in northern climates, should be seen at close quarters and hidden from a distance; examples of the misuse of flowers can be multiplied, but one of the most interesting is in the village of Broadway, Gloucestershire, where the traditional green and grey Cotswold village scene is spoilt by the overflow of flowers from the gardens onto the roadside; pretty in themselves – they are mostly not of a garish kind – they nevertheless destroy the essential tranquillity of the scene.

Nor is it only in planting that lessons are learnt from observation of nature; the student of informal design must study the structure of the earth itself, especially where it is laid bare by the elements – the mountains, the rivers and the shore of the sea. The Japanese even describe one way of placing a group of stones as 'like *chidori*', or sanderlings, the little birds that fly in clouds along the edge of the sea and alight in patterns in which order and chance play equal part.

In the actual process of design the landscape architect uses the same technique as the architect; the same synthesis of the various requirements of the programme into a satisfying unity. His chief temptation is to forget the third dimension. On his large and unwieldy plans the scale is so small that elevations and sections show hardly any height at all, and tend to be ignored, while the plan is often designed as if it were itself an elevation, to be seen from the air. But in a garden, from eye level, the third dimension is everything; seen from eye

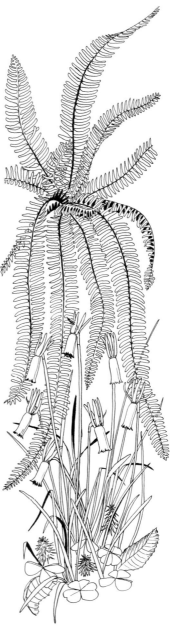

Blechnum spicant
Narcissus cyclamineus

34

Campanula latifolia

level the patterns of the plan flatten out unrecognizably, while fences, walls and trees stand in ranks one behind the other. An extra six inches on the height of a wall at eye level cuts off the view of acres of ground; a path with an imperceptible curve on plan becomes sharply serpentine, or unpleasantly angular; square paving slabs become sharp lozenges or acquire strange diagonal patterns; water uncompromisingly asserts its horizontal level, and if the ground near it has an insistent fall, the water itself may appear sloping; the trees which appear as green cushions on the plan rear themselves to eighty feet and more, creating huge barriers and enclosures of space, but allowing clear views for miles between their trunks at eye level. None of these things can be properly forecast on plan only, nor fully in elevation and section; the landscape architect must design in perspective. So also, of course, should the architect; but whereas one can get an approximation of a building's appearance from elevations, they are quite useless for gardens. A facility for sketching rapid and fairly accurate perspectives without geometry is invaluable, and dozens of these are needed in even the smallest designs; all the important objects must be placed in the plan by setting them up in geometrical perspectives and working back from these to the plan.

The effect of light on vegetation is very different from its effect on architecture; instead of regular surfaces which reflect light in a regular and predictable way, plants have an infinite variety of textures, all tending to absorb more light, and therefore to look darker, than hard surfaces, but still with a great range of tones – from the blackness of yew to the whiteness of poplar or whitebeam in the wind. Leaves and flowers are also often transparent, so that plants can be lit up from behind by a low sun to show brilliant colours against darker trees, rocks or buildings. The sun at various times of day can therefore be made to produce a whole series of different effects from the same material.

Lastly, the landscape architect must never hope for quick results. Always one's client wants to see something quickly; even architects, one finds, tend to imagine vegetation as something that can be installed by the yard in permanent and unchanging form. But generally quick-growing herbs become weeds, quick-growing shrubs become over-grown and ungainly, and quick-growing trees quickly decay and become dangerous. Most plantings which look mature after three or four years are in decay or rampant in ten or fifteen. The best that can be done is to have carefully prepared temporary planting plans, in addition to the permanent one, of plants which will make an interim show and be removed before they become a nuisance. This means, of course, leaving explicit instructions to the client on the after-care of the design; and this is, in any case, a wise thing to do. The calamities which befall buildings at the hands of clients or their successors are nothing to those which await gardens, which are always regarded as legitimate objects for digging up, replanting and every sort of well-meant destruction; some of this can be forestalled by a careful explanation of one's aims to the right person, if he can be found.

35

I have already expressed my conviction that the landscape architect needs to be not less but something more than an architect. It is today inconceivable that a system of training for such a person could be established without the universities and other centres of higher education. Already a start has been made, and one hopes that those in charge of these adventurous projects will look not only at the curricula of the schools of architecture and town planning which are their forerunners, but also at their mistakes. School training must always carry with it the danger that the student may work too much on paper and too little with earth and plants; but it has the invaluable advantage of directing his attention to first principles while he is young enough to adopt them. Should this training be a normal undergraduate course? Or should it be attached to a school of architecture, either by means of specialization in the later years, or by the addition of a post-graduate course of one or two years? There is so much in common between the two professions that it is difficult not to agree with those who say that the landscape architect must share as much of the architect's training as covers the common ground; as much, at least, as is devoted to the training of the visual imagination and the faculty of design; which means almost the whole of the five-years' course at the schools of architecture. Landscape students would be unlikely to spend so much time in a school of architecture without wishing to qualify as architects, so that such a training would inevitably end as a post-graduate course; producing landscape architects fully trained as architects with post-graduate training in botany, ecology, and horticulture. The alternative, an undergraduate course in all these subjects and the theory of landscape design, is not likely to be much shorter than five years if the theory of design is given its proper weight, and any attempt to shorten it by omitting the more architectural aspects of design would be wrong. For although the landscape architect's constructions are technically simple, his problems of scale and proportion, light and perspective are all more difficult than the architect's; and, in any case, as is well known, the same principles are involved in the design of the smallest as of the largest structures, and it is often as hard to design a flight of steps as a cathedral.

Almost as important as training landscape architects is the education of the public to enjoy, cherish, and respect their works, and especially those of the public who, as councillors or officers of public authorities, have the appearance of town and country so largely in their hands. The borough engineer, for example, holds a huge responsibility for his town's visual character, and after every one of his well-meant improvements bricks are thrown at him from every quarter and especially, of course, by architects. He has my sympathy – he is not trained in landscape design, and he may find the right kind of advice from landscape architects not easy to obtain; indeed, he may have only the vaguest ideas of what they do. Moreover, he frequently has real grounds for his persistent view of his fellow human beings as a mob of ruffians, waiting only for a chance to deface his works, to commit a nuisance or to commit suicide. Landscape architects and others interested in the appearance of their towns should therefore not only press for the use of proper professional advice but should help to propagate their ideas amongst all those in charge of the town. Form civic societies and bring in the architect and the borough engineer; hold exhibitions, write letters to the press, and, above all, try to find out what is projected in the way of public works, so that helpful advice can be given, or preventive action taken, *in time*. Remember also that borough engineers and other officers, like the rest of us, are much more susceptible to polite and constructive advice than to abuse, of which they get plenty and to which they are thoroughly immune. So write polite letters, and write more.

The destruction of trees and other plants by children and youths, often rather stupidly called vandalism, makes any kind of free landscape treatment an impossibility in many places. Here, again, the first answer is education, and the second persistence in replanting and replacing destroyed plants until the children get tired of destruction or learn better. Where these two courses have been enthusiastically followed, as in Bermondsey, London, the children have so quickly abandoned their interest in destruction as to confirm my opinion that it is mainly the novelty of trees in such a place which attracts their destruction, and that the children's interest decreases – in accordance with what might be called a law of diminishing vandalism – with their familiarity.

By such public education one might hope to see an improvement in civic manners sufficient to allow of a landscape, especially in towns, less railed off, less tidy, less generally buttoned-up than is now so often found. For the municipal habit of making everything safe, of railing off water with railings unclimbable by everyone except the children they are meant to deter, of shutting up parks at night, of lopping to the stumps every tree that could conceivably drop a branch at the crack of doom, of elaborate, unusable keep-off-the-grass gardens, has for long prevented the application of the English tradition of informal landscape to our town open spaces; one has to go to Stockholm to get an idea of what an eighteenth-century landscapist might have done if he had been given a town instead of a gentleman's park to play with.

37

Lilium canadense

The pictures in this book show a selection of garden designs – the larger fields of landscape work have been excluded – which, in spite of great variations in national character, in type and in size, seem to me to possess a common touch of the contemporary spirit. My own view – which I have freely allowed to sway my choice – is that the modern garden should find its inspiration in the contemporary scene; that if it looks backward for a precedent, it should turn not to the Renaissance gardens of Europe, in which princes and kings glorified themselves by subjecting nature to a symmetrical pattern, but to the gardens in which from time to time man has come to terms with nature and made her partner to his design. For nature will come, if not as partner, as destroyer, crumbling stone and overgrowing all artificiality with moss and fern and ivy. How much, indeed, of the charm of even the lovely Italian gardens lies today in the hugely-grown cypresses, the crumbling basins, the filmy overgrowth of weeds with which nature has reasserted herself? Many of these gardens were made, of course, in the springtime of the Renaissance, and have none of the brutal grandeur which Europe later learned to make of the simple Italian symmetries, at Schonbrunn, Karlsruhe, or Versailles. But we should turn to the enclosed courtyard gardens of Southern Spain, modest and private paradises of stone and water and greenness; or to the village greens of England; or to the parks of the English landscape movement; or, above all, to the gardens of China and Japan, which, in a climate not unlike our own (which is the best climate in the world for gardens), achieve a miraculous degree of unity with nature; not, of course, to copy any of these, but to find that common attitude of reverence for and partnership with nature which informs them all.

38

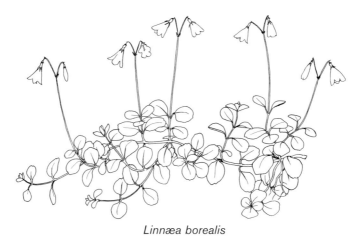

Linnæa borealis

Section Two
Relating architecture to landscape through elements and materials

Introduction

The essays in this section look at the dimensions of time and space – and therefore movement through space – and at physical materials and qualities. Mara Miller looks at how Japanese gardens structure time both by highlighting different scales of time (geological, seasonal, biological and historical) and by contrasting different experiences of time (mathematical, individual, social). This is achieved through diversity of perceptions – visual, tactile, etc. – and through variety of movement in terms of rhythm and pace in relation to those perceptions. Jan Woudstra looks at the material qualities of the Scandinavian Modernist tradition of detailing outdoor spaces. This involved both detailing (outdoor lighting and paving and so on) and the siting of buildings in the landscape in relationship to existing vegetation and geomorphological forms. It also involved the development of outdoor spaces for public recreation, including the invention of new typologies such as playgrounds. In the light of this Scandinavian example, Woudstra discusses new problems that have arisen today: in particular the globalisation of standard factory-produced detailing for outdoor spaces. Jacques Leenhardt explores the textural qualities of the Latin American vegetation used by Robert Burle Marx. He also discusses the specific spatial qualities that Burle Marx developed from his experience of painting, drawing and print-making in terms of verticality and horizontality and in terms of the relationships between colour, form and texture. Burle Marx's exploration of the activity of painting and silk-screen printing also relates to his investigations into the counterpointing of freedom of movement versus the static point of view. Leenhardt analyses Marx's use of size, scale, distance and materials in relation to the tension between legibility of the overall plan and movement through the (only partially visible) plan. Leenhardt thus analyses the different components of the dynamic experience of space in a Roberto Burle Marx landscape or garden.

41

Mara Miller

Time and temporality in Japanese gardens

Since at least the time of Frank Lloyd Wright, Japanese architecture and the Japanese integration of buildings with their surroundings have fascinated modern architects and designers. Although the Japanese term for 'nature' considered as a whole, *shizen*, was taken from the Chinese language (about fifteen hundred years ago),[1] and many of the themes, motifs, and concepts used in garden design were also adapted from China,[2] Japanese gardens are utterly unique in techniques, principles and effects.[3] Yet this uniqueness does not limit their appeal in any way – it arouses the deepest responses in people all over the world, as the proliferation of Japanese gardens in North America indicates.[4]

There are a number of reasons for this. The formal qualities alone are compelling (Fig. 1). The combination of natural materials and rational structure is especially appealing in an increasingly mechanical age (Fig. 2). The tranquillity they impart can transform lives. They are inspired places for parties (especially effective as places for socialising when guests don't know each other well) – a capacity that is often overlooked in the West.

One of the most distinctive and least studied characteristics of Japanese gardens is the way they structure time. In this paper I will outline several (though not all) of the ways that Japanese gardens structure time, with an emphasis on those that are unique.

The mere fact of structuring time is not unique to Japanese gardens – gardens everywhere do this; it is one of their most important contributions. While it has rarely been analysed by scholars or designers, most visitors feel it, experience it, intuit it, in all gardens, whatever their style or country of origin. The different 'styles' or cultural traditions assume the task of making clear the structure of time in their various ways, and they do it on several levels. The most basic is making visible contrasting scales or orders of time – seasonal time, geological time, the different varieties of biological and historical time, etc. The Japanese Garden by Koichi Kawana at the Denver Botanic Garden, for example (Fig. 1), juxtaposes the brief yet predictable cyclic life of leaves with the fragility of moss and lichen, indefinitely extended in time, and with the century or more of a large pine, the aeons of the rock, and the few centuries of human history represented by the rustic fence.

A section of water at the stroll garden called Kikoku-tei at the Higashi-honganji Temple in Kyoto shows a similar – and again typically Japanese – way a garden may juxtapose many different kinds of time (Fig. 3). (A 'stroll garden' is a garden one walks through, as opposed to a garden meant to be viewed from a verandah.) Perhaps the first thing we notice is the interplay of light and shadow – an image of ephemerality superimposed upon running water, itself an icon and a symbol of change not only for Heraclitus but also for Buddhism since ancient times. (An early Japanese Buddhist term for the phenomenal world is *uki-yo*, or 'floating world'.) The photograph is misleading, of course, for the movement of both the water and the shadows has been frozen, and indeed with no ripples on its surface it is difficult to recognize as water at all, so clear is it. (The presence of fish would inform us, but it was a hot day and the ornamental carp were in the shadows and did not show up in the photograph.) That it is a stream and not a path is evident from a number of indications, however. Some are based on the laws of visual perception: the reflections on the surface of the water of both a blade of grass *and* its shadow (mid-way up on the left, in the sun). Others require some familiarity with the conventions of Japanese design: the formlessness of the 'path' and lack of deliberate texture, the abrupt edges of large rock, too large to be suitable for path edging; and towards the top of the photograph, a big flat rock whose upper surface, along the same plane as the rocks to its right and left, makes a bridge perpendicular to the stream. The water flows past the steep sides of the rocks, a subtle reminder of the slow erosion of rocks by water everywhere, of the glacial pace of geological change. In the context of these large unchanging rocks, the transience of the water is the more noticeable, its quickness the more apparent.

Geological time, the time of the earth and its components – rocks and water, mountains and hills, rivers, ponds – is contrasted in this garden with biological time, or times, that is, the contrasting lifetimes of fish, leaves and grass – and ourselves. The garden makes the most of these contrasts, creating a rhythm of its own by the contrasts of still rocks and tree trunks with moving water, fish, persons. Indeed it determines to a great extent the speed of human visitors through it by means of such devices as stone bridges like this one, and paths of uneven stepping-stones.

The photograph, still though it is, therefore, is an image of an image of time. Two-dimensional though it is, it illustrates not only three-dimensional reality but the fourth dimension as well. We must be cautious, and aware: we are easily misled by our technology. We come, sometimes, to believe the superficial messages of our photographs, which easily mislead us into thinking about gardens as if they were primarily visual, simply because the photographs themselves convey primarily visual information.

The juxtaposition of time scales in such a way creates a temporal composition, a rhythmic pattern, that makes perceptible different scales of time. It makes us aware of the very passage of time itself – an inner awareness called temporality. As an artform, gardens do this not only on the level of individuals, but for societies as a whole; indeed we may count as one of the most important functions gardens have, one of their most important achievements, the dissemination of particular forms of temporality, or

1 Pine, rocks and rustic fence. Japanese Garden, Denver Botanic Garden. Designed by Koichi Kawana.
(Photograph Mara Miller)

2 Stone lantern and water basin with bamboo pipe. Japanese Garden, Denver Botanic Garden. Designed by Koichi Kawana.
(Photograph Mara Miller)

3 Stream bed in July. Kikoku-tei, Higashi-hongan-ji Temple, Kyoto.
(Photograph Mara Miller)

subjectively experienced time, throughout a population, so that these forms of time are no longer idiosyncratic, purely individual. One of the ways a garden designer may exhibit her/his genius is through the original apperception of a new form of time, which is then expressed in the design of the garden and thence disseminated to its visitors and throughout the society. There are countless examples of such original perceptions of time in garden design. The Zen juxtaposition of rocks and moss eschewing seasonal cycles of leaves and flowers was such a radical innovation, as were the several experiments with the integration of versions of a historical past into the present: the introduction of a discontinuous classical past into Italian Renaissance gardens via statuary, the appropriation of ruins into the eighteenth-century English landscape garden, the insertion of what is seemingly a farmer's fence into our contemporary Japanese urban garden.

Now time is a very abstract thing, constantly with us yet hard to know. So before we start out, I would like to point out that in this chapter I will be referring to four basic and equally common but profoundly different notions of time: physicists' time, objective time, subjective time, and temporality.

'Physicists' time' or 'scientific time' is the time studied (most of the time) by physicists and used by other scientists; it is quantifiable, uniform, and divisible into units

46

Iris

(seconds, minutes, hours, days) of equal duration. It is also directional (philosophers speak of 'time's arrow', which never reverses course or repeats); it 'moves' from the present into the future (at least ordinarily), and the trajectory of its arrow begins with a past, moves through the present and into the future.

Physicists' time is the least important for garden design. It is a form of time gardeners and garden lovers must reckon with constantly: considering the number of days till germination, the number of hours of sunlight needed to bring a plant to fruit, and so on. (These things can be calculated with remarkable precision, but they are rarely of aesthetic interest.) For the most part, in this paper, we will take the existence of scientific time for granted, and lay it aside. Gardens, of course, exist in this time, as do we, but insofar as time is scientific, it may be taken for granted: it is the same regardless of style or design, and therefore it is unproblematic for gardens.

More important to garden design is 'subjective time', that is, time as it *feels* to us. The fifteen minutes of a physicist and the last fifteen minutes of a student's schoolday may be very different fifteen minutes indeed. (Although, of course, physicists also experience quarter hours that drag on as if they were an hour or two.) There are three issues here. First, this is partly a difference between felt or experienced time (of our impatient student) and measured time (of our physicist). The physicist's time is purely quantifiable and objectively quantifiable; the student's is barely quantifiable – all quantification feels inadequate, and must give way to the qualities of the time, which are utterly subjective. Second, such quantification as is feasible not only varies widely from individual to individual, but within the experience of a given individual also varies from one time to another. Finally, the individual's experience of time may also vary, or 'stretch', in ways that are widely shared and predictable, and that therefore have something of an 'objective' quality to them. In her autobiography, the novelist Doris Lessing describes this last phenomenon thus:

> The main reason, the real one, why an autobiography must be untrue is the subjective experience of time. The book is written, chapter one to the end, in regular progress through the years. Even if you go in for sleights of hand like flashbacks of *Tristram Shandy*, there is no way of conveying in words the difference between child time and grown-up time – and the different pace of time in the different stages of an adult's life. A year before you are thirty is a very different year from the sixty-year-old's year.
>
> When scientists try to get us to understand the real importance of the human race, they say something like, 'If the story of the earth is twenty-four hours long, then humanity's part in it occupies the last minute of that day.' Similarly, in the story of a life, if it is being told true to time as actually experienced, then I'd say seventy per cent of the book would take you to age ten. At eighty per cent you would have reached fifteen. At ninety-five per cent, you get to about thirty. The rest is a rush – towards eternity.[5]

47

The various subjective experiences of time are sometimes referred to as temporality. It is often discussed, for we frequently become aware of the contrast between it and either scientific time or other people's subjective experience. Insofar as it is purely subjective, however, it is rather difficult to convey. Lessing in the above quotation is talking *about* it, not trying to get us to experience it in her way. Poems, film, and prose fiction, on the other hand, do try to recreate for us a specific experience of subjective time: *Remembrance of Things Past* does just that (among other things). Music, too, excels at this – as do gardens.

'In between' scientific time and purely subjective temporality are a variety of forms of 'objective' time. Particularly for modern technological societies, 'objective time' and physicists' time overlap considerably, for our general understanding of time is largely based on the studies of physicists and measured by instruments they have devised. I, however, would like to use the term 'objective' to denote something that is a little harder to get at than physicists' time, something less commonly recognised, but experienced everyday: namely, a widely shared form of subjective time – *any* widely shared form regardless of the specific content or structure.

By 'objective time' I mean that which is experienced and understood by many people (although not necessarily every single person). Scientific time applies to everyone, and regardless of whether we understand it or not. It may well be beyond the range of our experience. But objective time is the *experience* of time common within a society. As *experienced* time, *felt* time, it may be said on the one hand to be *subjective*. But given that this particular form of experience is also widely shared, it is also *objective*. (This is a category of time for which our usual dualistic way of thinking is not especially helpful. Perhaps we should just say that the terms 'subjective' and 'objective' as used here are not mutually exclusive.) It is both taken for granted, that is, operant on a pre-reflective level, and rational in the sense that it is capable of being understood by most people, given some discussion or explanation.

For example, in the eighteenth century in England it became necessary for the purposes of development of capital and industrialisation to have a relatively large population that could plan and think for the long term – longer than say, traditional agriculture usually called for, which is about one year or less. Investment, however, presupposes the ability to carry out a plan over a long period of time without seeing any results and delaying gratification. While the new English landscape garden served diverse purposes, one of these was inculcating a habit of planting, and therefore planning, on a scale hitherto quite rare, the scale of the lifetimes of large trees – for the next generations. In a different vein, Louis XIV's juxtaposition at Versailles of themes from the four seasons with the course of the sun through the sky reconciled familiar daily and annual changes with the seemingly eternal constants of the celestial realm – helping to justify his monarchy.

Some of the ways that Japanese gardens structure time and disseminate temporality are shared with other garden styles all around the world. In Ming and Qing China as in Renaissance Italy, seventeenth-century France, eighteenth-century England, the use of historical quotations and allusions in gardens helped to make the past present, to integrate an understanding of the relevance of history for the present day. Similarly,

48

4 Pond at the end of irises and the beginning of water lilies. Japanese Garden, Denver Botanic Garden. Designed by Koichi Kawana. (Photograph Mara Miller)

Japanese gardens even today, such as the one at the Denver Botanic Garden, use rustic fences (Fig. 1) of the type farmers used to make, and stone lanterns (*ishi-dohroh*) in historic shapes (Figs 2, 4) in order to bring the collective historical past into the present awareness of modern individuals.

An even more widespread form of objective time than (linear) historical is the cyclical form of time, the eternal recurrence analysed by Mircea Eliade. This is the time of the seasons, of the life cycles of animals dependent on the seasons, of agriculture. It is the kind of time experienced by many societies not under the sway of 'time's arrow' of physics. Yet modern and post-modern technological societies, too, are familiar with cyclical time: the cycles of the liturgical year, of the school or fiscal year, of the seasons, of holidays, perhaps of our own calendar of birthdays and anniversaries.

Gardeners, too, integrate cyclical time of the plants' internal calendar with scientific unrepeatable time: we plant the peas according to some larger, more-or-less reliable, recurring scheme. Cyclical time is one of Nature's forms of time, dependent upon the seasons. It has profoundly affected the planting of gardens, as an example from eleventh-century Japan shows. Here Prince Genji, the hero of Japan's greatest work of literature, the eleventh-century novel *The Tale of Genji*, has built a new mansion, with separate quarters for the several wives and ladies with whom he lives – each of whom has not only her rooms, but her own garden:

49

> The new Rokujo mansion was finished in the Eighth Month and people began moving in. The southwest quarter was assigned to Akikonomu as her home away from the palace. The northeast quarter was assigned to the lady of the orange blossoms..., and the northwest quarter to the lady from Akashi. The wishes of the ladies themselves were consulted in designing the new gardens, a most pleasant arrangement of lakes and hills.
>
> The hills were high in the southeast quarter, where spring-blossoming trees and bushes were planted in large numbers. The lake was most ingeniously designed. Among the plantings in the forward parts of the garden were cinquefoil pines, maples, cherries, wisteria, *yamabuki* [*Kerria japonica*, a yellow-flowering

shrub related to the rose], and rock azalea, most of them trees and shrubs whose season was spring. Touches of autumn too were scattered through the groves.

In Akikonomu's garden the plantings, on hills left from the old garden, were chosen for rich autumn colours. Clear spring water went singing off into the distance, over rocks designed to enhance the music. There was a waterfall, and the whole expanse was like an autumn moor. Since it was now autumn, the garden was a wild profusion of autumn flowers and leaves, such as to shame the hills of Oi.

In the northeast quarter there was a cool natural spring and the plans had the summer sun in mind. In the forward parts of the garden the wind through thickets of Chinese bamboo would be cool in the summer, and the trees were deep and mysterious as mountain groves. There... were oranges to remind the lady of days long gone. There were wild carnations and roses and gentians [*katani*, referent not certain] and a few spring and autumn flowers as well... Since the Fifth Month would be its liveliest time, there were irises along the lake...

And finally the northwest quarter: beyond artificial hillocks to the north were rows of warehouses, screened off by pines which would be beautiful in new falls of snow. The chrysanthemum hedge would bloom in the morning frosts of early winter, when also a grove of 'mother oaks' [*hahaso*, thought to cover several

50

Iris

varieties of oak][6] would display its best hues. And in among the deep groves were mountain trees which one would have been hard put to identify...

Murasaki's spring garden was out of its season but very beautiful all the same...[7]

In spite of the thousand years between us, and the enormous legacy of cultural differences between any of us and the courtiers of early eleventh-century Japan, any modern gardener finds much of this passage familiar: the need to consider placement of new plants in the garden, for instance, since southern and northern exposures receive different amounts of sunlight, and eastern and western ones different amounts of wind; the desire to screen off utility buildings like Genji's 'warehouses' and our sheds and garages; a love of water features such as ponds and waterfalls; the recognition that certain plants will hold special associations for different individuals, and that plants have a capacity to bring up the past; and a fascination with wild plants and with seasonal changes of colour.

Still, this passage is somehow 'distinctively Japanese' in several respects: the sense it conveys of intimate interaction with the environment, the virtual elimination of a sense of a fundamental dichotomy between human beings and nature, the way it focuses on the changes of seasons, all of which are in evidence on virtually every page of the novel. This novel went on to influence the next thousand years of Japanese culture, but it also reflected an intimacy with nature that was already present. The keen appreciation of seasonal change, for instance, appears in the earliest literary evidence, the poems of a poetry anthology called the *Manyoshu*. Nature was interesting not only for the major seasons, winter, spring, summer, fall, but also for times of transition from season to season (hence the love of plum blossoms, which appear at the very end of winter), and for shorter, more specific times of particular flowers' blooming, such as the irises of the Fifth Month.[8] Summer is not thought of as a single season, but as a series of transitions from irises and hollyhocks (each of which traditionally had their festivals) through lotuses and waterlilies (Fig. 4) through the coming of the crickets and locusts to the early autumn grasses and flowers. This photograph of the pond in the Japanese Garden of the Denver Botanic Garden could illustrate the Lady of the Orange Blossom's garden in the northeast quarter from *The Tale of Genji*, for its irises at the edge show a particular moment of summer. Equally distinctive is the Japanese focus on very short-lived flowers like chrysanthemum and cherry blossom, which draw attention to transience – a basic principle of Buddhist philosophy. Although in general Buddhists recognise the transience of life as a source of sorrow and pain for humanity, Japanese Buddhists have focused its peculiar beauty and made it into an advantage. The cherry blossom is treasured *because* it is short-lived; the chrysanthemum is prized most at the moment when it begins to die. The literature reveals not just enjoyment of the beauty of cherry blossoms, and a valuing of their beauty all the more for its brevity, but something else: a way of perceiving the world, and of grasping its events in terms provided by nature and the garden. An eleventh-century diarist records time by reference to the cherry blossoms: a friend who is leaving promises to return when the cherries bloom the next year. Here the flowering marks the passage of time, but also a quality of time, for the friend is remembered at the next cherry-blossom season with a particular poignance, and for that diarist (the author of *As I Crossed a Bridge of Dreams*) the cherry blossoms retain throughout her life the memory of her friend who had moved away. This way of using cherry blossoms to mark the passage of time, the association of cherry blossoms with friendship and with particular qualities of memory and a particular quality of awareness of temporality, persists in twentieth-century life, too: it can be seen in Jun'ichiro Tanizaki's novel *The Makioka Sisters* and the several movies that have been made of it.[9]

I have referred above to the flat-topped series of rocks in the upper left of Fig. 3 as a 'bridge'. Its flat surfaces and solid stability invite our weight; to see, in this case, is to imagine what it is to walk there. It would be a unique experience, as walking in most Japanese gardens is. It would establish for us its own rhythm, its own speed, which become our rhythm, our speed. To walk in a Japanese garden is to participate in the rhythms of that particular work of art. We are not voyeurs, nor audience, but essential components of the work itself. We can be seen, but our participation is not primarily visual, but rhythmic. And it is kinaesthetic as well. For the rocks have a particular feel beneath our feet, which is not merely haptic, textural, but affects our balance. Our weight comes down upon our feet differentially depending upon the idiosyncrasies of the individual surfaces.

We become more aware of the placement of our bodies in space, on the surface of the stones, of the earth.

We become more aware of the idiosyncrasies, of the specialness, of the 'this-ness', of this moment.

This is one form of Buddhist mindfulness – the immersion in the present moment, ignoring past and future. It is the second form of specifically Buddhist time in this garden. It has brought us to this mindfulness, this Buddhist garden.

In the particular moment during which this photograph was taken the heat was sweltering. The image gives us some clues: the trees are in the full leaf of summer, their sharp shadows in the bottom of the stream bed conveying an idea of the brightness of the midday midsummer sun. Kikoku-tei, like most of the gardens in Kyoto, and indeed in Japan, which has extremely hot and humid summers, was surely designed as much to give relief from the heat as for visual pleasure.[10] The tactile pleasure and organic relief it gives, as you walk in and out of the shadows, is extraordinary. The slow sound of the water, called up by the photograph, is also cooling.

And so this picture, like the experience in the garden itself, places the viewer also in relation to the diurnal and seasonal cycles, that is, with respect to the interrelations of the earth, the sun, the moon, the stars.

One of the most famous of Japanese gardens, Katsura Detached Imperial Villa in Kyoto, is renowned for night views, especially its Moon-Viewing Platform. Built ca. 1630, it was inspired by *The Tale of Genji* of six hundred years earlier. In the novel, Genji and his friends and lovers often gather to look at the moon, discuss the beauties of the season, and compose poetry. In the garden based on the novel, guests can see the

5 Teahouse in a garden forest. Saiho-ji Temple, Kyoto. Reconstructed ca. 1339 under the direction of Muso Kokushi. (Photograph Mara Miller)

moon as they are led along the verandah; they expect, of course, to see the moon reflected in the pond lying at the edge of the verandah. But when they reach the edge, surprise! – there is no view of the moon. The verandah and pond have been arranged specifically to thwart the literary expectations of the visitor, to provide not a predictable experience, but an utterly fresh one. The literary and historical past permeates the entire setting and the event; it is dependent upon a particular time of day, or rather, night, and of the month, since this would only be done with a full moon. One is brought up short, moreover, against one's own preconceptions about the experience – and cradled in the forethought of the designer and host, who has anticipated one's expectations in this subtle and delightful way. Finally, can one imagine going through this without becoming aware of previous guests who have also had this experience (of not having the expected experience)? The layers of temporal awareness become a kind of cushion against so many kinds of loneliness and anxiety....

Yet another way of structuring temporality is achieved by the tea garden, such as the one at Saihoji Temple (Fig. 5), a variant of the stroll garden. Originally developed during the early modern period (late sixteenth century) for the tea ceremony, the tea garden is a space in which the guests spend some time and through which they walk before entering the tea hut, where they join the host to drink tea. Every tea garden is unique, but the one pictured, at Saihoji, is particularly unusual in being situated within a specially created forest.

Most gardens (worldwide, and regardless of style), like many other works of art, are designed to be complete and in a sense 'self-sufficient' experiences in and of themselves; they have what the Polish philosopher Stefan Morawski calls the 'relative autonomy of art'.[11] They sweep us up into their own world – like fiction, like the movies, like painting. Now tea gardens do, like all these other examples, take our attention completely; they create their own world into which we enter, however temporarily. But they have a distinctive mode of their own: they are designed to effect a transition – physical, mental, emotional – between one part of the real world, namely our everyday lives, and another, the world of the tea ceremony, which is both actual and virtual, both reality and a work of art that functions by its own rules.

53

In addition to the forms discussed above, tea gardens set up two specific forms of temporality, both functions of their transitional character. First, we enter them not figuratively, as is the case with so many of the other arts, but literally; each is of a given length, and they are intended to be walked through, from beginning to end and at a certain pace. This pace cannot be fast, because the stones are nearly always unevenly spaced and with irregular surfaces, so that attention must be paid. But one does not dawdle, either, and there are no seats along the way to spend half an hour in reverie. At the end of the path at the teahouse, there is a place to sit, from which the garden can, of course, be seen; once the guests arrive, the host may regulate how long they spend there. But the timing of the walk itself has certain parameters, not too fast, not too leisurely.

The second aspect of this is that the time taken along the tea garden path is a time of transition from one world to another, which has its own set of rules. The mind should be free of the anxieties, angers, resentments, worries, that accompany life

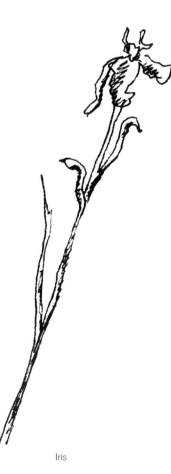

Iris

outside the tea ceremony – life on the subway or highway one must take to arrive there, for instance. By setting up an environment of extreme simplicity and great natural beauty – and by arranging stepping stones of such a kind and in such a way that they demand our attention – the mind of the guest focuses on the present moment exclusively. It is again a form of Buddhist mindfulness, an immersion in the present (which the physicists would call 'specious' or illusory), an elimination of time's arrow, of the past, of the future. Yet this is a very different organisation of temporality than that effected by the *karesansui*, or dry rock garden developed by Zen Buddhism during the Muromachi period (the latter part of the Middle Ages), where time lies outside the familiar trichotomy of past, present and future, and the Western dichotomies: directional versus recurrent time, and human time (which is limited) versus the Absolute or infinity (which is not limited). Zen gardens often limit their materials to rocks, sand, and sometimes moss, eschewing the plants whose changes mark the seasons, days and years, and whose lives seem to mimic our own human lifespans. Yet paradoxically the effect is not to eliminate variety, but to create an unchanging canvas for a different set of changes: the sands and walls of such gardens form the perfect backdrop for shadows of the clouds and the lightplay of the sky.

While every garden is unique in its effects, gardens do in general fall into meaningful categories of style or genre – in Japan, the Zen *karesansui*, the literary stroll gardens, tea gardens, etc. – with regard to the types of effects they achieve. There are, however, a few gardens that are *sui generis*, standing utterly alone. One such is the Kinkaku-ji, or Temple of the Golden Pavilion, a small man-made forest in north-western Kyoto housing a three-storied gold-leafed pavilion perched on the edge of a large pond. Kinkaku-ji has with justification been called the most beautiful building in the world. Its unique position is reflected in its history and its role as a muse for other arts as well as its physical form, for its supreme beauty was so great, allegedly, that it became intolerable for a young monk who lived there in the aftermath of World War II and he burned it down; the story (and the transcript of his trial) inspired the eponymous novel by Yukio Mishima, subsequently made into a movie, and later inspired an opera by Philip Glass – which has itself been made into a movie. There is a kind of poetic logic to this process of grounding so transcendent a work in the mire of historical contingency and human emotion, as though its perfection can only be completed if it can indeed incorporate the most sordid and tragic events the human mind can throw at it. Yet it was, in a sense, born out of just such sordidness: the *shogun* (generalissimo or military ruler) who had it built had it leafed in gold for the usual purposes to which gold is put – a somewhat obvious and materialistic display of wealth, ostentation, vanity, a desire to out-do any competition. Those who delight in the more typically Japanese taste for the subtle, the restrained, and the natural (or seemingly natural) are prepared in advance to dislike Kinkaku-ji for its obviousness and its commonness in spite of the fact that its expense alone makes it an extreme rarity. Yet like the Buddhist symbol of the lotus, the purity and perfection of whose beauty arises from the mud of the pond bed, Kinkaku-ji surpasses its humble, even dirty, history, the materialism and the crass desire for fame and eternity and an absolute hold on reality from which it arises.

55

For Kinkaku-ji turns out to be not at all obvious, nor are its effects to be predicted without seeing it in person, as it were. For gold, in such quantities and unworked, at such vast flat expanses, turns out to be quite different than anticipated. It is not gold at all, but an interplay of varying shades of greens and golds; not a building, but the medium for the reflection of the forest; not eternal and unchanging, as we expect gold to be, but dynamic, everchanging, from moment to moment, as clouds and breeze-swayed branches obscure or reveal the sunlight; not the flat surface of its outer walls, but the projection screen for the depths of the forest's boughs, brought closer and then farther by the breezes. Not only does the building reflect the forest, but the forest takes on the golden hue of the building; it is lit not only by the sunlight but by the golden light of the pavilion. The reflection of a building on the pond upon which it is situated is an effect long admired by the Japanese – it was used at the Byodo-in in Uji during the Heian period – and it inevitably brings to mind two cherished Buddhist images: the reflection, which like a dream and indeed like our ordinary everyday 'reality' may be mistaken for true reality which is apparent only to the enlightened mind, and the metaphor of the clear and dust-free mirror, which like the ideal enlightened mind takes in the reality of its surroundings but never attempts to hold onto them. But at Kinkaku-ji not only does the pond reflect the building, the building reflects the pond, whose ripples cavort across the surface making delightful patterns upon the plain walls.

The result is a perfect interpenetration of building with environment, in which the artificial is integrated with the natural, hard wood and metal with liquid and air and light, geometric rational plan with teasing unpredictability of natural forms, reality with shadows and reflections, the seemingly eternal with the fleeting and constantly changing.

This, of course, is in the sunlight. Surely bright moonlight would have similar effects – completely different though they would be. And in the winter? This is a garden that demands to be seen in every season, at every time of day or night, under all atmospheric conditions. Photographs capture the stillness, give the impression of stability and endurance that is completely misleading, and so could not be included here. No garden has ever captured so perfectly the images of flowing time as Kinakaku-ji.

The varieties of temporality and temporal structure in Japanese gardens far exceed those that could be indicated in this brief paper. Awareness of the subtle possibilities that await us in this form, however, brings three great benefits. First, we may avoid, in building future gardens along the Japanese model, the simple amassing of typical features associated with the style, such as lanterns, pagodas, water basins, cherry trees, etc., the combination of which can prove overwhelming and can never provide the serenity of a garden organised along Japanese principles. Second, we may enjoy Japanese gardens on their own terms. Finally, we may learn to use some of the insights of Japanese culture not only in building our own gardens but in facing our lives and solving the problems of the next millennium.

Notes

1 Hubertus Tellenbach and Bin Kimura, 'The Japanese Concept of "Nature"', in I. Callicott and J. Baird, *Nature in Asian Traditions of Thought* (Albany: State University of New York Press, 1989), pp. 153–181.

2 I am thinking here of such motifs as the rocks or islands in the shapes of tortoises and cranes, Chinese symbols of longevity and therefore of good fortune, and the Taoist-inspired Islands of the Immortals, and the themes of plants favoured by Confucian scholars for their virtues – the pine, bamboo, orchid, plum.

3 I must emphasise here that there are a number of distinct genres of Japanese gardens – stroll gardens, tea gardens, scholars' gardens, monastic dry rock gardens, etc., each with its own set of principles and effects. For further references on Japanese gardens, see the list of books at the end.

4 The *grande dame* is of course the Japanese Tea Garden at Golden Gate Park in San Francisco, but recently more authentically structured Japanese gardens have been built in Atlanta, Boston, Denver, New York, San Jose, St. Louis and Vancouver, among others.

5 Doris Lessing, *Under My Skin: Volume One of My Autobiography, to 1949* (New York & London: HarperCollins Publishers, 1994), p. 109.

6 The modern Japanese and Latin equivalents were provided by the translator, not the author of the present article.

7 (Lady) Murasaki Shikibu, *The Tale of Genji*, translated by Edward G. Seidensticker (New York: Alfred A. Knopf, 1991), pp. 384–385.

8 Japan used a lunar calendar.

9 Jun'ichiro Tanizaki, *The Makioka Sisters* (New York: Alfred A. Knopf, 1957).

10 For a study of the problems inherent in trying to use photographs for the purpose of understanding gardens, see Mara Miller, *The Garden as an Art* (Albany, NY: State University of New York Press, 1993), pp. 47–50.

11 Stefan Morawski, *Inquiries into the Fundamentals of Aesthetics* (Cambridge, MA: Massachusetts Institute of Technology Press, 1974, 1978). This is in some ways comparable to Kant's notion of aesthetic disinterest and Bullough's notion of aesthetic distance. For a discussion of problems that arise when these notions are applied to gardens, see Miller, *op. cit.*, chapters 5 and 6.

Some recommended books on Japanese gardens

Brooklyn Botanical Garden. 'Japanese Gardens.' *Plants & Gardens: Brooklyn Botanical Garden Record*, 41, no. 3, Autumn 1985.

Hayakawa Masao. *The Garden Art of Japan*. Translated by Richard L. Gage. New York & Tokyo: Weatherhill/Heibonsha, 1973.

Holborn, Mark. *The Ocean in the Sand. Japan: From Landscape to Garden*. Boulder, CO: Shambhala, 1978.

Itoh Teiji. *Space and Illusion in the Japanese Garden*. New York & Tokyo: Weatherhill, 1973.

Morse, Edward S. *Japanese Homes and their Surroundings*. New York: Dover, 1961.

Newsom, Samuel. *A Thousand Years of Japanese Gardens*. Third ed. Tokyo: Tokyo News Service, Ltd., 1957.

Nitschke, Gunter. *Japanese Gardens: Right Angle and Natural Form*. Köln: Benedikt Taschen, 1993.

Ohashi Haruzo. *The Japanese Garden: Islands of Serenity*. Tokyo: Kodansha International, 1986; distributed through Harper & Row, NY.

Slawson, David A. *Secret Teachings in the Art of Japanese Gardens: Design Principles, Aesthetic Values*. Tokyo & New York: Kodansha International, 1987.

Stein, Rolf A. *The World in Miniature: Container Gardens and Dwellings in Far Eastern Religious Thought*. Stanford, CA: Stanford University Press, 1990.

Jan Woudstra

Detailing and materials of outdoor space: the Scandinavian example

During the second half of the eighteenth century William Chambers' famous thesis on oriental gardening was instrumental in spreading the Chinese influence in garden design across Europe. It brought exotic detailing and frivolity in particular to the design of buildings, but also ideas on planting design. In Scandinavia for example the oriental influence could be felt from the late eighteenth and throughout the nineteenth centuries. Chambers appears never to have visited China, and the information for his thesis derived from a mixture of second hand sources and his own ideas based on tradition. In contrast, during the twentieth century Scandinavian design was influential on the rest of the world, primarily due to visiting architects and landscape architects returning to their own countries and applying similar principles.

In 1960 the landscape architect and architect Elisabeth Beazley published what has become a standard reference work entitled *Design and Detail of the Space Between Buildings*. This book has been quoted to be 'one of the most useful and readable books on landscape construction of the period, not least because it combined landscape context with a wealth of in depth knowledge of landscape detailing'.[1] In the introduction Beazley analysed and listed the problems regarding the treatment of the space between buildings. Unfortunately her observations are still as current today as when they were written. Her main conclusions were that there was much lacking in our twentieth century efforts, but that there were some outstanding examples of good new work, 'outstanding because they are straightforward, robust, simple and well detailed' (Fig.1). Of these criteria she noted that: 'These virtues should be the rule, not the rare exception.'

She continued:

There is a strange resignation on the part of the general public, who are often oddly confused about what they like and what we can now do. Though enjoying the past tradition they do not seem to realise that a new and equally good one can, and in fact gradually is, taking its place. The present attitude towards outdoor design is one of either apathy or perverse preciousness, both of which are quite illogical. When the importance of exterior design is compared, in terms of the number of people affected, with that of the interior design of any building, this

59

Jan Woudstra
Detailing and materials of outdoor space;
the Scandinavian example

1 The twentieth century trends of design of outdoor space contrast with the early nineteenth century, which had continued within a well-established tradition. A builder or craftsman would carry out any work. He would work with local materials, know the scope of these and the constraints. In this way he would lay paving, build steps, or place gates, seats and fences wherever they were required. Since all this had to be done with local material in order to be cost effective, the scope for variation was limited, and there was a natural association of any built features with the surrounding landscape. This might be slightly different in the surroundings of stately homes, where money might be raised for special features. But even here the bulk of materials would have been local.

The introduction of trains during the nineteenth century made transport cheaper. This particularly affected stone transport and it was now possible to obtain non local materials for a reasonable cost. However, in general the distance of transport from any railway station to the site was limited. Hence for example it is possible in London to predict the type of stone within a certain radius of each railway station. Besides a wider availability of natural materials, increased industrialisation also meant that additional manmade materials became more widely available.

Example of an alleyway in Stockholm.
(Drawing by Laurence Pattacini)

attitude is even stranger. Consider the millions who 'know' and genuinely admire Oxford but who have never been inside a college (meaning indoors), or the hundreds who walk down some street or across a square daily on the way to work, without ever entering the houses that surround them. Extraordinary care may be lavished (and quite rightly) on the design of the inside spaces themselves and the colours and textures and the durability of their materials. But the outdoor spaces tend to be treated either as a sort of no-man's-land where economy is the key-note, or as somewhere not good enough in itself to be designed on the same principles as the rest – a space to be prettied in the name of amenity.

That is one side of the picture; the other, though equally dour, is the bleak 'serviceable' approach which takes the standard object or a standard dimension and uses them with utter inflexibility. The layout of most council estates was once a good example of this; in many cases it still is...[2]

From these remarks it is clear that in the ensuing years little has been learned, since many of the mistakes she observed are still being made. Following her critical introduction Beazley proceeded with chapters on paved surfaces, trim of paved surfaces, walls and fences, and a final chapter about planning. Examples for discussion are mainly from England and quite a number from abroad, from Scandinavia, the Netherlands and one or two from the United States. Remarkably Beazley's monograph remained the only British book in print dealing with landscape detailing for almost thirty years.[3] Until fairly recently it had only been partially replaced by books incorporating landscape detail, such as Cliff Tandy's *Handbook of Urban Design* (1970), or others which brought the discussion down to a garden scale, such as John Brookes' *Room Outside* (1969) and Peter Shepheard's *Gardens* (1969). The latter two also draw their examples from a wide range of foreign gardens, both historic and contemporary. Of all the countries included these authors most admired the Swedish and Danish approach to design and detailing.

This long tradition of quality detailing is illustrated by a paper that was presented in 1937 by Sven A. Hermelin, the president of the Swedish Association of Garden Architects, at the first International Congress of Garden Architects, held in Paris. A lengthy passage of this was quoted in Christopher Tunnard's *Gardens in the Modern Landscape* (1938), which expressed both contemporary philosophy and aesthetic principles of the modern practice with information on detail and may therefore be worthwhile quoting in full:

The utilitarian style has strongly influenced the construction of domestic buildings; they are often asymmetrically planned, have large windows exposed to the sun, and, if possible, are sufficiently free from screening to permit of distant views.

Ordinarily, the garden is planned in such a way as to form a direct relationship with the house, access from one to the other being everywhere facilitated. The garden thus becomes a part of the dwelling. Its arrangement is decided more for the activities of the people – especially of children – than for flowers. It allows for seats and benches resting on paved areas which relate to the

2 A middle-rise housing scheme in Uppsala (Sommarro development, Lindbergsgatan) designed by landscape architect Ulla Bodorff in 1946 represents the archetypal Swedish modernist housing. Buildings are set in undulating landscapes with rocky outcrops; both vegetation and natural features have been carefully preserved. Although the ideology has now changed many of these contemporary housing schemes are as appropriate today as when they were first designed.
(Drawing by Laurence Pattacini)

house, and lawns as extensive as possible, though not always mown. Paths and walks are reduced to the minimum and often consist only of stepping stones between which grass or creeping plants are allowed to grow, thus conserving a homogeneity between the units of the plan. Pools for the children are much appreciated and, when possible, they are made deep enough to allow for bathing. In general, trees are not numerous in these gardens; most people prefer to have flowering shrubs. When herbaceous plants are used they have a definite part of the plan devoted to their culture, and need not, as formerly, be confined to the conventional flowerbed. There is little room in gardens now for the bedding plants which for so many years have enjoyed such a wide vogue.

The utilitarian style of building has exercised a profound influence on gardens, which it appears to be ridding of conscious symmetrical planning. The arrangement of gardens is freer and more mobile than formerly. One does not look for axial construction and the monumental planning of former styles, which could never be prevented from looking severe, above all when close to the house, the hard lines of which can be softened by subtle plant arrangements. One strives to create a contrast between the disciplined outlines of terrace walls, paved spaces, pools, etc., and a free and luxuriant vegetation designed to produce a happy decorative effect and to give the impression that it is the work of nature or of chance. It is pleasant to leave an existing gnarled pine in a paved courtyard the aspect of which is otherwise strictly architectural, or to arrange matters so that trees with heads of interesting shapes appear to detach themselves from the smooth walls of the house, their rigidity being softened by the foliage. It is admissible that between the paving stones of courtyard space should be left for isolated plants to give the impression that they have grown there spontaneously.[4]

Tunnard interpreted this quotation as evidence 'of the break with tradition which has taken place in Swedish gardens since the advent of a rational architecture in the Scandinavian countries'. Although Tunnard approved of the discarding of 'axial and symmetrical planning, ostentatious decoration', he criticised what he considered 'the romantic conception of nature', warning that 'nature worship' has, in the past, proved 'dangerously stultifying to the free development of garden design'. Nevertheless his own design for the architect Serge Chermayeff's house near Halland displayed exactly these criteria with a strong Swedish flavour, which he said he disliked. This illustrates how influential the Swedish style had become.

Swedish design evoked images of buildings set in undulating rocky landscapes with a careful sensitive treatment, preserved vegetation and natural features. This was noted by Elisabeth Beazley who wrote:

They also showed a genius for the siting of buildings and the design of the landscape setting. They showed how splendid modern architecture could look in just the sort of landscape town-dwelling Englishmen most like: wild nature and left wild by design with birch and pine among outcropping rock, and short grass running down to lakes or rivers or inlets of the sea. Even where the natural landscape was less attractive, a genius was shown for making the best of it in the least pretentious manner...[5] (Fig. 2)

It proved the closeness of the Swedes to nature. This was sometimes hard to understand by British architects of whom the following discussion was recorded about the Stockholm town hall designed by Ragnar Östberg. In 1949 a group of well-known architects, discussing international influences in architecture, addressed the issue of the Virginia creeper which had been planted against the facade of the inner courtyard. G. Grey Wornum noted: 'Now the creeper he planted in the big courtyard obliterates it a great deal.' F.R. Yerbury responded: 'Everyone asked Östberg why he wanted to hide the wonderful brickwork, and he always answered: "Ivy" (actually it's virginia creeper) "is so pretty".' J.M. Richards, who was in sympathy with climbers, replied: 'The use of plants and creepers in modern buildings is one of the things we are still learning from

Scandinavia; we may be getting tired of some of the fashions imported from there, but not this one.' Hugh Casson, avoiding a debate between Wornum and Richards on the subject, but being in sympathy with the former, noted: 'In Scandinavia, creepers seem to be used more inside than outside. Every window is so strung with ivy you can hardly see out of it.' This debate clearly shows the contemporary concern of British architects to be able to fully express the architectural shape unobscured by vegetation.[6]

Some of the most inspiring detailing was produced by the Stockholm Parks Department, which under the directorship of Holger Blom became world renowned for the creation of quality public space, which in its creation had made the best use of the existing natural features. At the same time they showed how landscape architecture was able to 'give a good setting for every activity of life'.[7] To assist him with the design work Blom employed several leading landscape architects, including Sven A. Hermelin, Ulla Bodorff and Walter Bauer, of this group; however, Erik Glemme has been most closely identified as the designer who was responsible for an extensive output.[8] These designers contributed to beautiful spaces, each planned entirely on its own merit. They also designed temporary structures in the parks to serve as news and ice cream stands, cafés, etc. In the design for kiosks Eric L. Bird saw 'touches of frivolous gaiety' in the design of a kiosk and a 'little sentimentality' in the design of a bird table. Bird continued to note that there was no '"be-modern-and-like-it" attitude, nor any outworn classic conceptions…'[9] Buildings in parks are features that easily become out of date and therefore are regularly replaced; in order to pre-empt this they were light temporary structures, and the temporary nature was emphasised by the materials and by the fact that they were demountable.

A similar approach was adhered to in the design of lighting in parks and gardens. Instead of the customary lampposts more intimate lighting at low level was introduced, in flower and mushroom shapes. These interestingly shaped types of lighting were photographed at the café at Norr Mälerstrand, and were likewise introduced to Britain at the Festival Gardens.[10] Garden furniture was a standard inclusion in garden design in the early twentieth century, with both architects and landscape architects supplying models for wooden chairs and benches.[11] In Stockholm the Parks Department produced a range of furniture, including metal wire chairs and tables for outdoor seating areas.

The Stockholm Parks Department was well geared towards appropriation of open space, and particularly noted for the layout of temporary open spaces, by means of what the landscape architect Frank Clark referred to as 'Holger Blom's famous portable gardens – those precast concrete circular plant containers…'[12] Soon after the Second World War these planters were noticed by foreign delegations and tested in towns in other countries, where they became regular features in the urban landscape. For example the first planters in the Netherlands were produced from a drawing provided by Blom in 1947, and were positioned in The Hague in 1948.[13] A few years later in London they featured at the Festival of Britain at the South Bank Exhibition in 1951.[14] These and similar planters became features in most western cities, and it is remarkable how these often fairly coarse designs remained popular for such a long period.

Another popular planter was based on the famous wooden bowls designed as

3 Wooden bowls in the Tivoli gardens (top). These bowls were designed as a prototype for a concrete bowl, and indeed during the sixties and seventies they might be found everywhere. However it is ironical that the earlier wooden model has survived many of the later concrete copies.

Cast concrete copies in Bournemouth of the wooden Tivoli bowl (bottom). This example clearly shows the erosion of the finer detail of the original, with a rounded instead of a curved rim. Their position alongside an elevated road makes them appear like a poor apology for an unsympathetic setting, which is emphasised by the fact that they remain without plants, even though Bournemouth prides itself on being a Floral winner.
(Drawing by Laurence Pattacini)

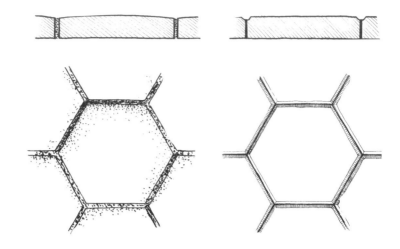

4 The application of diagonal walks coincided with the use of hexagonal paving materials. Here an original concrete tile at the Bellahøj development in Copenhagen, used by the landscape architect C.Th. Sørensen. The tile itself is cambered, with rounded edges, and has a very attractive slightly course texture (left). The modern replacement tiles (also used at Bellahøj) lack any of these qualities, and have a hard, dull appearance instead (right). Whilst produced at the same size and materials, the overall appearance is severly affected, showing the importance of profile and texture.
(Drawing by Laurence Pattacini)

small bubbling fountains in Tivoli Gardens in Copenhagen. They were designed by the landscape architect G.N. Brandt (and not C.Th. Sørensen as is sometimes suggested) in 1943. The idea for the design was based on an example of a parterre with small fountains he saw whilst on a visit to the 1927 Garden exhibition in Liegnitz in the former Silesia. During this trip he also visited the Fürstenstein estate of the Von Pless family, where such a parterre had been created by the architect Von Walcher just before the First World War. Brandt's initial idea had been to copy these bowls in concrete and to sink them in the ground, so that the surrounding plants would be reflected in the water. However, wartime restrictions on the use of cement left no option but to produce them in wood, with the final design achieved in co-operation with the architect Poul Henningsen. The bowls were constructed using old methods of barrel construction with two galvanised steel metal straps.[15] Despite being a prototype for a concrete bowl the originals have remained there as wooden bowls until today. During the sixties and seventies these large dish-shaped bowls could be found reproduced as planters in concrete or asbestos in virtually every major town in the western world[16] (Fig. 3).

The special qualities of Swedish planting design were also being recognised; whilst H.F. Clark had noted that 'The free planting of flowers and shrubs follows the teachings of our own William Robinson so closely that it must be more than a mere coincidence'.[17] George Chadwick described it in a similar fashion and provided the evidence: 'the use of giant Petasites and rhubarbs for foliage effect, the naturalising of tulips in the long grass in Humlegarden, the cow parsley and meadow plants or the Astilbe and Heracleum and

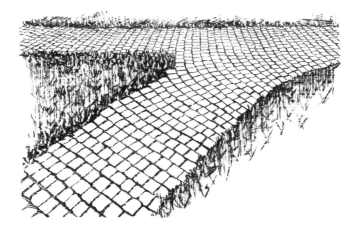

5 Granite setts are one of the favourite paving materials throughout Scandinavia. They are used with great effect in town centres, and in landscape schemes where a certain quality is required. Here an example of a path in the Mariebjerg cemetery, Gentofte near Copenhagen by G.N. Brandt (1926–1936). It shows the effective and beautiful manner in which this material is applied and a path junction has been resolved. This material is simply laid on a bed of compacted sand, without use of cement or hardcore as is common in Britain, and without use of edging or drainage. These have become superfluous by laying the path with a slight camber with the edges at the same level of the grass. (Drawing by Laurence Pattacini)

other streamside plants in Tegnerlunden, the waterside planting along Norr Mälarstrand'.[18] Brenda Colvin however felt that the Germans 'had an extremely sound grasp on the ecological aspect of landscape architecture' and that 'German landscape teaching had had a marked influence on the continent'.[19] Whatever the case Swedish planting design was quoted as exemplary in a discussion between Sheila Haywood and Kenneth Booth on the subject.[20]

The Scandinavian example was not just restricted to planting design, or landscape features, but also included ideas on paving. The main purpose of paving is to provide a dry hard surface to walk on comfortably. Sylvia Crowe rightly observed that additionally a floor pattern might be used as a unifying background, as shown with Swedish examples, and also that it might at times be directional. This was explained as follows: 'A path leading with certainty to one point can be emphasised by the direction of the coursing or by a change of material, such as a flagged path leading across an area of setts or cobbles.'[21] The latter is frequently seen as a quality of Danish design (Fig. 5).

One of the most famous examples of a unifying or organisational type of paving is that at Vällingby, near Stockholm, designed by the Parks Department supervised by Holger Blom (Fig. 6). The English architect Frederick Gibberd described this in his book on urban design:

The floor design is one of the most interesting in Europe. Formed almost entirely of granite sets in blue, grey and dark red, it is in a wide circular pattern which, in

6 The Stockholm Parks Department became world renowned for its leader (Holger Blom), its policies, provisions and quality of design. One of its examplary inner city parks was Tegnerlunden, which was discussed and published abroad (see for example Peter Shepheard, *Modern Gardens*, 1953, pp. 124,125). Now after more than fifty years a progression of gradual modifications have changed the original character; gravel walks have been tarmacked; informal waterfalls have been spoiled by excess of concrete and now lie dry. Sweden has unfortunately shared an international lack of political interest in funding public parks during the 1980s and '90s, ultimately resulting in the dismantling of the Parks Department as a separate organisation. However, the parks survive, and with a greater interest previous mistakes can easily be repaired.

(Photograph 1997; compare this with a similar picture in Shepheard's book)

7 Erik Glemme was the star designer
of the Stockholm Parks Department;
he liked experimenting with forms and
shapes. Many of his paving designs
were innovative and remain unique in
the way he was artistic, yet responded
to the site, and his artistry never
became domineering. This example for
the town centre at Årsta shows the
overall simplicity of his design.
(Drawing by Erik Glemme for kv
Grängen, 1949)

places, embraces the carriageways and the circular fountains in the main square.
Existing trees are incorporated in the design, and the detail design, such as
fountains, seats and lamp standards, is excellent.[22]

Whilst some examples of directional paving can be found in Sweden (Fig. 7), it was
Denmark that became exemplary for this type of treatment. In design terms this meant
the application of diagonal walks, and coincided with the use of hexagonal paving
materials (Fig. 4). Danish influence in the immediate post-war years was significant in
the Netherlands, where several designers admitted being influenced by Danish examples.
Designers such as Wim Boer and Mien Ruys used diagonal walks in their designs, but
later rejected Danish influence as being too formal.[23]

69

Denmark and Sweden managed to achieve and retain their reputation for
children's playgrounds from the wartime to well into the 1970s. In the building boom of
the 1920s in Denmark many blocks of flats were built, and due to new ways of financing
new housing it was possible to set aside open space. For the first time landscape
architects were employed for the landscape work, which included the design of
playgrounds.[24] One of the early landscape architects involved was C.Th. Sørensen, who
saw that the aim of these facilities was to provide children in towns with the same
opportunities for creative play as those in the country. Returning to observe the use of
the playgrounds he designed, Sørensen was taken aback by the fact that they remained
unused, whilst the adjoining building sites were used for play. This is the reason why
Sørensen, writing in his 1931 *Parkpolitik i Sogn og Købstad* (Park policy in parish and

8 The Stockholm Parks Department never became specifically known for its playing facilities, but this was just considered to be part of its policies and field of work. In fact many good custom-built pieces of play equipment, which were also sculptural, were positioned in the new housing developments. Here just such an example, which is functional and has a pleasant form, designed by Erik Glemme. (Drawing for kv Grängen, Årsta, 1949)

town), suggested the establishment of so-called 'skrammellegepladser' (waste material playgrounds), where children would be able to play with old cars, boxes, and timber[25] (Fig. 9).

It was not until 1943 that the idea was picked up by the architect Dan Fink and the first waste material playground was established in Emdrup, with John Bertelsen as a play leader. Supervision was to be kept to a minimum, encouraging each child's individual potential. The Emdrup playground became an immediate success, and after the German occupation foreigners flocked to see what had been created. The idea was exported and reinterpreted as the Robinson playgrounds (after Robinson Crusoe) in Switzerland, and adventure playgrounds in Great Britain.[26]

Lady Allen of Hurtwood had visited Sørensen in 1945; inspired and enthused she returned to England to spend much of her working life fighting for playgrounds. Her writings included *Design for Play* (1962), *Playparks* (3rd edn 1964), *New Playgrounds* (1964), *Adventure Playgrounds* (n.d.), and the seminal *Planning for Play* (1968). For some time she was vice-president of the International Playgrounds Association, of which Sørensen was the founding chairman from 1961 to 1964. One of the playgrounds she instigated on the Danish model was the Notting Hill Adventure Playground in 1966. It was once considered to be destined to become a classic of the type, but the cuts in local government spending have generally meant that playgrounds have not been maintained.[27]

Danish adventure playgrounds are generally surrounded by earth mounding and extensive planting, not only for aesthetic and microclimatic considerations, but also to prevent 'the adult world from penetrating too much' and thus to provide a sheltered play

9 Immediately after the war Denmark received a worldwide reputation for its adventure playgrounds, which had been initiated by the landscape architect C.Th. Sørensen. These showed a real concern for and understanding of children's needs. In Sweden the younger generation was also well catered for with provisions made in separate playgrounds, with Arvid Bengtsson as the international champion. Child's play has lately become more integrated, and minimum provision is found everywhere. This example of a rather tense reclining female figure in Odense, which doubles both as a piece of public art and as a slide, is an example of how this is done. Elsewhere, such as in Britain, this would most likely be perceived as shocking, particularly if the Scandinavian dictum 'playing is learning' is taken literally. (Photograph 1997)

10 Globalisation has also arrived to those corners once considered as bastions of good design. Here the pavilion at Norr Mälerstrand, Stockholm, designed by Erik Glemme. In the foreground a full set of the original 1930s metal wire chairs, with to the immediate left picnic park benches dating from the 1970s 'recreation era'. More obtrusive are the plastic garden chairs, which dominate the scene by their bulk and brightness. (Photograph 1997)

72

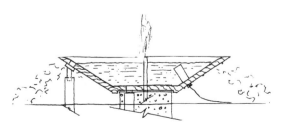

11 The presumed form of the Tivoli bowl as published on a drawing in Alan Blanc's book *Landscape Construction and Detailing*, 1996 (top), and a survey of the actual construction by the landscape architect Vibeke Fenger in 1997. It shows that Blanc knew the bowls only from photographs. (Redrawn by Laurence Pattacini)

environment. Sørensen also encouraged the keeping of animals on these playgrounds, but these can only be seen in Danish examples.

In Sweden it was Arvid Bengtsson, the head of the parks department, first in Helsingborg and later in Göteborg, who managed to spread the word and provide exciting play equipment (Fig. 8). One observer, guided around Göteborg by Bengtsson, noted that

> The Swedes do not have any difficulty with an obvious fact – our children will be our successors in a remarkably short time. In their first years they are being formed into either dignified successors or into annoying and frustrated boys and girls, with some time later severe objections against us, the older generation, who have the strings in their hands. Outside the education within the family the playing of children in groups is particularly educational, because 'playing is learning', thus maintain psychologists.[28]

Scandinavia led a movement away from mechanically perfectionised equipment into play which required more fantasy and personal creativity, encouraging more 'natural' play. This meant also that play equipment was created with a 'childlike simplicity and originality'. This particularly included natural materials such as de-barked trees for climbing on and wooden building blocks.[29] Bengtsson had observed children in towns and noted the reduction of playspace due to a doubling of cars after the war by the end of the 1950s. Cars had taken playspace for parking. This and the above philosophy formed the main arguments by which he managed to carry through an extensive programme of building playgrounds in Helsingborg, supported of course by public opinion. This included a variety of playgrounds, including the adventure playgrounds based on the Danish model.[30]

Despite the inspirational examples with regard to good detailing, Sweden lost its lead in the early 1960s and Denmark slightly later, not due to the quality of its detailing, but because its architecture was considered outdated. All over Europe the rise of popular gardening on television and in magazines, as well as gardens centres, has meant a certain globalisation-universalisation of detailing and materials. The availability of prefabricated materials has meant an increasingly uniform appearance of gardens throughout western Europe. Whether they are in urban or rural areas, on rocky ground or a low clay soil, they all contain the same paving material, the same lighting and the same furniture. One of the best examples of this globalisation is the plastic garden chairs, now commonly found in every corner of Europe, including the corners which were once considered the bastions of good design (Fig. 10).

Unlike the 1940s, when much of the design work was carried out by landscape architects and architects, now this is often done by building contractors. It is not unusual for engineers to determine the detailing in the townscape, guided by economists and approval from planners, none of whom have followed courses in design. Due to this situation, the competitive stance between architects and landscape architects for their share in design of outdoor space is even more ironic. At least there is a common idea about shape and form, and perhaps it is now time for both professions to acknowledge

Jan Woudstra
Detailing and materials of outdoor space;
the Scandinavian example

each other's strength, and work together towards a better and more beautiful environment based on the best examples such as that of Sweden and Denmark. Indeed the continuing popularity of this tradition can be proven by the inclusion of Brandt's Tivoli bowl in Alan Blanc's recent publication on landscape detailing. In this Blanc took a little bit of artist's licence with regard to the exact construction of the original bowl (which he mistakenly attributed to Sørensen). In fact the bowls consists of wooden slats held together by steel straps with an external thin copper dish shell. Included in the copper shell are a small pump and lighting, producing a delightful effect. It is therefore likely that Blanc had not seen these bowls but derived the information from secondary sources. The exact design was unknown; all that remained of the original was the approximate form. It shows that similar to the oriental influence during the eighteenth and nineteenth centuries, the Scandinavian example has reached a new symbolic or legendary meaning in the late twentieth century[31] (Fig.11).

1 Alan Blanc, *Landscape Construction and Detailing*, London: B.T. Batsford, 1996, p. vii.

2 Elisabeth Beazley, *Design and Detail of the Space Between Buildings*, London: The Architectural Press, 1960, pp. 11–12.

3 Beazley's book was republished in 1990 as *Beazley's Design and Detail of the Space Between Buildings*, substantially expanded by Angi and Alan Pinder; the new edition does however lack many of the original inspiring photographs which helped to explain the issues.

4 Christopher Tunnard, *Gardens in the Modern Landscape*, London: The Architectural Press, 1938, pp. 77,78.

5 E. Beazley, *Designed to Live In*, London: George Allen & Unwin, 1962, p. 104.

6 F.R. Yerbury *et al.* 'Round the table; round the world', *The Architect's Journal*, 109 (1949), pp. 70–82.

7 'International Federation of Landscape Architects', *Journal of the Institute of Landscape Architects*, No. 25 (1952), p. 14.

8 For a fuller account see: T. Andersson, 'Erik Glemme and the Stockholm Park System', in M.Treib, *Modern Landscape Architecture; A Critical Review*, Cambridge, Mass. and London: The MIT Press, 1992, pp. 114–133.

9 E.L. Bird, 'Swedish architecture in 1946. Part III: Stockholm's Parks and Gardens', *Journal of the Royal Institute of British Architects*, 54 (1947), pp. 410–415.

10 Ibid. This type of lighting never took off greatly in Britain, where budgets for public space have been progressively reduced since the Second World War, although Scandinavian types were adopted at the Span developments. In Germany such lighting has gained popularity in both public parks and gardens, and became well known abroad through post-war garden shows.

11 With the increase of the garden for leisure purposes during the 1930s the demand for furniture increased. Firms especially dedicated to the purpose marketed garden furniture. Well-designed furniture could now be obtained from shops. Heals in London, for example, marketed furniture designed by Christopher Nicholson; the designer Sybil Colefax also designed a range of garden furniture (see Geoffrey Jellicoe, *Garden Decoration and Ornament for Smaller Houses*, London: Country Life, 1936, pp. 82–83).

12 H.F. Clark, 'Space between buildings; the landscaping of Stockholm's parks', *The Architectural Review*, 102 (1947), pp. 189–198.

13 W.F. Koppeschaar, 'Bloemurnen; een Zweeds idee', *De boomkweekerij*, 2 (1946/7), p. 199; J. Muntjewerf, W. van Eijkern, 'Bloembakken', *Beplantingen en Boomkwekerij*, 23 (1967), pp. 75–79.

14 Gordon Russell, 'The design of garden accessories', *Journal of the Institute of Landscape Architects*, March 1954, pp. 2–4.

15 G.N. Brandt, 'Tivolis Springvandterrasse', *Havekunst*, 24 (1943), pp. 69–76.

16 The bowls were included for example in: Sylvia Crowe, *Garden Design*, London: Country Life, 1958, p. 124v.; K. Hoffmann, *Garten und Haus*, Stuttgart: Julius Hoffmann Verlag, 1956, p. 146.

17 *The Architectural Review*, 102 (1947), p. 190.

75

Jan Woudstra
Detailing and materials of outdoor space;
the Scandinavian example

18 G.F. Chadwick, *The Park and the Town*, London: The Architectural Press, 1966, p. 310.

19 *Journal of the Institute of Landscape Architects*, No. 25 (1952), p. 12.

20 S. Haywood, K. Booth, 'Planting design', *Journal of the Institute of Landscape Architects*, 29 (1954), p. 6.

21 Sylvia Crowe, *Garden Design*, London: Country Life, 1958, p. 158.

22 Frederick Gibberd, *Town Design*, London: The Architectural Press, 1959, p. 198.

23 Bonica Zijlstra, *Mien Ruys een Leven als Tuinarchitect*, Amsterdam: Nederlandse Tuinenstichting, 1990, pp. 67–68.

24 Lady Allen of Hurtwood, *Planning for Play*, London: Thames & Hudson, 1968, p. 9.

25 C.Th. Sørensen, *Parkpolitik i Sogn og Købstad*, Copenhagen: Nordisk Forlag, 1931, p. 54.

26 Gerda Gollwitzer, *Kinderspielplätze*, Munich: Georg D. W. Callwey, 1957, pp. 78–79.

27 Arvid Bengtsson, *Environmental Planning for Children's Play*, London: Crosby Lockwood Staples, 1970, p. 163.

28 D. Bouman, 'Zweeds groen', *Groen*, 26 (1970), pp. 190–197.

29 See for example V[an] A[lff], 'Kinderspeelplaatsen in Scandinavië', *Bouw*, 6 (1951), pp. 188–189.

30 See L.H. Blom, 'Kinderspeelplaatsen in Helsingborg (Sverige)', *De Boomkwekerij*, 15 (1959), pp. 206–207; 211–212.

31 Alan Blanc, *Landscape Construction and Detailing*, London: B.T. Batsford, 1996, p. 175.

Jacques Leenhardt

Playing with artifice:
Roberto Burle Marx's
gardens

It is tempting to talk about Burle Marx by starting with what appears to be the most extraneous aspect of his life: Brazil. Burle Marx indeed is from Brazil, in a number of ways. He is from a country whose name derives from *Haemoatoxylum braziletto*, a tree with wood the colour of embers that has been prized since early antiquity, and that Europe used to import from Asia in the Middle Ages. The Portuguese were delighted to find abundant supplies of it when they landed on the coasts of South America. The life of Burle Marx, like that of Brazil, has been closely bound up with wood and the forest and with plants such as coffee and hevea which made and broke the country's social and economic destiny, as well as with nature and its lushness.

And yet there was nothing automatic about Burle Marx's encounter with his own country and its extraordinary flora. When he came into the world in 1909, Roberto Burle Marx was born into a country that was still scarred by a long period of cultural dependence. At that time, everything that was beautiful or good came from Europe: manners, taste and style. If people wanted to maintain their position in Rio de Janeiro or São Paolo society, they had to denigrate the products of the land in which they lived. It did not occur to anybody that native plants could be used for decorating the gardens of the aristocracy, even though, in 1908, dom João VI, driven away from Portugal by the arrival of Napoleon, had planted the magnificent Botanical Garden in Rio de Janeiro which still today is the pride of the Cariocas – the inhabitants of that city. Botanical science may well have been interested in native plants, but the floral decoration of private and public gardens comprised only roses, carnations and gladioli imported from Europe. It took other stimuli than those emanating from local fashionable society for Burle Marx to discover the infinitely varied vegetation of the different regions of Brazil.

Born in São Paolo of a recently arrived German immigrant father and a mother whose family of French and Dutch origin had settled a long time back in the state of Pernambouc in the north-east of the country, Burle Marx was also a son of old Europe. A family trip to Berlin in 1928 was an opportunity for him to discover what he was unable to see in Brazil because it was too close and taken for granted: tropical flora.

The Botanical Gardens of Berlin-Dahlem had followed the fashion for hothouses for tropical plants that had developed in the latter half of the nineteenth century. The

Jacques Leenhardt
Playing with artifice:
Roberto Burle Marx's gardens

1 Study for a garden, pastel, Berlin
1929.

scientific legacy of the great Humboldt and all the eighteenth-century botanists and travellers who had enthralled the court and the city with their cargoes of exotic fruits, flowers and animals had become the subject of renewed public curiosity thanks to colonial expansion. Illustrated magazines carried reproductions of etchings depicting the wonders of nature in the Amazon, or in Africa, and towns vied with each other to build the most splendid hothouses.

It was on making sketches at the Dahlem Botanical Garden, which was particularly noted for a collection of rare flowers from Brazil, that the young Burle Marx discovered the magnificence of his country's flora, which seemed to him doubly exotic: far from their native soil in neat rows in Prussian hothouses, they took on a paradoxical aura.

On his return to Rio, after having spent a year and a half in Germany painting and studying singing, Burle Marx enrolled at the Fine Arts College and began his career as a painter. While music and literature have always been present in his work, it is unquestionably painting that played the biggest part in the development of his landscape art. Burle Marx has never in fact stopped painting since the 1920s, and a knowledge of his pictorial work sheds a great deal of light on his garden landscapes.

On his eightieth birthday, in 1990, a major work[1] was published, charting the painter's development. His early work portraying the city and its structure, its buildings and its people, displayed realism. In this respect, Burle Marx fitted into the prevailing current in Brazil at the time, which depicted a social and cultural reality that had been neglected for too long.

The Brazilian artistic panorama of the day was dominated by the Modernists. Although they were very different from each other, they all shared the same desire to rediscover what was truly Brazilian, and included artists such as Lasar Segall, Vicente do Rego Monteiro, Candido Portinari and Tarsila do Amaral. Burle Marx followed in their footsteps with a style that was a mixture of a certain expressionist interest in the city and the people who live in it, and an awareness of local colour, very far removed however from exoticism. The complexity of influences that he allowed to seep into his work meant that Burle Marx kept a certain distance from the excesses of formalism created by the modernist wave that erupted in São Paolo as a result of the Modern Art Week held in

2 Series of superimposed garden
plans, Silk screen and acrylic on
canvas, 1984.

1922. His brand of Modernism expressed itself rather through the opening up of a new field of art, when he responded to the call of the innovative architects and town planners of the day.

That was when he moved away from celebrating objects, or people, typical of his work during the 1920s, to concentrate on composition, which he had experimented with in his many still lifes. He translated the lessons he learned from the post-cubist tradition and from his interest in the organisation of space directly into his work, which was beginning to develop in the direction of landscape design.

It is important to remember the cultural explosion that was taking place at this time, and its main consequence: all the various art disciplines were driven by an urgent need for a new direction, and overlapped with each other. Burle Marx sustained an ongoing interest in new music and in literature. He read in depth Euclides da Cunha's major work, *Os Sertões*, which provided an essential literary and sociological study of the climate, the flora and the peoples of the desert region of the interior of the Brazilian north-east. This work, vibrant with an entirely novel experience in literature, probably acted as a reminder of the German Engler's theories on the ecological park, which Burle Marx had encountered in Berlin. Written from a perspective influenced by both Darwin and Taine, it invokes a way of life remarkably in harmony with nature that is specific to the *sertão*. Euclides da Cunha's language and thinking restore to Brazilian culture the mystery and richness underlying the simple, tough and brutal lives of the people who live in the desert regions of the *sertão*.[2]

The Modernist cultural explosion was in fact expressing a new way of looking at things with a vision that did not sweep away the past, but tried on the contrary to appropriate it to create, at last, a culture that was truly Brazilian.

From the end of the 1920s, under the influence of this cultural awakening, Burle Marx began to draw the town and the gardens, workers and people strolling, imposing a balance and an order on the flood of impressions assailing him. This desire for control, typical of art as it was conceived at the time, remained the hallmark of his entire œuvre and his entire life, as is illustrated in the way he made connections between architectural structures and plant forms from the time of his *Study for a garden* (Berlin 1929).

Jacques Leenhardt
Playing with artifice:
Roberto Burle Marx's gardens

3 Ministry of Education
and Health, Rio de
Janeiro 1938.
Le Corbusier's
architectural project,
Architect Lúcio Costa.
Garden restored in
1982.
(Photograph © Jacques
Leenhardt)

Analysis of the sketch he made for a tropical garden in Recife, shortly after his
return from Europe, shows clearly that he was trying to use a system of
correspondences and resonances between shapes, colours and materials that he had
developed in the field of painting to create new aesthetic effects.

So, for example, in his drawings, fountains and palm trees echo each other's
shapes. Similarly, he plays with the vertical and the horizontal, the two human sight lines,
and also with greenery and concrete forms, the sky and walls of brick or *azulejos*,
decorative blue tiles. These systems of contrast constantly reaffirm the presence of art in
the poetic realm of the garden by multiplying the indications of the presence of artefacts
in an area assigned to nature. From the very early days of his career, Burle Marx thus
combined the art of the painter with that of the urban and natural landscape designer, to
build a body of work that was to bring the garden into the world of modernity.

In the latter stages of his career, this organic connection is still in evidence, but
this time it is rather the landscape artist who influences the painter. In his paintings of the
1970s, there are shapes silk-screen printed onto the canvas that are actually garden
plans, graphic representations of paths. It was from these printed plans, sometimes
superimposed one on top of the other, that the painting itself was built up in a second
stage. By making this distinction between the silk-screen plan and the 'free' movement
of the brush, the hand and the body, the idea emerges that Burle Marx transposed the
experience of gardens into the activity of painting, an experience marked both by the
restrictions imposed by the paths and the freedom of the eye to rove, which gives the
body an imaginative and sensory ubiquity.

Town planning and gardens in Rio de Janeiro

Since the beginning of the nineteenth century, Rio de Janeiro had been the theatre of an
intense town planning revolution. As soon as he arrived from Portugal, dom Pedro had
brought over a mission of French scientists, engineers and artists. The architect
Grandjean de Montigny adapted classical building styles, while the gardens continued to
imitate European models, both in form and in the choice of trees, with French-style
flower beds, or romantic English gardens. The court established in Petropolis imagined

4 Safra Bank, São Paolo, garden wall, 1990.
(Drawing by Sasha Birksted)

its nobility was enhanced by the civility of English roses and European conifers, just when, paradoxically, Europe believed its civilisation was augmented by the glory emanating from its colonies and was including more and more exotic plants in its hothouses and winter gardens, as can be seen from the abundance of South American flora in the ten-volume journal by Louis Van Houtte, published in Ghent between 1845 and 1855, *Flore des serres et des jardins de l'Europe*.

Then, in 1858, Auguste François Marie Glaziou arrived in Rio, where he set up as a hydraulic engineer. Through his work, which gave him the opportunity to travel up and down the country, he discovered Brazilian flora and its unique diversity. This revelation fascinated him to the extent that he organised countless trips into the interior of the country and collected no less than 24,000 species for his herbarium. After Glaziou's return to France, his collection was finally kept at the Paris Muséum d'Histoire Naturelle. This passionate activity earned Glaziou the attention of dom Pedro II, who soon made him head of parks and gardens for the city of Rio. In this new post, Glaziou had the chance to redesign the major gardens, in particular those of the Praça da Republica, of the Campo Sant'Ana and of the Passeio publico, which had been created by the master Valentim at the time of the viceroy Luis de Vasconcelos.

Glaziou's gardens, in particular the way he drew on his exceptional knowledge of botany to further an aesthetic based on forms that were both precise and fluid, are crucial to our understanding of the roots of Burle Marx's work.

In his approach to space, Glaziou in fact represents an original combination of two main traditions then fashionable in Europe: the picturesque of the English-style garden and the formalism of the French. As we know, landscape painting experienced an unprecedented wave of popularity, culminating in works such as those of Daubigny or Théodore Rousseau. For them, nature's beauty was proportionate to its resistance to all human efforts to impose on the landscape. The waning influence of Romanticism gave a 'wild' connotation to the word 'nature' that owes something to Chateaubriand. However, the movement in the latter half of the nineteenth century which spurred all categories of artists to assert their professional autonomy had given rise to a new demand: even if the artist claimed to efface himself before nature, he still had to signal that self-effacement

5 Vertical plant installation, Gustavo
Cisneros's residence, Caracas,
Venezuela 1980.
(Photograph © Jacques Leenhardt)

clearly! In other words: the artist must draw attention to his art, and therefore make it visible. It is this need to trumpet a know-how over and above the requirements of an ideology based on 'a feel for nature' that prompted the search for effects described as 'gardenesque' by John Claudius Loudon, who took his inspiration from the term 'picturesque' formerly used by Quatremère de Quincy.

Glaziou seems perfectly to have grasped the implications of this coexistence between form and nature's right to exuberance. He took his cue from Jean-Charles Adolphe Alphand, appointed by Haussmann as head of Parisian parks and gardens whose character he changed completely, as exemplified by the Buttes Chaumont. For the gardens of Rio de Janeiro, Glaziou designed wide avenues surrounding generous flower beds. The one he designed for the Campo Sant'Ana could in fact be described as a French version of an English-style garden, unless it is the opposite. The emphasis was on the legibility of the overall design, which was in a way reinforced by masses of green or by mounds of huge rocks, whose visual value Glaziou had probably appreciated on studying Alphand's Buttes Chaumont.

From this legacy, characterised by the diversity of contributory influences, Burle Marx succeeded in developing an extremely individual style combining the art of colour, geometry and botany, and governed by an acute awareness of the user of the spaces he created.

Although it would be mistaken to speak of the 'functionalism' of the garden, it is remarkable that Burle Marx has always paid great attention to those for whom his gardens are designed. This again probably derives from the Brazilian version of modernism which developed during the Twenties. Burle Marx does impose his own ideas, at all costs. One is very much aware of the craftsman, alongside the artist, who bows not only of course to nature, but also to human pleasure and comfort.

This attention to the needs of the public also puts him on a par with architects and town planners, in that his wish was not only to compose beautiful gardens for individuals, but also to work for everyone and consequently to work in the city for the public gardens. In this respect, his meeting with Lúcio Costa, who remained a friend throughout his life, was decisive.

Lúcio Costa had been appointed to teach at the Rio school of fine arts at a very young age. In the Thirties, he gave his student Burle Marx his first commission: the garden for the house of Alfredo Schwartz, which he was in the process of building with Gregori Warchavchik. Costa and his partner were fervent admirers of Le Corbusier, and in 1936, when Costa won the competition for the new Ministry of Education and Health, he was fortunate enough to involve Le Corbusier himself in the final design of his building. Again, he invited Burle Marx to join the team, which included Oscar Niemeyer, another key figure in Brazilian architecture, with whom he also worked frequently.

Burle Marx returned from Recife, where he had been in charge of the city's parks, and was commissioned to design two gardens for Costa and Le Corbusier's building: one on the ground, in the spaces created by the emphasis on verticality recommended by Le Corbusier, and the other, which was part of the original plan, on the roof of the low wing (two stories) of the main building (eighteen stories high). Burle Marx designed for the

Jacques Leenhardt
Playing with artifice:
Roberto Burle Marx's gardens

6 Sculpture and installation using round
pebbles. Garden of the Museum of
Modern Art, Rio de Janeiro.
(Photograph © Jacques Leenhardt)

first time a composition of rounded shapes which fitted together like a huge organic jigsaw where each component in turn is made up of other shapes fitting into each other, this time obtained not from cutting out shapes, but through the interplay of the plant species themselves. The design was best appreciated from the top floors of the ministry. Today, unfortunately, only the large shapes designed by Burle Marx remain. We know of it thanks to a 1938 gouache on card which clearly shows the important role of Burle Marx's talent as a painter in the presentation of his projects. The plantations themselves however are unrecognisable due to neglect. The relationship between the trees used and their alternation, the contrast between tall and low plants and the different colours, echoed in the shapes, have all been lost.

The gouache, which shows Burle Marx's original intention, is immediately astonishing in that the colour green is virtually absent. The artist seems to want to offer the users at the ministry a truly abstract painting, a painting that was not only to be contemplated, but inside which people could also walk.

Distance and contemplation

This attention to shape, which could be described as Burle Marx's formalism, if this term were not inappropriate here because it conveys the idea of the pursuit of form for its own sake, develops its full impact in the work he executed much later, but which is closely related: the terraced garden of the Safra Bank in São Paolo (1982). Technical constraints meant that he was unable to add much soil, and could therefore use few plants, and so he chose to make a rock garden, with bold designs over the entire surface. To do this, he used a huge variety of gravel, stone and ceramic paving slabs, stones washed smooth from the river bed, pozzolana, etc. The little vegetation he did plant constitutes only a fine network of green focus points, installed in concrete tubs, which emphasise the curves of the overall layout or provide vertical elements when required.

The most surprising feature of this garden layout is that visitors, who seem to be guided by the lines of the design along a sort of pre-planned route, in fact spend their time crossing the 'paths' created by the materials. So walkers are alternately or contradictorily subjected to two logics: one that attempts to force them to follow the path traced by the materials, and the other that wants the body to establish its itinerary in the space according not to the lines on the ground, but to the elements that attract the eye based on the interplay between colours and light and shadow. This space is thus a fairly unusual experience of the freedom of feeling and movement, an experience which is undoubtedly one of the garden's particular charms.

In its way, the layout for the Ibirapuera park (1953), a gigantic complex housing the buildings for the São Paolo biennale, designed by Niemeyer, and the Museum of Modern Art, reflects a similar preoccupation. Unfortunately never executed, this project included a suspended walkway designed to give the visitor a distanced view of the flower beds. It would have created the impression of walking on the surface of a painting, represented by the planted area, three metres below.

This way of translating the dual aesthetic register of the experience of the body

7 Water gardens and sculptures,
Army Ministry, Brasilia, 1970.
(Photograph © Jacques Leenhardt)

and that of visual perception into space is undoubtedly one of the hallmarks of the Burle-
Marxian conception of the garden. The richness of the aesthetic experience of a space
through which the walker moves in fact implies that the various levels of perception
collide, in both the visitor's mind and body. As in the theatre, the spectator must feel an
integral part of the show, be living among living beings, but at the same time,
paradoxically, he must be given the feeling that he is 'at the theatre', in other words,
watching an event and outside it, but distanced from it, according to Bertolt Brecht. The
paradoxical character of the double register of vision and physical experience therefore
constitutes the foundation itself of a true aesthetic of the landscape and of the garden.

Verticality and horizontality

The experience of the garden is entirely made up of rhythms. As an experience of the
body, it obviously brings into play the structure itself of the body: verticality. Man in
nature, and consequently in the garden, is always a mobile vertical moving in relation to a
fixed horizontal. The horizon is in fact imposed by the very structure of the space, except
in the specific case of high mountain landscapes, which figure prominently in Romantic

painting and in Chinese art. Contrary to 'natural' horizontality, verticality is necessarily created by artifice. By artifice, I mean the capacity for framing the landscape, which the walker does almost automatically, as does the photographer, even an amateur.

Artificiality is again to be found in the art of the landscape designer who 'builds' his verticality from plant elements such as, to take a prime example, the palm tree. And again, in the same register are the constructions on which plants requiring little soil are planted. Depending on the space available and the nature of the materials making up the environment, Burle Marx thus made the most of a pre-existing wall (Safra bank), or he himself created a construction (Parque del Este, Caracas).

Burle Marx invented a range of strategies to force the eye to take account of verticality. If necessary, he did not hesitate to build metal structures to support cascades of *Bromeliaceae*. There is a splendid example in the Petrobrás garden in Rio, or again, in his own garden at Sítio. On the terraces leading away from the veranda, echoing the vertical posts supporting its roof, he installed tubular metal frames which, once covered with plants, can also be seen as plant sculptures.

Verticality is not therefore simply a matter of plants, even if the palm tree has always been an essential feature in Burle Marx's gardens. On occasion, he uses simple blocks of stone, sometimes recovered from demolition sites, even concrete sculptures. On the other hand, the ceramic sculptures of the artist from the North-East, Miguel Santos, in the garden at Sítio evoke the connection between the garden and the canopy of heaven, a reminder that man has his feet on the ground and his head in the poetry of the clouds.

Apart from the dimension of verticality, the space of our perception is also affected by our size, in other words by the relations of proportion that it dictates. While the eye continuously sees what is close and what is a long way off, without its vision changing its emotional nature, the body, on the other hand, experiences a limited space on a human scale, and a space that is infinitely open in completely different ways. The emotional quality of spaces thus varies considerably depending on whether the space in which we are located is closed or open, as analysed by Bachelard in his *Poetics of Space*.[3] Mastering this relationship of scale between the body and space is an essential element in the conception of the garden, which becomes particularly clear when the scale of landscaped spaces is such that it runs the risk of losing this balanced proportion.

Burle Marx demonstrates his mastery of this problem in the conception of the public park in Caracas (Parque del Este Rómulo Bétancourt, 1958). He created closed areas, places that are restful for the eye and the body, with spaces enclosed by boldly coloured constructions against which the plants stand out. Elsewhere he uses built walls covered in *azulejos*, the traditional Portuguese ceramic tiles.

Brazilianising culture

Brazil had developed its own painted tile industry, which is in evidence throughout its history of decoration. Major artists such as Candido Portinari made extensive use of them in buildings of very modern conception such as the famous Ministry of Education and Health, and Oscar Niemeyer used them for the Pampulha chapel in 1942.

Jacques Leenhardt
Playing with artifice:
Roberto Burle Marx's gardens

8 Alternate squares of *Stenotaphrum secundatum* and *Stenotaphrum secundatum* var. *variegatum*, Edmundo Cavanellas' residence, Pedro do Rio, Rio de Janeiro, 1954, Architect Oscar Niemeyer.
(Photograph © Jacques Leenhardt. All rights reserved)

Burle Marx was very close to Portinari, who had taught him at the federal university of Rio de Janeiro. As a painter in the Thirties, he had developed in a way that had much in common with the modern version of figurative painting, to which Portinari had given a 'national' dimension with his large frescos. The influence of Picasso was reworked, as it was by the Mexican muralists, in a spirit that sought at last to build a specifically Brazilian and Latin-American artistic tradition.

The revival of folk tradition was a general preoccupation in the Twenties and Thirties. Whether they were more tempted by formal modernism, or keen to give its own domestic character to figurative art which European influence had for a long time stymied, all the artists were trying to 'Brazilianize' art. Burle Marx went down the same route, not only in his painting but also in his botanical research, which led him to discover the native flora. Similarly, his fondness for folk art traditions, and particularly for the ceramics of the North-East which he collected all his life, inspired him to include folk art sculptures in his landscape compositions. He also designed *azulejos* with abstract patterns, sometimes akin to Kandinsky's aesthetic, in which once again the ancient traditions of rural craft were combined with a modernist aesthetic.

These constructions, whether they were decorated or not, were another of Burle Marx's many means of creating a dynamic, humanised space. Like the *fabriques* that ornamented the gardens of the eighteenth century, walls, pergolas, even sculptures which provided a focal point for the eye, they outline spaces proportioned on a human scale.

But they do not belong to the Romantic register which can be found in *Le Désert de Retz* or in the paintings of an artist like Hubert Robert. Even if Burle Marx did sometimes use materials from a demolition site, as he did at Sítio, his residence forty-five kilometres outside Rio, these constructions have nothing to do with the poetry of ruins. On the contrary, it is a question of conserving decorated materials and, as such, vectors of a history destroyed in the frenzy for demolition that grips developing societies. On site, these constructions, made of blocks of granite from nineteenth-century buildings, provide vertical supports for the plants and spatial frames for the eye. As we have already seen, Burle Marx is always careful not to let the garden obey the natural law of the ground and the horizon. And finally, these structures, which break up the space, are sometimes simply accumulations of blocks of stone, true 'chaoses' like those once used by Glaziou, and which Burle Marx repeated in the Parque del Este.

89

Beyond the need for the landscape artist to find a way of marking the horizontal space with elements that force the eye upwards, it should be noted that the intervention of these *fabriques* in a new style also has the function of stimulating the gaze by importing something foreign to the site. Burle Marx pushed this thinking to extremes. The fragments of English bank architecture in his garden are an extreme example of the desire to make the site visible from the non-site. The same applies to those stones worn smooth by the river which he assembled in rigorous enclosures near the Rio de Janeiro Museum of Modern Art, at the Cisneros' residence in Caracas and again in his own garden. These heterogeneous elements are displaced references which 'distance' the native elements of the landscape and dynamise them, sometimes giving them a dramatic force able to sustain the natural power of the environment.

Jacques Leenhardt
Playing with artifice:
Roberto Burle Marx's gardens

9 Architectural fragments in garden at Sitío Santo Antonio da Bica. (Drawing by Sasha Birksted)

Arte Povera, Land Art and the art of the garden

The use of raw materials such as rocks, natural or imported, or simple concrete shapes that Burle Marx designed himself and which are therefore more akin to sculpture (Army Ministry, Brasilia, 1970), establishes an unexpected relationship with the minimalist art of the Sixties. Burle Marx probably did not think of his own work as a visual artist in the categories used by the artists of the Arte Povera movement or the minimalists. The latter in fact took as their starting point the problematic of the material and the object which was to do with challenging the gallery and museum space. But it is no coincidence that from these premises they too often found themselves using natural raw materials, first of all in traditional spaces such as galleries, and then in non-institutional places, and finally, quite simply in the 'natural' environment.

The developments of minimalism in Land Art also show the convergence of formal and 'materiological' preoccupations (as Dubuffet would have said) within the movement which, in the Sixties, delivered a powerful blow to easel painting.

The connection between an aesthetic of the material – earth, stone, coal, plaster, sand etc. – and a new conception of the space of the work, a space seeking to break free from the restrictions of gallery walls, introduced a new type of relation between the spectator and the work. It was a question of appealing anew to a sensibility which had in a way been 'atrophied' or 'reduced' by the traditional frontal relationship imposed by the contemplation of a picture from a fixed point, established since the Renaissance by the system of representation in perspective. The institutional space of this perception had been the museum or gallery room, as a setting for the picture and as a coding of the relationship between the spectator and the picture. The new possibilities that the Land Artists were trying to explore, in terms of site and physical experience of space, were in fact also central to the work of a landscape artist such as Burle Marx.

Generally speaking, one could say that the Sixties designated the open space of nature and that of the garden as an essential challenge. In truth, the garden constitutes

10 Contrast between rocks and plants, Ralf Camargo residence, Teresopolis, Rio de Janeiro. (Photograph © Jacques Leenhardt)

a type of extreme situation with regard to the problematics of Land Art. For that very reason, the garden is an artistic space which demonstrates the network of aesthetic relations which had gradually developed between Arte Povera, Land Art and landscape design. Gilles A. Tiberghien, in his work on Land Art, summarises this relationship as follows:

> One of the essential functions of art was to 'schematize' our glance, to give it a form of representation of nature, varying according to the time period and the culture, which determines our aesthetic judgement. From this point of view, gardens could be considered as an 'application' of these schemes, which a certain number of Land Art artists have renewed under other forms, yet still within a wholly classical perspective. This is somewhat true of the work of Nancy Holt, Christo, Walter de Maria, of the first ephemeral works by Heizer and Jan Dibbets, and photographs by Richard Long.[4]

A consideration of the role played by the Japanese garden in this development convinces us that there are many connections between the most creative landscape artists of the Forties and Fifties and Land Art.[5]

91

Robert Smithson suggested describing the relationship to the spatial scale based on two antithetical notions: the site and the non-site. In this way he was trying to measure an unmeasurable, in other words to create awareness of the gap between the persons located in the space whose proportions they are conscious of, and the infinite world. Everything that our perception and our memory can register and do is therefore 'non-site', a sort of abstraction, for the true world is both too infinitely big and too infinitely small with regard to what we can and are able to perceive of it. Writing about his approach, he said: 'There is a central point which is the "non-site"; the site is the hazy boundary where all intellectual markers are abolished and where, metaphorically speaking, the dominant impression is of an oceanic gulf.'

Jacques Leenhardt
Playing with artifice:
Roberto Burle Marx's gardens

11 Garden of the Museum of
Modern Art, 1984.
(Drawing by Sasha Birksted)

All that comes within the power of our urge to control is little compared with the size of the world. We can never grasp anything but non-situated realities, torn away from the scale of the world by the limitation of our conceptions. Underlying this argument is the famous saying of Pascal: 'The eternal silence of these infinite spaces terrifies me', and we know Smithson read Pascal's writings avidly.[6] Once again, the artist is confronted with infinite spaces and with the question of his place, and therefore that of his work, in this immensity.

The question clearly comes into play at the two levels of real space and the metaphysical feeling of being lost in the immensity. Smithson often states that if only the site is real, only the non-site, i.e. the trace of it shown in the work of art, is able to permit us to grasp something of the site, perhaps its absence or, better, its evanescence or, as he says, its 'evaporation'.

92 The garden, a series of artifices

One of the themes under which this question can be examined is surely the artificiality of the garden. In this respect, it is close to the work of art, especially if, as with Burle Marx, this artificiality is constantly emphasised through the use of forms that are geometric and therefore hardly natural. The form of the rock crystal has been of continual interest to philosophers and artists. Burle Marx uses it, in particular for the blocks of concrete which he arranged on the lake in the garden of the Army Ministry in Brasilia. We know that Tony Smith, Donald Judd and other exponents of minimalism and Land Art, and of course Robert Smithson (*Granite Crystal*, 1972), also made use of the ambivalent form of the rock crystal, which in itself constitutes an oxymoron for a system of perception and thought which usually opposes the natural and the geometric.

There is another area where the landscape gardener and the land artist meet, which is that of temporality. A garden is not so much ephemeral as evolutive, although the disappearance through neglect of many gardens designed by Burle Marx and other

12 View of the Banco Safra rock garden, Banco Safra building, Avenida Paulista, São Paolo, 1985.
(Photograph © Jacques Leenhardt)

landscape gardeners reminds us of this essential characteristic. The garden requires long-term care and demands of the artist both foresight and monitoring, at least when that is possible. The same applies to major installations *in situ*, those which improve public spaces such as rehabilitations of abandoned industrial sites which were sometimes turned over to artists for them to give the place a facelift.

The fact that some artists accepted commissions to rehabilitate industrial wastelands, often abandoned quarries, determined the orientation of their creations towards the work of landscape artists like Burle Marx, even if there were clearly differences in their approach as there were in the results. We should note that some of the artists called upon in this spirit took a sceptical view of the use of their work by operating companies which themselves had little regard for the environment.[7]

In the gardens of Burle Marx, the tactile qualities of rocks nearly always prove to have an importance on a par with those of plants. These rocks are probably sometimes part of the site. Burle Marx places plants in their crevices, as if they grew there naturally. The choice of river-washed stones, with their round shapes calling out to be touched and caressed, creates a climate of intimacy quite contrary to the usual qualities associated with rocks. Elsewhere, these rocks can play a more strictly visual, almost theatrical role. According to Chinese tradition, nature provides the elements for a true rock drama.

However much care Burle Marx devotes to preparing his site, he does not always draw up detailed plans. He sometimes dives straight into the natural vegetation, leaving it as it is, then taming it gradually. This was his approach to the summer residence of Nininha Magalhães Lins in Rio de Janeiro. For him, intervening in the little that remains of the Mata Atlantico, the forest of Brazil's Atlantic coast characterised by a huge variety of trees over a limited space, was a question of imposing order on this luxuriance. He wanted to bring out the salient features that were already present, starting with the river, which he set out not so much to restrain as to 'design'. His proposed plan simply emphasised the changes in level with a series of waterfalls, creating successive pools.

93

Jacques Leenhardt
Playing with artifice:
Roberto Burle Marx's gardens

These pools were sometimes surrounded by low walls, an opportunity for the landscape artist to mark out some planted areas clearly for the eye.

Burle Marx's technique generally consists in not mixing types of tree in a given space. And so he organised clumps of *Crinum asiaticum* along the banks of the river, or terraces of *Bromelia vriesea* on piles of rocks.

As a backdrop to these carefully planned areas, Burle Marx left the forest in its original state, thus creating a new contrast, sometimes emphasised by an abundance of epyphitic orchids (*Dendrobium nobile*) hanging from the trunk of a larger subject. The skill resides in the arrangement of contrasting forms and colours. While the orchids highlight the verticality of a trunk, they stand out at the same time against a dark green background of climbing *Philodendron* whose mass they soften.

Mirrors of the sky

One of Burle Marx's secrets is undoubtedly his mastery of aquatic surfaces. There is no need to evoke the importance water has always had in the design and creation of gardens. From antiquity to the Villa d'Este, at Versailles and today, pools, ponds, lakes and fountains have always been highly symbolic, but also functional. Water is life, but it is also the noise of its splashing, the light it captures from the sky and reflects from beneath the foliage, a mirror to nature whose image is reflected upside-down.

Last, and for Burle Marx this is certainly not least, water provides a moist or aquatic milieu that is suitable for the flora of the Amazon. And so, whenever possible, he uses the lake as a botanical focus. Who has not noticed the pleasure with which he installed, in a very open space that is suited to their sumptuous display, the *Victoria amazonica*, those giant water lilies which he was so delighted to discover, amid many other Brazilian species, in the Marnier-Lapostolle gardens at Saint-Jean-Cap-Ferrat on the Côte d'Azur. The moment he has the opportunity, Burle Marx creates a water garden in which he can make real 'plant pictures' such as at Vargem Grande, no doubt sometimes thinking of the saying ascribed to Monet: 'Giverny is my finest picture.'

The landscape artist often has to work within very narrow confines. A vertical staircase or a waterfall can, supported by a wall, create an effect of depth where there are only a few metres at the most. The changing mirror of the water cascading down like a sheet of light creates a luminous focus which opens up a vista. That is one of the subtle ploys used by Burle Marx in certain circumstances, with particular attention paid to the perfection of the surface of the water. On reaching the pool, the tumbling, glistening liquid is transformed into a bubbling iridescent mass of water. There, for example, in the garden of the Cisneros residence, a profusion of aquatic plants arranged around the pool soften the effect of the waterfall. In this narrow, shallow pool, a double row of little jets of water, barely higher than the water level, subtly create an unexpected sense of space.

The pools designed by Burle Marx, when they are not natural ponds, nearly always have strongly accentuated geometric shapes. Straight lines, often broken, denote the edges, which are sometimes slightly rounded at the corners. The most striking example is the Triangular Square designed for the Army Ministry in Brasilia. The pyramidal

13 Brazilian water lilies.
(Drawing by Sasha Birksted)

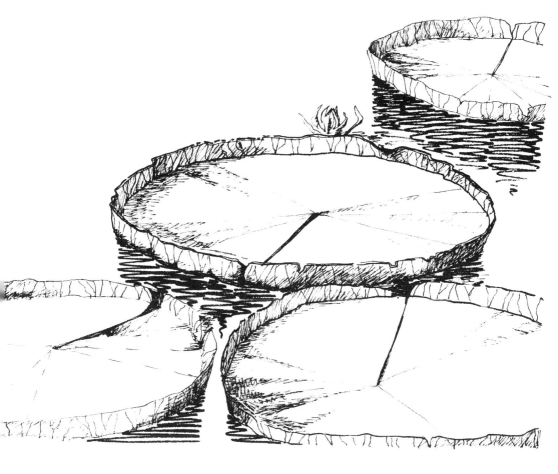

Jacques Leenhardt
Playing with artifice:
Roberto Burle Marx's gardens

14 Olivio Eames garden, São Paolo.
(Drawing by Sasha Birksted)

structure of the concrete sculptures and the obelisk rising up in the background are reminders of the overall triangular shape of the garden.

The aesthetic use of water is not only confined to the shape of the lake. Burle Marx makes the most of the banks to install a wall to serve as a backdrop for a border of *Canna glauca* (fazenda Vargem Grande), or a bed of giant arums (*Typhodorum lindleyanum*) breaking the straight lines of the edge.

Brazil's rich aquatic flora enables him to ornament his ponds with submerged borders. Often he preserves the geometrical shapes he so delights in, thus giving a precise outline to the areas of vegetation that emerge on the surface of the water. Elsewhere, he has used these submerged areas to create a contrast with other borders adjacent to them, above the water level. This enables him to confront different species, water plants or otherwise, which are all reflected in the mirror of the pools. Those surrounding the Ministry of Foreign Affairs in Brasilia give a very good idea of the resources used in these arrangements to create an infinite visual variety.

96

Transforming space

It is sometimes surprising to note that Burle Marx has not been afraid to destroy what could be seen as the harmonious disorder of his gardens with brutally geometric lines or shapes. There is probably no systematic use of such ploys, but it does seem that he finds these contrasts a means of signalling, often in very limited spaces, the power of organisation battling against the power of nature.

This need to indicate the artifice of the 'natural' space of the garden takes on many other forms. For example, there is the garden of *Bromeliaceae* for which a particular area had been reserved within the general layout of the park of the immense fazenda Vargem Grande. The plants are set out as in display units, constructions of local stone resembling a built stonework rock garden. This enabled Burle Marx to create concentric borders, like graded pyramids with a circular section, which provided an

15 Colour plans, Odette Monteiro's house, Correas, Rio de Janeiro, 1948.
(Photograph © Jacques Leenhardt)

impressive visual terracing. Furthermore, these constructions, which are sometimes as high as three metres, enabled him to block a view of little interest, while dramatising an exceptional collection of one of the plants he loved best: *Vriesa imperialis*.

There is no end to the means he uses to create the constantly fluctuating impression that the visitor is both inside nature and inside a work of art. The most radical form that this desire to designate the garden as artifice could take is perhaps in the garden designed in 1954 for Edmundo Cavanellas' house outside Rio de Janeiro, built by Oscar Niemeyer. The landscape artist's desire to enter into a dialogue with the architecture is very clear. Burle Marx worked with a building that had supple but extremely rigorous lines and his garden echoed the two characteristics of the building: sinuous lines dominated in the part of the garden facing west, while a stricter geometry governed the part of the garden facing east. Here there is a lawn planted in the form of a chequerboard. One square is sown with *Stenotaphrum secundatum* and the next with a different coloured variety of the same species (*Stenotaphrum secundatum variegatum*), so that the impression of artifice is taken to extremes. It is reinforced further by the presence of two bands of squares of equally contrasting colours, but planted with a variety of taller herbaceous plants which emphasises the significance of the process by creating a difference in level.

This way of drawing attention to the fact that the garden is contrived must however be seen in the light of Burle Marx's central preoccupation, which is the legibility of the design. To force the eye to pay conscious attention to the shapes afforded, not only does Burle Marx design them clearly and enliven surfaces which could appear monotonously uniform, but he will, if necessary, emphasise the outline of a form. At Tito Lívio Carnasciali's house (Rio de Janeiro, 1946), a tiled path makes a fairly closed curve and then continues in a straight line. In the bend, as Burle Marx did not want to cut the tiles at an angle, the grass bordering the path is cut in a series of right angles shown clearly in the contrast between the dark green of the grass and the white tiles. To soften

97

Jacques Leenhardt
Playing with artifice:
Roberto Burle Marx's gardens

16 Odette Monteiro garden.
(Drawing by Sasha Birksted)

the disappearance of this motif when the path becomes straight, attenuating the transition from curve to straight line, and to prepare the eye to penetrate the shady area that follows, Burle Marx has changed, over a few square metres only, the way the tiles are laid. Large joins planted with grass blur the white geometry of the path and establish a visual link with the different elements of the new environment. That such a small technical modification can play such an important part in a remote corner of a garden is truly a mark of the scrupulous attention to detail that Burle Marx employs at every stage of his approach.

One could make a connection between this attempt to establish a powerful aesthetic relationship between the architecture of the house and the creation of a lawn in the form of a chequerboard, and the solution once used by Guévrékian for the garden of the Vicomte Charles de Noailles at Hyères in the south of France (1927–1929). Burle Marx probably did not design the chequered surfaces with concrete borders as Guévrékian did. But the solidity of the structures is no less apparent, thanks to the rigour of the planting process, which reveals a desire to present a nature that has been forced.

In addition to the gardener's affirmation of geometrical laws, which he imposes on nature, this process creates another aesthetic effect: it enlivens the entire planted area. Often, lawns are simply neutral areas, green spaces as they are called today, which the eye roves with boredom, seeking an element that attracts the attention. Burle Marx never allows such boredom to surface in his gardens. He works on surfaces, even if he does not plant a flower bed or border. In the same way that he uses many different types of stone, gravel and paving in his mineral gardens, in sown areas he varies types of herbaceous plants so as to create shapes. The geometric example of the Cavanellas residence is paralleled by the lawn adjacent to the Museum of Modern Art in Rio de Janeiro, where two varieties of different coloured grass make up an interlacing pattern of curves like a jigsaw puzzle.

The pattern on the ground animates the surface even more for the eye, which is prevented from straying beyond the lawn by a row of palm trees enclosing this area. Here we rediscover the art of determining spaces. For an area to be readable, for it to offer the eye the minimal unity that enables an aesthetic action to unfold, it is important for the eye to be able to grasp it as a whole, as a relatively independent space worthy of demanding attention. Without ever losing the idea of the garden as a whole, and therefore as a landscape, sub-entities need to be created, almost paintings, in the sense of defined special areas.

A few metres from this lawn, employing the same approach, Burle Marx used a structure of square borders regularly placed on either side of the paths paved with stones, meeting at right angles. Contrary to what happens at the Cavanellas residence, the spectator does not immediately perceive a chequerboard structure. The carefully designed squares do not have sides measuring one metre, but six, so that the visual scale is such that the logic governing the layout is not evident at first glance. For it to become visible, for want of being totally legible, for the eye never absorbs it in its entirety, this structure must be the subject of an overall sensual experience, which brings

Jacques Leenhardt
Playing with artifice:
Roberto Burle Marx's gardens

into play the body moving through space. The walker can only *feel* its presence, never *grasp* it. This geometry with a deferred reading introduces us to one of the fundamental principles of the art of gardens, which has always been extremely important to Burle Marx: time. The dimension of time is part of the art of gardens. First, of course, in that the garden evolves as the plants grow and, consequently, the relationship which is established at the beginning with the plant is merely an incomplete foretaste of what the garden will be like when it reaches maturity. It is hard to speak of a definitive state, when talking about gardens, for the life span of each species varies and it is necessary to continually prune, trim and replant.

But in fact the most essential time in terms of the experience of the garden and the landscape is that of the walker. The prime function of the spatial organisation of the elements is to give a rhythm to the walk, taking as its beat the alternation of walking and rest, of strolling and pauses, for which the benches placed at various intervals provide the requisite comfort. The structure of the garden therefore anticipates the sequential experience of the walker, subject to the various angles and framings that have been created for him. His walk will therefore be constructed in time as a series of alternating perceptions structured by selected viewpoints, and the procession of visual sequences taken from different angles under constant modification.

The description of a garden can therefore be given according to three different concepts, which the experience itself brings together. The visitor can be aware of the general layout from the start, as for example at the Parque del Este in Caracas, where a map at the entrance shows the general organisation of the spaces. This abstract knowledge more or less accompanies the walker, whether he is aware of such a plan, or because the structure of the place has provided a dominant or panoramic viewpoint which informs him of the general layout. The Vargem Grande fazenda, for instance, due to its topography, offers a plunging view which makes it easy to take in the overall layout of the garden at a glance.

The second concept the walker can form is linked to the installation of viewpoints (indicated for example by benches) which break up or frame the landscape from angles preferred by the landscape artist. It can be, however, that the visitor himself chooses a viewpoint by simply stopping. He will then choose a particular arrangement of forms and colours, close or far off, which arouse pleasure in him. Such an activity, and the pleasure that goes with it, are in a way associated with the power of composition. The walker is in control in this free game of configuring 'his' landscape, a highly aesthetic and independent freedom, if not of the work of the landscape artist, then at least of the insistent invitation constituted by a consciously placed bench.

The third concept in the perception of the garden, and perhaps the most important, remains that which the visitor forms through walking. It is perhaps exaggerated to say that in this instance it is a concept, for the walker then finds himself completely subjected to the sensory experience created by his environment. If on the other hand we look at things from the landscape artist's point of view, this experience which depends on the senses (this percept) has indeed been conceived. It is unquestionably the outcome of a carefully considered landscape conception. The time taken to walk around has been integrated into this conception, like the time for the spectator to move in a kinetic work of art.

Burle Marx has always paid particular attention to these dynamic aspects of perception. The sequence of elements making up sensation is of prime importance to him, in that he knows that composing a garden is not simply the same as composing a painting. The dynamic of the walk implies that the painter also makes room for what we could imprecisely call the 'film director', or the kinetic artist. Like the film director, in fact, the landscape artist must be able to organise the articulation of still shots and the sequence of shots in time. The landscape artist is therefore also a specialist in the double movement caused by the movement of the spectator. The construction of the garden's images starts with the experience of the mobility of the point of view.

The dialectic of the walk is in fact made up of two elements: landscape images, which are always framed and more or less immobile, in the construction of which a wealth of previous experiences is invested, and a sequence of mobile elements, which are hard to control. These elements become, for the walker, significant and pertinent features which impinge on his consciousness. They may come from the memory or from the movements of his body themselves. A particular shape, seen in a particular light, a particular flower or tree thus takes on, in a moment awakened by a particular tendency of the mind and the senses, an autonomy and a uniqueness that will remove them, for a while, from any vision of the whole.

It is unfortunately not possible to entrust this phenomenology of the walk to literary description. It would take a different skill. But anyone who has experienced Burle Marx's gardens will have no doubt that a preoccupation with the dynamic experience of space is an essential dimension of his work. Thus we come full circle and return to Euclides da Cunha and Guimarães Rosa on whom we should call to describe, ultimately, the experience of this work of art and nature, of nature and art, that is the garden at its peak.

Text reproduced by permission of Actes Sud
English translation © Ros Schwartz, 1997

Jacques Leenhardt
Playing with artifice:
Roberto Burle Marx's gardens

1   L. Coelho Frota and G. de Hollanda, *Roberto Burle Marx, uma poetica da modernidade*, Minas Gerais, Groupe Itaminas, 1989, p. 53–54.

2   *Os Sertões*, critical edition by Walnice Nogueira de Galvão, Editora Brasilense, São Paolo, 1985.

3   Gaston Bachelard, *Poetics of Space*, London, Beacon Press, 1969.

4   Gilles A. Tiberghien, *Land Art*, Art Data, London, 1995, p. 199. Translation Caroline Green.

5   Even though the institutional worlds of Land Art and landscape gardening remained mutually exclusive, at the theoretical level the two were often integrated. So Smithson, for example, referred to the landscape artist Olmsted, author of the layout of Central Park in New York: 'Inherent in the theories of Price and Gilpin, and in Olmsted's response to them are the beginnings of a dialectic of the landscape. [...] The picturesque, far from being an inner movement of the mind, is based on real land; it precedes the mind in its material external existence. We cannot take a one-sided view of the landscape within this dialectic. A park cannot be seen as a "thing in itself" but rather as a process of ongoing relationships existing in a physical region – the park becomes a "thing-for-us".' Robert Smithson: 'Frederick Law Olmsted and the Dialectical Landscape', in *Artforum*, February 1973, reproduced and translated in *Land Art* by Gilles A. Tiberghien, *op. cit.*

6   Cf. his article 'A Museum of Language in the Vicinity of Art' in which he comments on *Portend* by Ad Reinhardt, p. 73 in *The Writings of Robert Smithson*, ed. by Nancy Holt, New York University Press, 1979.

7   'But it would perhaps be a misguided assumption to suppose that the artists hired to work in industrially blasted landscapes would necessarily and invariably choose to convert such sites into idyllic and reassuring places, thereby socially redeeming those who had wasted the landscape in the first place.' Robert Morris, *Earthworks: Land Reclamation as sculpture*, Seattle, Seattle Art Museum, 1979, p. 16. (Cited by Gilles A. Tiberghien, *Land Art, op. cit.* p. 119).

Relating architecture to landscape through geometry, form and scale

104

Introduction

This section, though necessarily also involving materials and dimensions as discussed in Part Two, focuses on form, geometry and scale. Jan Birksted analyses the ways in which internal and external spaces can be structured to create unity of interior and exterior spaces. At the same time, the example of the Maeght Foundation also describes a series of spaces with totally different spatial qualities, designed by artists such as Miró, Giacometti and Braque, who were fascinated by the shaping of space and the handling of materials. The example of the Maeght Foundation also offers a model of site-specific design. Thomas Deckker also discusses an example of site-specific design but from the opposite spectrum: here the architecture highlights the landscape through opposition and contrast. Interestingly, both the examples described by Jan Birksted and Thomas Deckker are imbued with political significance in the form of a social ideal and a political vision. Jan Birksted's example involves a single building in the landscape. Thomas Deckker's examples extend to suburban, suburbanised and urban marginal sites. Caroline Constant's discussion of Prague Castle and of Prague involves a bigger urban environment, one with complex historical meanings to be dealt with symbolically through materials and geometry. Finally in this section Augustin Berque's discussion of Tokyo extends to a metropolis. Augustin Berque analyses the way in which Tokyo is structured and how it grows: it is without hierarchy and without centre, and thus forms an apparent opposition to the Western tradition, which we find perfectly described by Caroline Constant's discussion of Prague Castle. Here the design by Plečnik aims to link a single building and its garden, Prague Castle, to the city lying beneath and beyond it in a total visual and spatial harmony.

106

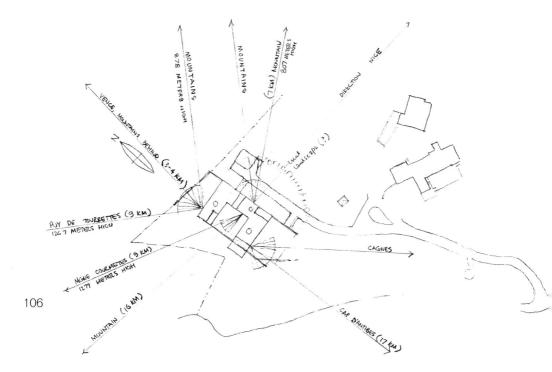

Local Landscape (?)

MOUNTAINS
878 METERS HIGH

MOUNTAINS

(7KM) MOUNTAIN
807 METERS HIGH

DIRECTION NICE

VENCE MOUNTAINS BEHIND (3-4 KM)

N

PUY DE TOURRETTES (9 KM)
1267 METERS HIGH

NGNE COURMETTES (9 KM)
1277 METERS HIGH

MOUNTAIN (16 KM)

CAGNES

CAP D'ANTIBES (17 KM)

1 Site plan by Sert of the Maeght
Foundation with views.
(Courtesy of the Loeb Library, Graduate
School of Design, Harvard University)

Jan Birksted

External interior/internal exterior spaces at the Maeght Foundation

> One clear image will stand in my mind forever: the Parthenon. Stark, stripped, economical, violent; a clamorous outcry against a landscape of grace and terror. All strength and purity.[1]

Le Corbusier's words have set a standard for placing architecture in the landscape. Like the Parthenon, the Maeght Foundation – designed by one of Le Corbusier's closest friends within the Modern Movement, Josep Lluis Sert – also lies elevated on a hilltop and set against a similar landscape: the sparkling Mediterranean in one direction and hazy, sometimes snow-capped, mountains in the other. Like the Acropolis, it is enclosed by a wall to form a *temenos*, a space of purity and harmony. André Malraux, in his inaugural speech on 28 July 1964 at the Maeght Foundation, echoes Le Corbusier's feeling:

2 The Giacometti Terrace at the Maeght Foundation.
(Photograph Jan Birksted)

It was by a night such as tonight that they listened to the silence which followed the last chisel at the Parthenon.[2]

The Acropolis may be a religious *temenos* while the Maeght Foundation is an artistic *temenos*, but even the Maeght Foundation has an origin in religion since it was conceived in memory of a child, Bernard Maeght, who died prematurely of illness – and it was located at the very site of the rediscovered ruins of an ancient chapel dedicated to this child's patron saint, Saint Bernard.

His parents, Aimé and Marguerite Maeght, were art dealers. Aimé Maeght had first worked as a lithographic printer. Pierre Bonnard had noticed his skill and care during the printing of a Bonnard poster. Later, when Aimé and Marguerite Maeght started their own business, Bonnard lent them paintings to sell on a commission basis, and other artists living in the area followed suit, such as Matisse. Bonnard and Matisse then encouraged them to move their business from Cannes to Paris, where, in 1947, they met Miró whose work they started to exhibit, in addition to the work of Léger and Braque, Kandinsky, Giacometti, Calder, Chagall and others. During holidays, Aimé and Marguerite Maeght would return to their house in the hills above the village of Saint Paul in the south of France, where they invited gallery artists such as Braque, Miró and Ubac, who came to stay and to work, as well as writers and poets such as René Char, Pierre Reverdy and Jacques Prévert. When the Maeght Gallery started to publish books and catalogues, these writers and artists would collaborate on the images and the texts of these publications. From the very beginning, there was a collaborative atmosphere at the Maeght Gallery.

But it was then that their son died. Georges Braque suggested to them rebuilding the chapel in memory of their son – but, even more, he suggested they should start something '*plus grand que vous*', 'larger than you yourselves'. The idea of an art foundation slowly took root and developed in their imagination as a place where artists could work – specifically not a traditional museum. But this private and personal story is overlaid by large-scale historical circumstances; the historical context was ripe.

108

After a period of economic stagnation and of political instability, De Gaulle was elected President of France in 1958. De Gaulle supported the European Economic Community, ratified in 1958, which resulted in an economic surge of such magnitude that it has been described as France's 'second industrial revolution of the 1950s and 1960s'.[3] De Gaulle felt that 'an increase in influence also required a flourishing cultural life'[4] and André Malraux was appointed Minister of Cultural Affairs. Malraux stressed 'the need to make the most distinguished examples of high culture accessible to as many people as possible [and to] bring national and international standards to the provinces.'[5] The Maeght Foundation project fitted both the Gaullist agenda and Malraux's own 'intensely idealized, and even mystical, notion of what role culture should play in modern society'.[6] Thus Malraux personally supported Aimé and Marguerite Maeght with their project when problems arose such as planning permission.

In addition, the themes and issues involved at the Maeght Foundation were topical to French cultural life in the 1960s. A passionate debate was taking place between

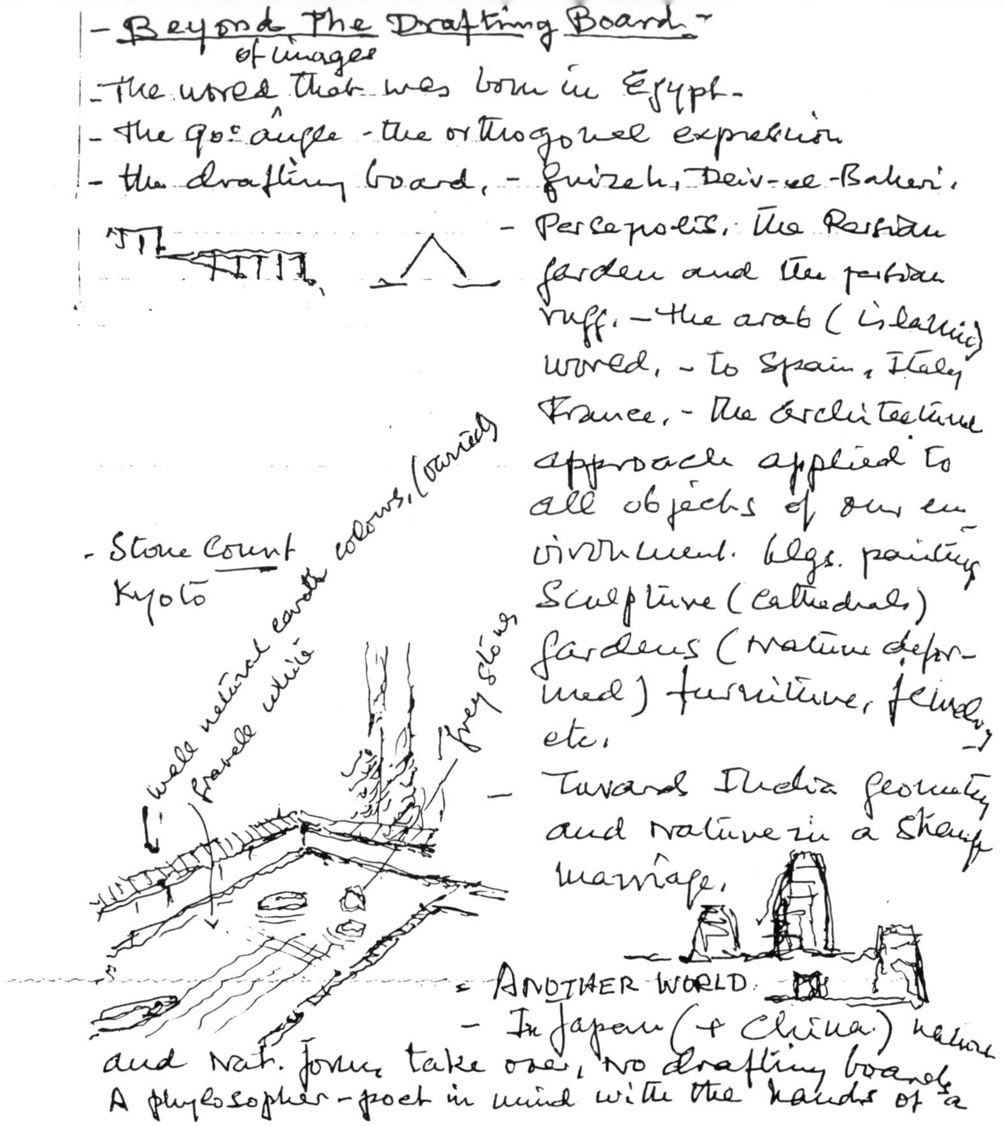

- Beyond the Drafting Board -
  of images
- The world that was born in Egypt.
- The 90° angle - the orthogonal expression
- the drafting board, - Guizeh, Deir-el-Bahri.

- Percepolis, the Persian garden and the persian rugg. - the arab (Islamic) world, - to Spain, Italy France, - the architecture approach applied to all objects of our environment. bldgs. painting Sculpture (Cathedrals) gardens (Nature deformed) furniture, jewels, etc.

- Stone Court Kyoto

well natural earth colours, (varied) pebble white

grey stone

- Toward India geometry and Nature in a sharp marriage.

= ANOTHER WORLD.
- In Japan (+ China) nature and Nat. forms take over, no drafting boards A phylosopher - poet in mind with the hands of a

109

3 Sert notes about garden design and architectural design.
(Courtesy of the Loeb Library, Graduate School of Design, Harvard University)

Sartre and Merleau-Ponty concerning the 'radical questioning of the ocularcentric bias of the dominant tradition'.[7] Their main source of inspiration was Husserl and Heidegger. Heidegger rejected the objectifying gaze which he claimed results both in a distanced perspectival object-to-subject relationship between humans and world, and in a unidimensional visual relationship to that world. Thus Heidegger contrasts two forms of vision: 'abstracted, monocular, inflexible, unmoving, rigid, ego-logical and exclusionary; the latter is multiple, aware of its context, inclusionary, horizontal, and caring'.[8] Sartre claimed that 'vision produces profoundly disturbing inter-subjective relations and the construction of a dangerously inauthentic version of the self'[9] while Merleau-Ponty argued that vision, on the contrary, offers us evidence of both the richness and the reality of the world to which it connects us. For Sartre, vision involved a sense of distance and of control, whereas for Merleau-Ponty it involved 'an ecstatic decentering of the subject' and 'a sense of wonder'.[10] Merleau-Ponty also emphasised the interaction of the senses and the importance of the tactile.[11]

Within this political and intellectual context, the Maeght Foundation started to take decisive shape in 1960, when, on a visit to Miró in Palma de Majorca, Aimé and Marguerite Maeght took an immediate liking to Miró's new studio, designed by Josep Lluis Sert. Miró and Sert had previously collaborated in 1937 at the Paris Universal Exposition, where Sert, as a gesture against the fascist regime of Franco, designed the Pavilion of Republican Spain, for which Miró painted 'Peasant in Revolt', Picasso painted 'Guernica' and Calder designed the 'Mercury Fountain'. Sert, having left his native

110

4 Sert drawing of a Mediterranean
landscape around Marseille.
(Courtesy of the Loeb Library, Graduate
School of Design, Harvard University)

Catalonia due to Franco's dictatorship, was now settled in America, where Aimé and Marguerite Maeght visited him to discuss their project and to commission him to design the Maeght Foundation. Here again, similar to the collaborative atmosphere at the Maeght Gallery, we find, like overlapping circles, a series of existing friendships and collaborations as the basis for new ones: Maeght and Miró, Miró and Sert, Sert and Maeght...

Sert had left Spain due to Franco's régime and had lived in Paris, where he met many contemporary artists such as Braque, Piccasso, Léger, and Calder. After emigrating to the USA at the outset of the Second World War, Sert had published his book *Can Our Cities Survive?* which made him a spokesman for the new tendencies in modern architecture. Sert's interest in large-scale urban planning and his advocacy of regionalism, both climatic and socio-cultural, informed his projects. In these schemes, Sert attempted 'a fundamental contribution to urban design in the way that it integrated social, economic and cultural, as well as natural factors into the physical plan... a new regional phase in modern urban design, leaving the rigidity of the initial universalist phase behind, replacing its utopian continental outlines with specifics and values based on the particular'.[12] Sert's 1948 scheme for Chimbote in Peru, for example, had combined modern architecture with a subsistence economy and with existing geological features both natural and man-made, such as an ancient and complex system of fresh-water channels. The project for the Maeght Foundation was clearly one which fitted in with Sert's regional concerns, with his concern for art, and with his existing friendships with those very artists who were represented by the Maeght Gallery. In this respect, Sert had written:

> If the architect is obliged to be aware of the subject and materials of the piece to be exhibited – and of its content, intensities, textures – the artist, too, has to have a heightened sensitivity to and understanding of the space, its sequences and relationships. In all of this, light is of primary importance, as are, we ought to add, the relationships between open and closed spaces in buildings to be used for exhibitions.[13]

111

Once again, we find a unique marriage of circumstances and of existing friendships.

After initial designs, outlines of the buildings were moved around the site and the many different levels were studied so they could be made use of both inside and outside the buildings. Sert had planned to use exposed concrete, but when he realized how many stones were available on site both in the ground and from old ruined buildings and terrace walls, and when he discovered a local factory producing hand-made wood-baked bricks, he decided to incorporate these two local materials.

During this period, discussions were also taking place between Sert and Miró, Braque, Calder, Chagall and Giacometti about the lighting and exhibition conditions inside, as well as special commissions for the Foundation. Building started on 5 September 1960. Even then, discussions continued: 'When Sert and the artists met at Saint Paul, new discussions would start up during the dinners and these conversations

5 The entrance pine-grove to the Maeght
Foundation with the Cloister and the
Town Hall linked by the central corridor.
(Photograph Jan Birksted)

would then continue during site visits even when the buildings were beginning to be laid
out. Full-size replicas of Miró's statues were placed in situ on the unfinished terraces to
make sure that their proper place in terms of scale, relationship to each other and to the
architecture, had been found.'[114] Sert describes how

> it was decided that utmost use would be made of the sloping site. The garden
> extensions would be part of the museum itself. The artists represented in the
> Maeght Gallery would contribute pieces especially designed for the gardens,
> courts and interiors. The plan of the Maeght Foundation would resemble that of a
> small village, and volumes would be many and differentiated. The outside spaces
> around the buildings would be well defined so as to be used as extra exhibition
> rooms or patios.[15]

The outcome of this design process was the Foundation Maeght as it is today. When you
look at the plan, you will see that the entrance from the north opens into a pine grove –
shaded, green and cool – enclosed by a wall. To the right lies the re-built chapel
dedicated to Saint Bernard. To the left, lies a quadrangle of low buildings with a

112

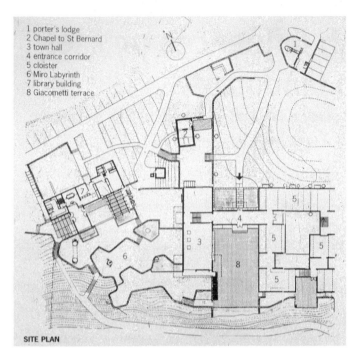

1 porter's lodge
2 Chapel to St Bernard
3 town hall
4 entrance corridor
5 cloister
6 Miro Labyrinth
7 library building
8 Giacometti terrace

SITE PLAN

6 Plan

courtyard in the centre; this has been nicknamed 'the Cloister.' Different room heights in the Cloister are due to different floor levels, following the site levels. Some window-sills are level with the ground where parts of the Cloister are dug into the terrain. To the right lies a large three-floor building surmounted by two parabolic rain-collectors. This wing, which has been baptised the 'Town Hall', consists of one very large exhibition room and a lecture hall and bookshop and offices, as well as service rooms.

The entrance to the Maeght Foundation is a corridor which links the Town Hall to the Cloister. But this entrance corridor also separates the entrance pine-grove to the north from the south-facing paved terrace called the 'Giacometti Terrace', with its panorama towards distant sea and mountains. The north-facing wall of this entrance corridor is a double screen of white glazed volcanic stone and of glass. The south-facing wall is solid masonry. This corridor is clearly articulated both from the Cloister and from the Town Hall by vertical windows at the masonry junctions, which emphasize its separateness. Here we begin to see how the Maeght Foundation is structured. First, every space is clearly separated by its own materials and spatial qualities, that is, every space is clearly articulated, therefore clearly defined with its own specific character. Secondly, every element and every space is clearly contrasted to another element or

7 The courtyard with Braque's pool in the Cloister.
(Photograph Jan Birksted)

8 Layers of light and space in the Braque rooms.
(Photograph Jan Birksted)

114

another space with a differing character: the north and south corridor walls contrast, the Cloister contrasts with the Town Hall, the northern pine-grove contrasts with the southern Giacometti Terrace. These oppositions continue. The corridor terminates in the Cloister by a glass door that gives directly unto an exterior courtyard; but in the Town Hall it opens into an internal vertical staircase. The multiplication of such oppositions in plan and in section continues throughout the Maeght Foundation. In the Cloister, daylight is filtered from above; it is lateral and direct in the Town Hall. The structure and the materials also contribute to these oppositions. The load-bearing walls of the Cloister contrast with the expressed frame-and-infill structure of the Town Hall. And these oppositions continue outside, in the views unto the surrounding landscape, as well as in the gardens. Views from the Cloister are inwards. Views from the Town Hall are outwards. Not only does the northern entrance grove contrast with the southern Giacometti Terrace, but the eastern

Cloister courtyard – central, level, visible – contrasts with the Miró Labyrinth – marginal, terraced, hidden.

So every observation is matched by an opposing one. Unity is constituted by specific oppositions: solid versus transparent, a sequence of rooms versus a megaron, stairs built into the ground versus open-tread cantilevered stairs rising to the roof, horizontality versus verticality, enclosure versus panorama, paved terrace versus planted courtyard, and so on. But this is not all: in addition to this comprehensive system of contrasts, there is another important character to the Maeght Foundation.

Some exhibition spaces in the Cloister were designed in discussion with Braque to exhibit his paintings. Braque rejected the Renaissance rules of perspective as laid down by Alberti.[16] Instead of perspectival space, Braque spoke about 'tactile space':

> ... in the still-life, you have a tactile, I might almost say a manual space... In tactile space you measure the distance separating you from the object, whereas in visual space you measure the distance separating things from each other.[17]

It is Braque's notion of 'tactile space' and of 'manual space' that we see in his last paintings, the Studio Series, painted with thickly textured paint and structured spatially into layers of folded space. It is exactly these characteristics we also find in the Braque rooms. The daylight is indirect and subdued. In the smaller rooms, it lights up the edges, and leaves the centre in shadow. Over the length of the longer rooms, shadow and subdued light alternate due to the barrel-vault roof construction. These exhibition spaces themselves appear to be constructed of layers of folded space.

Secondly, in the Giacometti Terrace, we also find a personal vision of space. Giacometti described the memorable, indeed visionary moments that transformed his life and art:

> On that day – I still remember exactly how I walked out into the Boulevard Montparnasse – I saw the boulevard as I had never seen it before... Everything was different. The depth of space metamorphosed the people, the trees...[18]

115

> He shot up in front of me... He seemed immense to me, all out of proportion to normal size. An unknown person sat there, so that I no longer knew whom I was looking at and what I saw.[19]

And central to Giacometti's sculptural concern with space and distance, size and perspective, mass and immateriality, is the importance of movement since weight is a function of movement and gravity.[20] And it is precisely this spatial quality that is found in the Giacometti Terrace. The strong directionality of the Giacometti terrace – oriented by its length, its panorama, and its water cascade towards the horizon – creates both a strong and a single sense of direction which highlights by contrast the varying movements and directionalities of the individual sculptures, and a strong unified enclosure which highlights the different sizes and varying scales of the individual sculptures.

9 The Miró Labyrinth.
(Photograph Jan Birksted)

Thirdly and lastly, is Miró's garden, the 'Labyrinth'. From the Giacometti Terrace, an abrupt and narrow opening in a rubble wall leads into the Miro Labyrinth. Here, strange beasts – the 'Solar Bird', the 'Lunar Bird', the 'Goddess', the 'Lizard' – intermingle with trees and plants on different terraced levels. Some grow directly out of the soil, others stand in water, some spout or gush water, others crawl up stone walls. They peep over the terrace parapets, stare down from the walls, glare around corners, hide in nooks and crannies. These are not simply Miró sculptures in a garden or landscape; they are the inhabitants of a Miró world. In the Labyrinth, as in his paintings, Miró develops his notion of 'fields of space'[21] in which objects merge with the background instead of the traditional figure/ground relationship. As one sits on one of the stone benches in the Labyrinth, a feature common to all these beasts and creatures appears: silence and immobility. It is this feature which is central to Miró who himself said:

> Immobility strikes me. This bottle, this glass, a big stone on a deserted beach – these are motionless things, but they set loose great movements in my mind... Immobility makes me think of great spaces in which movement takes place which do not stop at a given moment, movements which have no end.[22]

So, just as the spaces and the light of the Braque rooms in the Cloister matches Braque's work, and the Giacometti terrace matches its Giacometti sculptures, so the Miró Labyrinth embodies Miró's concept of space. These spaces extend the vision of their works of art, and thereby complement and complete them. These different spaces are designed with specific spatial and experiential qualities so that a variety of spaces is created.

Let me now summarise this. First, we saw how the Maeght Foundation is systematically structured as a sequence of contrasting spaces, whether interior spaces or exterior spaces. Both interior and exterior spaces play an equally active role in the structuring of the Maeght Foundation. The oppositions themselves involve both internal and external features, thus already overcoming any split between interior and exterior.

117

Secondly, each one of the spaces, in addition to being contrasted with another space, has its own specific and unique spatial character, as imprinted by Braque, or Giacometti, or Miró, etc. As a result, any basic opposition between interior space and exterior space is replaced by a spectrum of different qualities incorporating both inside and outside spaces: some interior spaces are external in character; some exterior spaces are internal in character. The very notions of 'external space' and of 'internal space' become not descriptions of where they are, but descriptions of their spatial qualities; the notions of 'internal' and of 'external' become qualities attached to either interior or exterior space. In this way, the surrounding gardens, courtyards, groves and terraces, and the different views towards the landscape form with the exhibition rooms a complex and graded system of spaces encompassing internal interior spaces – the Braque rooms – external interior spaces – the Town Hall – internal exterior spaces – the Cloister courtyard – and external exterior spaces – the Miró Labyrinth.

At the Foundation Maeght, the architecture and the gardens and the distant landscape are subsumed into an overall unified design based on site specificity, a systematic structure of spatial oppositions and the multiplication of spatial features such that the basic opposition between inside and outside is replaced by graded variations of internal and external experiences. At the Maeght Foundation, we find an alternative concept of the architecture/landscape relationship: one which does not pit architecture 'against a landscape of grace and terror', but where architecture and landscape crisscross and overlap to form a different 'intersection of geometry and geomorphology'.[23]

Notes

1   Le Corbusier, Fourth Meeting of CIAM, 1933.

2   André Malraux, Inaugural Speech, reprinted in *La Fondation Maeght*, a special issue of Derrière le Miroir (Paris: Maeght Editeur, 1974), p. 6.

3   Romy Golan, *Modernity and Nostalgia, Art and Politics in France between the Wars* (New Haven and London: Yale University Press, 1995), p. 66.

4   Hugh Gough and John Horne, *De Gaulle and Twentieth Century France* (London: Routledge, 1991), p. 116.

5   Brian Rigby, *Popular culture in Modern France, A Study of Cultural Discourse* (London: Routledge, 1991), pp. 133–134.

6   *Ibid.*, p. 133.

7   Martin Jay, 'Sartre, Merleau-Ponty, and the search for a new ontology of sight', in D.M. Levin, *Modernity and the Hegemony of VIsion*, (Berkeley: University of California Press, 1993), pp. 143–185, p. 143.

8   *Ibid.*, p. 148.

9   *Ibid.*, p. 149.

10 *Ibid.*, p. 166.

11 See Jay, *op. cit.* And Sartre explores both varieties of visual experience (retinal, perspectival) and of touch (touching objects, touching people, being touched, touching oneself) as central to his philosophy of existence in *Being and Nothingness* (London:

Routledge, 1958). See, Chapter Two, 'The Body'.

12 Jaume Freixa, *Josep Ll. Sert* (Barcelona: Editorial G. Gili, 1979), p. 55.

13 Sert, quoted in Freixa, *op. cit.*, p. 130.

14 Knut Bastlund, *Josep Lluis Sert, Architecture, City Planning, Urban Design* (London: Thames & Hudson, 1967), p. 170.

15 Sert, quoted in *La Fondation Maeght*, a special issue of *Derrière le Miroir (op. cit.)*, p. 87.

16 'The [visual] rays, gathered together within the eye, are like a stalk; the eye is like a bud which extends its shoots rapidly and in a straight line to the plane opposite' (Alberti, *On Painting* (New Haven and London: Yale University Press, 1966 [first published in 1435–6], p. 46).

17 Georges Braque quoted in E. Mullins, *Braque* (London: Thames & Hudson, 1968), p. 41.

18 Giacometti quoted in R. Hohl, *Alberto Giacometti, Sculpture, Painting, Drawing* (London: Thames & Hudson, 1972), p. 209.

19 *Ibid.*, pp. 138 and 149.

20 Again Giacometti said: 'A man walking in the street weighs nothing, much less anyway than a man lying down who has fainted. He is in equilibrium on his legs. One does not feel his weight' (R. Hohl, *op. cit.*).

21 See Barbara Rose, *Miró in America* (Houston: Museum of Fine Arts, 1982).

22 Miró, *Yo trabajo como un hortelano* (Barcelona: Gustavo Gili S.A., 1964), p. 40.

23 Elizabeth K. Meyer, 'Landscape architecture as modern other and postmodern ground', in H. Edquist and V. Bird (eds.), *The Culture of Landscape Architecture* (Melbourne: EDGE Publishing Committee, 1994), pp. 13–34; p. 17.

119

1 Plan of Prague Castle.

Key

1   First Castle Court
2   Columned Hall
3   Second Castle Court
4   Presidential Passage
5   Passage to Power Bridge
6   New Bastion Garden
7   Third Castle Court
8   Bishop's Palace
9   St. Vitus Cathedral
10 Golden Portal
11 Royal Palace
12 St. George Fountain
13 Obelisk
14 Bull Stair
15 Paradise Garden
16 Matthias Pavilion
17 Gate to New Castle Steps
18 Blind alley
19 Southern Ramparts Garden
20 Bellevue
21 Loggia
22 Aviary (no longer extant)
23 Winter Garden (no longer extant)
24 Moravian Bastion
25 Stair to lower garden
26 Alpine Garden
27 Pyramid
28 Slavata Monument (Obelisk)
29 Hercules Fountain
30 Spanish Hall
31 Stair to Stag Moat
32 Pedestrian footbridge

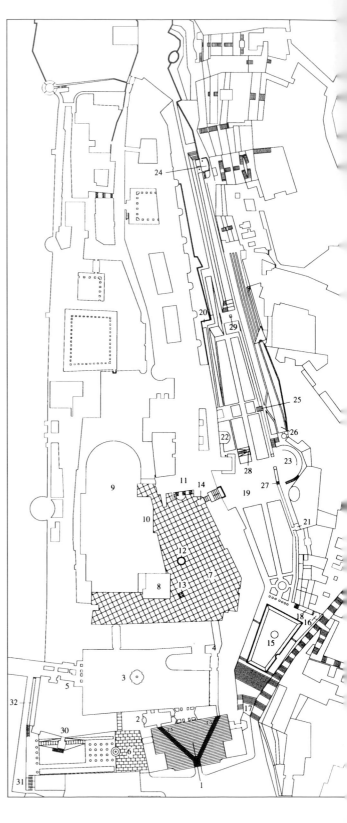

Caroline Constant

A landscape 'fit for a democracy': Jože Plečnik at Prague Castle (1920-1935)

> I don't want anything great, I want things
> small; these I will make great.
> Jože Plečnik[1]

Seeking to transform Prague Castle from a symbol of Habsburg domination into a 'castle fit for a democracy', in 1920 Tomáš Garrigue Masaryk (1850–1937), president of the newly created democratic republic of Czechoslovakia, appointed Slovenian architect Jože Plečnik (1872–1957) to serve as Castle Architect. Plečnik's protracted search for architectural forms capable of embodying the cultural spirit of his fellow Slavs led him, during the years following World War I, to transform the landscape of Prague Castle in a manner that is unique in twentieth-century architecture. Despite a conscious evocation of the milieu's cultural history in his designs, Plečnik encountered considerable criticism for his work in Prague Castle that ultimately led him to resign from his post. This paper examines the political motivations underlying the interventions Plečnik made in Prague Castle between 1920 and 1935 and suggests reasons for the opposition that this work sustained during both the early democratic and succeeding communist eras in Czechoslovakia.

Plečnik's architecture is difficult to classify. Like many of his Modern Movement contemporaries, Plečnik sought forms that were new, yet grounded in human experience and cultural memory. Unlike his functionalist counterparts, Plečnik anticipated the dangers of severing architecture from the nourishment of the past; he sought an organic relationship with history, whereby historic forms would continue to have meaning, albeit

121

2 Prague Castle viewed from Charles Bridge, Peter Parléř (from 1357). (Photograph Caroline Constant)

transformed, in the present. His method of incorporating historical references is largely without precedent. While eschewing established formal means, Plečnik produced elements that rely on specificity rather than abstraction. He based the unity in his work on discontinuities rather than connections; inverting the expectations of classical architecture to embody the whole in part, he posited a new relationship of part to whole wherein an individual form, while complete in itself, is understood as an element of an incomplete and implied whole. Starting from the symbolic potential of an architectural fragment, he initiated a process of reconstruction, a means to an end rather than an end in itself. This expanded power of the individual architectural gesture facilitated Masaryk's cultural aspirations – the construction of a national identity for the new democratic Czechoslovak republic.

From Vienna to Prague (1894–1921)

Plečnik's interest in his Slavic heritage was nourished in both his native Ljubljana and in Vienna, where he undertook his professional training and launched his independent architectural practice during the final decades of the Austro-Hungarian Empire. Pan-Slavism was particularly virulent in fin-de-siècle Vienna, owing to the minority status afforded the Slavs after Emperor Francis Joseph granted the Hungarian majority greater autonomy in 1867 to avoid splitting the Empire. After apprenticing in his father's furniture workshop in Ljubljana and completing a course of studies in cabinet making at the provincial trade school in Graz, Plečnik moved to Vienna in 1892 to work for the J. W. Müller Company. In 1894 he began his architectural studies in Otto Wagner's program at the Academy of Fine Arts, working in Wagner's atelier for a year before completing his courses in 1898. Awarded the Prix de Rome, he traveled to Italy, Spain and France before returning to Vienna at the turn of the century to work for Wagner and establish his independent practice. Although he carried out several important commissions in the Austrian capital, including the Zacherlhaus (1903–1905) and Church of the Holy Spirit (1908–1913), Plečnik moved to Prague in 1911. Archduke Francis Ferdinand's criticism of his church prevented its decorative programme from being completed; such official opposition to his work may have prompted the architect to abandon Vienna and its rising tenor of German nationalism in favour of Prague, where, in a more liberal political climate, critics looked favourably upon his work as a creative individual and a Slav.[2]

In 1911 Plečnik accepted the post of professor of architectural composition at Prague's School of Applied Arts, a position he held until 1921.[3] To avoid competing with Czech architects, he undertook only minor design commissions and devoted himself primarily to teaching, using the long vacations of the academic year to further his research on Slavic art.[4] This fruitful period of contemplation stimulated his belief in the Slav mission. Just as he encouraged his students to value their cultural roots, Plečnik made frequent visits to his native Ljubljana to probe the distinctive aspects of his own Slovenian heritage.

Plečnik's Slavic self-consciousness proved provident for his architectural ambitions. The murder of Archduke Francis Ferdinand in June 1914 and the subsequent collapse of the Austro-Hungarian Empire at the end of World War I led to the unification of Czechs, Slovaks, Germans, Ruthenes and Magyars in the democratic republic of

Czechoslovakia, with Tomáš Garrigue Masaryk as president. The arbitrary nature of this political alliance led Masaryk to a self-conscious search for a new national identity capable of surmounting cultural differences.

Prague Castle (Hradčany, 1920–1935)

After a competition held in 1920 for the reorganisation of the Southern Ramparts Garden in Prague Castle failed to elicit any promising proposals, the organising committee on which Plečnik served asked him to submit a design for the western portion of the site, known as the Paradise Garden. While developing a proposal that related to both the castle complex and its environs, Plečnik met President Masaryk, who appointed him Castle Architect. Plečnik's Slovenian roots were initially regarded as an attribute, as Chancellor Přemysl Šámal subsequently argued:

> He has the respect of the entire Czech artistic community, itself a guarantee that the building works might proceed without controversy. Had the works been entrusted to a Czech architect we would, given the well-known tendency of the art world to bicker, have unleashed a frightful welter of contradictory opinion, and we should not have got as far as we have today.[5]

As Plečnik had previously accepted an offer to chair the department of architecture in the recently instituted University of Ljubljana, he delayed his departure until the beginning of the academic year 1921–1922 and returned to Prague each summer until 1934 to expedite his commissions in the Czech capital, aided by his former pupil Otto Rothmayer, who remained in Prague to supervise the work. Masaryk entrusted his daughter Alice with overseeing the castle's reconstruction; the Masaryks' enlightened patronage and their support in the face of local opposition were vital to the process.

In Plečnik, Masaryk sought an architect capable of expressing in architectural form those values that he associated with the new Czechoslovak state.[7] In 1925 the president declared his aims:

> The purpose of this project is to render the Castle a seat of a democratic president. The complete reconstruction of the Castle's exterior and interior must be simple but artistically regal, symbolizing the notion of the state's independence and democracy. The nation looks upon the Castle as a national seat and therefore, in order that the Castle be transformed from an edifice conceived and executed in the spirit of the monarchy to that of a democratic castle, not only the President but also his government must be mindful of the changes.[8]

In this transformation Masaryk sought a pan-national acropolis embodying a new Slavic style, capable of fulfilling ceremonial as well as symbolic requirements:

> This is where in the artistic making of a democratic State symbolism and ceremony comes in. … [It] is necessary to think of a democratic garden and park,

etc. – all these are problems, and serious ones at that, which should involve the highest intelligences in the field of art. Ceremony is the expression of an idea to be received by the eye and the senses in general, and thus very important from the viewpoint of instruction and education.[9]

While Masaryk envisioned an architecture capable of engaging the citizenry in self-education,[10] he did not limit his vision to modifying the castle complex; he also sought to integrate the castle with its urban environs, as he professed in March 1920:

> I frequently observe with what reverence and loving devotion people come to the Castle to see the thousand years of our architectural history. So immediately after my return from abroad, I made arrangements for the necessary repairs to be carried out and for the various parts of the castle to be properly surveyed. My aim is to make the castle a worthy monument to our past. On the Letná, as on the northern and south-western part of the Petrín, I wish to lay out parks. ... To avoid continuing the irregular communication network of the old city without a plan and for the future I believe it is necessary to solve the problem of the regulation of and communications in this venerable part of Prague.[11]

This declaration became a manifesto for Plečnik, who accepted the appointment as Castle Architect in November of that year.

The existing architectural milieu was replete with political overtones. A feudal seat founded in 884–885 by the Přemysl ruler Bořivoj, Prague Castle came to embody the political, religious and cultural history of the emerging Czech state. During the fourteenth century Charles IV, German Emperor and King of Bohemia, transformed Prague into a seat of the Holy Roman Empire and began construction of the Gothic cathedral. Because the major building campaigns undertaken by Habsburg kings Ferdinand I and Rudolf II failed to give the castle the grandeur of comparable monarchic seats in Vienna or Paris, Empress Maria Theresa (reigned 1740–1780) engaged court architect Niccolo Pacassi to transform the medieval castle, a fortified city with its piecemeal Baroque development, into a palace – an embodiment of Austro-Hungarian domination. Despite its extensive physical embellishment, the castle became an empty symbol under the Habsburgs, who used it infrequently and only for ceremonial purposes. The complex thus fell into a period of decline that extended until the end of the Austro-Hungarian empire.

In pursuit of a 'democratic' means of expression, Plečnik sought to counteract certain manifestations of Habsburg rule. Through a relatively modest series of interventions, carried out incrementally, he amended the castle's imperial overtones by forging new connections, internally as well as externally, with both the city and its surrounding countryside. As a result of these changes, Prague Castle came to reflect the spirit of Charles Bridge (from 1357), which operates both as an extended threshold, removed from the space of the city, and as a monumental roadway linking Prague's Lesser Quarter, at the base of Hradčany (the rocky promontory on which Prague Castle is sited), with the Old Town across the Vltava River (Fig. 2).[12] Plečnik's concern with

124

issues of access and visibility was simultaneously physical and historic in nature. He countered a set of specific historic forms, with their attendant iconography, with elements that were equally precise in form, although smaller in scale and more ambiguous in meaning. To modify the imperial overtones of the eighteenth-century additions, he made frequent reference to the castle's prior history. His modifications to the first courtyard demonstrate his selective attitude toward that history.[13]

First Castle Court (1922–1923)

The form of the first court as a *cour d'honneur* opening to Hradčany Square emanates from Niccolo Pacassi's additions of 1763 to 1771. The space is dominated by the Matthias Gate (1614), a ceremonial entrance that originally overlooked the castle's western moat (Fig. 3). To provide an antechamber for the presidential reception suite, which is reached by a stair to the right of the portal, Plečnik proposed to close the gateway and fill its upper zone with glass. To counteract this subversion of its historic role, he bracketed the gate with a pair of flagstaffs that extend twenty-five metres in height, each cut from a single tree.[14] These rustic wooden flagstaffs with their gilded bases and tops are important indications of Plečnik's intentions. Their forms derive from both the pylons of Egyptian temple complexes and the flag poles in Venice's Piazza San Marco.[15] Such recourse to multiple precedents was a hallmark of Plečnik's work in Prague Castle; it was a means to imbue the complex with broader cultural relevance. Framing a rusticated facade of stone, the flagstaffs combine rustic simplicity and formal sophistication, thereby satisfying Plečnik's aim of overcoming distinctions between 'popular' and 'high' cultures.

Plečnik's courtyard paving reflects his intended entry sequence. He restructured the presidential entry route by inserting an open passage to the right of the Matthias Gate, while redirecting visitors through the Columned Hall (1927–1928) to the left of the historic portal. He created this lofty volume in the manner of a peristyle court by boldly opening up three storeys of the eighteenth-century structure that formerly housed the kitchens. This

3 First Castle Court, Prague Castle: Matthias Gate (1614); facades by Niccolo Pacassi (1763–1761); flagstaffs and paving by Jože Plečnik (1922–1923). (Photograph Caroline Constant)

hall, since modified, originally opened directly to both the first and second courts (Fig. 4).[17] Plečnik lined its plaster walls with false colonnades of grey stone and sheathed its ceiling in copper, held in place with a grid of brass tacks. Through its formal autonomy the Columned Hall provided a hiatus in the continuity of the Theresian complex, a threshold capable of preserving the entry court's historic appearance while simultaneously altering its processional sequence. As the gate's vitreous enclosure was never built, Plečnik's interventions in the first court only had the force he intended following Masaryk's death, when the Renaissance gateway was draped in black so that the public filed directly into the Columned Hall to observe the president's body lying in state.[18]

While Plečnik's proposal to close the Matthias Gate would have diminished the first court's hierarchical value, it was consistent with his broader aim of providing a variety of approaches to the complex to enhance accessibility, while granting greater primacy to the third court as an ceremonial anteroom for state functions. Although the incomplete state of these modifications led to misunderstandings concerning his intentions, the creation of thresholds out of boundaries remained an important strategy for transforming the castle from a symbol of Habsburg domination into a more democratic form of expression.

Second and Third Castle Courts

Plečnik's adjustments to the second court, while minor, concern issues of access that are also historically grounded. At its southern end he placed bollards to mark the presidential route, which proceeds through a second passageway to one of the castle's three original access points, the Romanesque White Tower, where Plečnik placed the stair and elevator serving the presidential suite. This top-lit vaulted hallway connecting the second and third courts invokes another aspect of the site's prior history – the open

4 Jože Plečnik, Columned Hall
(1927–1928), Prague Castle.
(Photograph Architecture Museum,
Ljubljana)

route, subsequently enclosed by Pacassi, that led to the Summer Palace of Rudolf II (Fig. 5).

Plečnik facilitated entry to the castle precinct by adding a vehicular entry to the second court from Hradčany Square through the New Bastion Garden; he also created pedestrian passages alongside the existing gate to Powder Bridge, built during the Renaissance to connect the second court with the Royal Garden across Stag Moat. His proposal for a second bridge, at a raking angle to the first and leading directly to the third court, would have augmented the approach from the north, an idea that was fundamental to Masaryk's urban objectives.

Plečnik's transformation of the castle's third court (1927–1932) was more radical, prompted by an archaeological survey undertaken as part of Masaryk's broader initiative to acquire a systematic understanding of the castle's early history. As the president subsequently argued, 'Only if we respect the heritage of our forefathers will we find our own path toward freedom and continuous development.'[19] The courtyard's existing structures are replete with historic significance: the Bishop's Palace, its oldest extant structure and seat of the Bishops of Prague from the tenth to the twelfth centuries; St. Vitus Cathedral, begun by Matthew of Arras in 1344, with its historically dominant Golden Portal (1385–1399), built for Charles IV by Peter Parléř of Gmünd; the Royal Palace, with ninth-century origins, enlarged under Charles IV (from 1333) and Vladislav Jagiello (from 1483); subsequent additions of the Summer Palace of Rudolf II (1583) and presidential offices, resheathed in Pacassi's facades. A wall separating the court's two primary levels was surmounted by the St. George fountain, marking the site of an early source of water for the complex.[20]

To enhance the third court's spatial unity without sacrificing the integrity of its

5 Jože Plečnik, passage to presidential apartments, Prague Castle.
(Photograph Caroline Constant)

127

existing buildings, Plečnik devised a warped ground plane capable of linking their diverse levels (1927–1932) (Fig. 6). He lowered the northern portion of the courtyard, exposing the foundations of an earlier basilica, while raising the segment to the east, revealing its original level in the Eagle Fountain that he created at the entry to the Royal Palace.[21] To preserve access to the archaeological remains, he covered the excavations with a structure of reinforced concrete that left those foundations nearest the cathedral exposed to view. His adjustments to the numerous doors that open onto the third court attest to the site's prior complexity, while his ramp (1928) descending to the Royal Palace court enables the diverse historic layers to be perceived with a new simultaneity. To reinforce the resulting spatial unity, Plečnik paved his courtyard surface in a gridded pattern whose geometry both originates with the entry to the governmental offices and aligns with the St. George Fountain (1373), which he elevated on a new base at its former site (1929–1930) (Fig. 7).[22]

6 Jože Plečnik, Third Castle Court (1927–1932), Prague Castle. (Photograph Caroline Constant)

128

7 Jože Plečnik, base to St. George Fountain (statue, 1353; base, 1929–1930) and obelisk (1928), Third Castle Court, Prague Castle. (Photograph Caroline Constant)

Plečnik also used the grid to rationalise the siting of an obelisk that he introduced to draw the visitor in from the western gateway. The obelisk was a major theme in his reorganisation of Prague Castle. Masaryk initiated the idea of erecting a monument to the Czech legionaries killed in World War I for another site in the castle grounds. After the solid granite shaft broke during transport to the site, the massive stone sat in the castle grounds for three years before the disconsolate Plečnik could adapt it to a different purpose.[23] In 1928, to commemorate the tenth anniversary of the founding of the Czechoslovak republic, he gave its broken end a suggestive shirred profile and erected the monolith on a concrete base in the third court.[24] Recalling the president's original impetus for the memorial, Plečnik sited the monolith over a pre-Romanesque burial ground, where the tomb of a noble warrior was excavated in July of that year.[25] Unlike its historic antecedents that terminate axial vistas, thereby controlling vision, Plečnik's obelisk deflects attention to the court's historic components.[26] Like many of his contributions to the castle complex, the monument destabilises meaning to ground it in the interpretive powers of the individual imagination.

Protruding from the southeastern corner of the third court is the threshold to a stair that Plečnik created (1929–1930) to connect the third courtyard with the Southern Ramparts Garden (Fig. 8). In its design and siting the stair combines references to the castle's mythic origins and early history with a novel means of access and visibility. Plečnik placed his stair near a Romanesque tower, one of three tenth-century castle approaches that originally provided access from the city to both the Royal Palace and the Cathedral's dominant southern portal. This role was undermined when the tower's rectangular form was embedded in palace extensions of the fifteenth century.[27] Rather than emulate the closed defensive form of the historic tower, Plečnik created an open stair within a caesura that he excised from Pacassi's eighteenth-century facades. He oriented the descent to a view of Vyšehrad, the rocky outcrop overlooking the Vltava that is the

8 Jože Plečnik, 'Bull' stair (1929–1930), Third Castle Court, Prague Castle. (Photograph Caroline Constant)

129

traditional site of Prague's earliest settlement.[28] In a gesture that affirms the moral and religious foundations of Masaryk's humanistic socialism, the stair also aligns with the cathedral's southern portal, which served as its primary entrance until the nave and facade were completed in 1929. This axis marks the medieval site for the coronation of Czech kings, a ceremony that evoked the mythic origins of Hradčany under the founders of the Přemysl dynasty, Queen Libuše and her consort, the peasant farmer Přemysl.[29] The form of Plečnik's threshold, projecting into the third court, evokes these mythic foundations.

According to the early twelfth-century chronicles of Cosmas, from a site on Vyšehrad Libuše envisioned 'a town the glory of which will reach to the stars' on a site where her subjects would find a man building a door sill (in Czech, *práh*) for his cottage. He was duly found on Hradčany, and the city was named *Praha* or threshold.[30] Plečnik created four columns, representing the mythic door sill, surmounted by four bulls that allude to the labours of the farmer Přemysl. While Plečnik sought broader connotations for such forms – in addition to their association with Minoan iconography, the bulls have both classical Athenian and vernacular Slovakian antecedents[31] – Damian Pešan's sculptural reliefs crowning the threshold reaffirm its association with the local myth: incised in gold on the exposed ends of the wooden roofbeams the figures of Queen Libuše and her consort soar in a trance-like state, holding aloft the cloth-like copper roof.

Prague Castle Gardens: Paradise Garden (Rajská Zahrada, 1920–1925)

Plečnik's strategy of forging new spatial connections to augment consciousness of the nation's history derives from his first undertaking for Prague Castle, the redesign of the Paradise Garden that lay just below the wing that he converted to house the presidential offices and apartments. The Paradise Garden originated in the mid-sixteenth century as a walled appendage to the Summer Palace built for Archduke Ferdinand of Tyrol; it was the first of a series of baroque gardens developed atop a former rubbish heap along the steep southern slopes of Hradčany. This self-contained and private enclave took the form of a Renaissance *giardino segreto* (secret garden) adapted to the sloping site. It included a circular gazebo built in 1617 for the Emperor Matthias on the exposed corner of the precinct wall; this was the first structure within the castle gardens to take advantage of the urban prospect, an important theme in Plečnik's modifications.[32]

Vestiges of a pair of monumental stairs uncovered beneath the garden's terminal segment in 1919 prompted Plečnik's design, which incorporates a broad staircase rising from a grassy sward to a gate that he inserted in the fortification wall.[33] To reinforce this transgression of the garden's historic boundary, he projected the stair's uppermost landing beyond the precinct wall so that it extends into the New Castle Steps that ascend from Prague's Lesser Quarter (Fig. 9). The central column separating the dual gateway is a characteristic feature of Plečnik's architecture; it serves both to thwart axial vistas and to engage the visitor in acts of interpretation.

On the central landing of his stair Plečnik intended to place the obelisk, its form seemingly extruded from the palace wall, which it resembled in profile.[34] Near the top of the shaft was to be an eternal flame, befitting its memorial purpose, with Jan Štursa's sculpture of the Czech lion and Slovak cross rising above the flames. After the monolith was damaged in transport to the site Plečnik devised a second, hollow version with an internal stair. He abandoned the idea of including an obelisk in this portion of the castle precinct after this second attempt also resulted in the shaft being damaged in removal from the quarry. For the garden's opening ceremonies he marked its intended site with a black cube crowned by a wreath, a memorial to a lost memorial. Set on the edge of the stair landing, the cube served as a temporary war memorial while simultaneously commemorating the obelisk's ill fate.

The Paradise Garden at the base of these stairs represents a radical interpretation of a traditional theme (Fig. 10). Emulating the historical evocation of paradise in the medieval cloister garden, Plečnik created a kerbed sweep of lawn dominated by a monolithic granite basin, marking the historic site of the baths of Ferdinand II, that hovers on a minimal support of two rectangular blocks.[35] Just as the obelisk is seemingly freed from the wall, so the basin, with its protruding bottom surface, is assertively free of the ground – a geometrically pure centre suspended over a reflective marble surface and set in a grassy carpet. Rather than terminate the garden sequence in the literal verticality of an obelisk, Plečnik used the basin's more suggestive form to transmute the dominant horizontal focus of the Southern Ramparts Garden to a vertical orientation. The basin's exceptional size (4.3-metre diameter) operates together with the viewing distance

9 Jože Plečnik, gate from New Castle Steps to Paradise Garden (1924), Prague Castle. (Photograph Caroline Constant)

131

10 Jože Plečnik, Paradise Garden (1920–1925), Prague Castle. (Photograph Caroline Constant)

imposed by the lawn to discourage any complete grasp of its volume; one can see into it only from the presidential offices and reception suite above. He reinforced the basin's association with the office of the president by aligning it with the doorway to the official reception rooms, which he elaborated with delicate gilt symbols of the Czechs and Slovaks (1922). This substitution of the role of a democratic elected official for the watchful eye of god in the traditional Paradise Garden conformed with Plečnik's vision of the president as the Christian Good Shepherd watching over his flock.[36] Plečnik refrained from idealising his representation of paradise by shifting the stone kerbing that edges the grassy sward to accommodate an existing yew, the oldest specimen in the castle gardens. Rather than reinterpret the garden's historic form, he contemplated the problem anew, representing paradise as an inaccessible ideal while deforming its edges to accommodate an element of nature.

Although a wall originally separated the Garden on the Ramparts from the Paradise Garden, at the time Plečnik took on the problem of revitalising this segment of the castle precinct the neglect of the intervening period had mitigated the formal contrasts between them. To further unify the garden sequence, Plečnik destroyed the wall, leaving three baroque piers as remnants of the historic boundary, which he transformed into a spatial entity by planting a row of conically trimmed hornbeams parallel to it. Terminating this threshold is a 'blind' alley that he excised from the constructed terrain alongside a projecting segment of the bastion beside the Matthias Pavilion. Here Plečnik provided visitors an opportunity to withdraw from the garden sequence, drawn to the vista afforded by this 'passage' with no other destination (Fig. 11).

11 Jože Plečnik, passage adjoining Matthias Pavilion, Paradise Garden, Prague Castle.
(Photograph Caroline Constant)

132

Southern Ramparts Garden (Na Valech, 1921–1927)

As with his modifications to the courtyard sequence, Plečnik's modifications to the Southern Ramparts Garden, lying immediately east of the Paradise Garden, concern issues of access and visibility that are both physical and historic in nature. Originally planted as a vineyard, the terrain atop the southern ramparts was developed after 1860 as an English park, with a series of paths meandering amidst an irregular layout of trees. Plečnik began his reorganisation of the Ramparts Garden by extending a path straight from a baroque fountain (1703) that he repositioned below the Paradise Garden to the ramparts' eastern gate. While giving the garden a certain unity, comparable to Pacassi's eighteenth-century facades, this walkway provided the foundation for the architect's numerous interventions along its length.

Plečnik's letters to Otto Rothmayer indicate his concern for the myriad views available from each intervention in the garden sequence. Rejecting the picturesque focus on a sequence of static vantage points, Plečnik structured circulation through the garden to take advantage of the multiple sights available in the urban panorama. He sculpted the ground plane to provide a variety of routes, while maintaining the large trees on the site, planted according to a picturesque concept of order, that contrast his more architectural development of the terrain.[37] To enhance visual connections with the city below, he selectively diminished the height of the rampart wall and created a series of overlooks and descents to the garden's lower levels. Few of these elements are completely new; in addition to the blind alley, Plečnik also added a Bellevue (1924) at the garden's highest point and a loggia (1926–1927) atop the lowered garden wall (Figs. 12, 13).

12 Jože Plečnik, Bellevue (1924), Southern Ramparts Garden, Prague Castle. (Photograph Caroline Constant)

133

13 Jože Plečnik, Loggia (1926–1927), Southern Ramparts Garden, Prague Castle. (Photograph Caroline Constant)

In his modifications to the Southern Ramparts Garden, Plečnik encountered a new challenge to the castle's intended democratic appearance. Reflecting the site's historic role of defence, the rampart walls countered the image of democratic accessibility to which Masaryk aspired; by isolating the castle visually, moreover, they emphasised the precinct's monumentality. Although both the Paradise and Southern Ramparts gardens originated during the Renaissance, when this narrow strip of land was created atop the debris from a fire that devastated the castle in 1541, their bounding walls bore differing cultural associations. Unlike the walls that originally lined the Renaissance garden, built to ensure privacy rather than provide military protection, the high walls of the southern ramparts were erected following the revolution of 1848, when the Prague citizenry sought to turn the Habsburg Empire into a constitutional monarchy.[38] In contrast to the Renaissance walls, which Plečnik shored up and preserved, he reconfigured the rampart walls by lowering their height and punctuating the linear sequence with a variety of forms, including granite spheres that recall those in the Royal Garden across Stag Moat.

Plečnik sought to overcome the bastions' defensive character by transgressing their historic boundaries and heightening visual relationships with the city. He differentiated between the bastion adjoining the Theresian wing of the Royal Palace, emanating from the period of Charles IV, and the nineteenth-century bastions that lined the rampart walls, associated with the hated period of Habsburg domination. Transforming the earlier bastion into an aviary (1924), he drew attention to its historic roots through a stair that descends to its Přemyslid foundations.[39] While maintaining selected aspects of the Habsburg bastions, he sought to transform their significance. The first became a semi-circular viewing platform above a winter garden, which Plečnik sheathed in glass to obviate the wall's defensive appearance (1923–1924).[40] He lowered the height of the Moravian Bastion (1922–1923) and covered it in brick to create a second viewing platform (Fig. 14). A slender obelisk topped by an ionic capital and golden orb marks the bastion's presence from afar; the streaks of lighting bursting from this gleaming sphere allude to a line from the former Slovak national anthem. An altar-like granite table shielded by a pergola provides a respite from the castle grounds. A pair

14 Jože Plečnik, Moravian Bastion (1922–1923), Southern Ramparts Garden, Prague Castle. (Photograph Caroline Constant)

of mottoes inscribed on the table base accentuate the humility that Masaryk brought to the office of president: 'A majority of people can be helpful to a single man, rather than an individual to the majority' and 'Four eyes see more than two'.[41]

Reiterating his transgression of the Habsburg bastions, Plečnik embellished an existing stair to a lower garden by opening up its side walls and inserting central columns. Pešan's evocative female head that Plečnik placed over the threshold (1924-1925) may be a further reference to the legendary Queen Libuše; such recourse to elusive iconography remained a hallmark of his work in Prague Castle.[42] This Siren-like figure beckons visitors to descend below the ramparts, where Plečnik organised the sloping terrain as a series of terraces, which he linked with diagonal ramps and planted as a vineyard to reflect the site's prior history. He gave the segment nearest the winter garden the rustic qualities of an 'alpine' garden by strewing boulders about one end, reiterating the thematic dialectic of primitive and classical by which he sought to make the castle's complex history palpable (Fig. 15).

Despite the linear form of the Southern Ramparts Garden, Plečnik offered visitors a variety of routes and amplified cross axes along its 400-metre length. In the vicinity of the castle's historic southern portal he created a monumental stair overlooking the Ramparts Garden, which contrasts with his more intimate 'bull' canopy in the third court (Fig. 16). He

15 Jože Plečnik, Alpine garden, Southern Ramparts Garden, Prague Castle.
(Photograph Caroline Constant)

16 Jože Plečnik, stair to third court, Southern Ramparts Garden, Prague Castle.
(Photograph Caroline Constant)

reinforced the threshold's Minoan allusions by including tapering columns at the landings that he modelled after those in the Palace of Minos. Plečnik reiterated the stair's visual linkage with the city's ancient origins by placing a pyramid along the wall (a reference to Rome's Pyramid of Cestius astride the Aurelian wall) that successively obscures and reframes views of Vyšehrad during descent to the garden below.[43] While such recourse to Mediterranean imagery remained controversial, it provided an effective counterpoint to the castle's Germanic aspects, furthering Masaryk's vision of a Slavic acropolis.

In his modifications to existing garden elements Plečnik stressed ideological affinities between Masaryk's democratic ideals and early Czech history. A pair of obelisks commemorating the second defenestration of Prague marks the spots where the king's governors landed when they were jettisoned from the windows of the Royal Palace by Protestant noblemen in 1618, provoking the uprising of the Czech Estates against the Habsburgs in the Thirty Years' War. To enhance the visibility of this first memorial, dedicated to Jaroslav Borita and visually obscured in a reentrant angle of the palace, Plečnik lowered the ground underneath the second obelisk, commemorating Vilém Slavata, to reveal the site's historic level. He reinforced the religious significance of this historic event in a number of ways. Beside the Slavata Monument he added a giant balustrade, oval in section, in a form reminiscent of an altar rail. Together the obelisk and the balustrade form a cross, like those Plečnik added atop both historic monuments, reflecting both the Catholic triumph in the Thirty Years' War and the religious foundation of Masaryk's humanistic socialism (Fig. 17).

Plečnik elevated the existing 'Hercules' Fountain on a new base that he decorated with symbols of the unification and concordance of the Czechs and the Slovaks, an issue that was both fundamental to Masaryk's political philosophy and associated with the region's first legendary rulers.[44] Plečnik felt special affinities with the Slovaks on account of their destiny as a 'non-historical nation', a fate they shared with the Slovenes.[45] Alice Masaryk encouraged his admiration for Slovak culture; through references to Slovakian folk art, which she viewed as 'the Crete of Slav art', she anticipated that the renovation of Prague Castle might counteract Czech materialism.[46]

17 Jože Plečnik, Slavata Monument, Southern Ramparts Garden, Prague Castle. (Photograph Caroline Constant)

New Bastion Garden (Na Baště, 1927–1932)

Plečnik's garden atop the new bastion recalls certain problems he confronted in the third castle courtyard. The site consisted of two segments at different levels: the castle's fourth courtyard, bounded by two wings of Theresian origin, and an extension to the earlier fortification wall, where a horse ramp provided access to the seventeenth-century Spanish Hall. Rather than unify the bastion's discrete levels, which were separated by a brick palisade, he drew upon their differences to heighten visual links with the adjoining Stag Moat, a natural ravine that reinforced the castle's defensive bulwarks when Rudolf II enclosed it to create a deer park. Plečnik used a stone wall traversed by a variation on Bramante's Belvedere staircase to mark the limits of the earlier fortification. He reiterated this historic division by further subdividing the garden into three main areas: a paved terrace in the lower court; a gravel upper terrace planted with a columnar grid of cypress trees; a grassy lawn with a ramped stair leading to the Spanish Hall (Fig. 18). Plečnik's paving in the lowest level is a rustic variation of that in his third court: granite strips marking the rectangular subdivisions frame pebbles set in grout. This geometric order contrasts with the lawn near the Spanish Hall, where remnants of a fortification wall from the period of Přemysl Otakar II (ruled 1253–1278) were discovered while construction was in progress. Here Plečnik distributed rough stones from the site in an irregular pattern around a primitive stone and wooden pergola that he created to shelter the historic remains. Such archaism was not only consistent with his additions to the other castle courts and gardens – the fir flagstaffs in the first court, the bull stair in the third, and the alpinetum below the Southern Bastion Garden – it also provided a visual transition from the castle's paved inner courts to the rough 'wilderness' of Stag Moat. Plečnik reiterated this primitive gesture in the far corner of the garden, where his stair of rough cyclopean masonry descending to the ravine contrasts both the smooth plaster arcade of his retaining wall and the precise profiles of its urn-like stone balusters (Figs. 19, 20).

To augment access to this remote segment of the castle sequence, Plečnik created internal passages linking the New Bastion garden with both the first and second

18 Jože Plečnik, New Bastion Garden (1927–1932), Prague Castle.
(Photograph Caroline Constant)

courts and a pedestrian footbridge leading to the bridge that crosses Stag Moat
(Fig. 21). This footbridge was part of a circulation route by which he proposed to link the
entire castle perimeter, transforming the precinct's formerly defensive perimeter into an
open circulation zone.

19 Jože Plečnik, stair to Stag
Moat, New Bastion Garden,
Prague Castle.
(Photograph Caroline Constant)

20 Jože Plečnik, parapet
overlooking Stag Moat, New
Bastion Garden, Prague Castle.
(Photograph Caroline Constant)

21 Jože Plečnik, footbridge to
New Bastion Garden, adjoining
Stag Moat, Prague Castle.
(Photograph Caroline Constant)

Bastion overlooking Stag Moat (1922–1924)

Outside the castle bulwarks, beyond Stag Moat, is a series of gardens and pavilions begun in the mid-sixteenth century by Ferdinand I. Calling this part of the castle complex 'the most beautiful architectonic poem of central Europe', Plečnik argued: 'There is no greater task than that of adapting them.'[47] In conjunction with his proposals for restructuring the vehicular approach to Prague Castle, he made numerous proposals for this segment of the castle landscape.[48] Although few of his suggestions for revitalising the Royal Garden were carried out,[49] Plečnik made an important contribution to a more remote site on the same side of Stag Moat. On an isolated spot that afforded a magnificent view back to the castle, President Masaryk placed a simple bench beneath a linden tree, where he could seek respite from his official duties. Plečnik amplified the inherent isolation of this presidential vantage point by erecting a bastion around the tree (Fig. 22). He elaborated the access route to enhance his patron's sense of removal from daily concerns within the castle precinct. After penetrating a wall that prohibits any outward prospect, the president would encounter a sequence of terraces that Plečnik created, rising on axis with the linden, to gradually restore the view. The architect used the tree as he would a central column, to deflect a dominant visual axis and engage the visitor in a myriad of vistas. The manner in which his bastion elaborates upon this simple presidential ritual exemplifies Plečnik's architectural objective: 'I don't want anything great, I want things small; these I will make great.'[50] The effectiveness of his piecemeal interventions in Prague Castle derives not only from their historic grounding, but also from his ability to apply such logic at scales ranging from the detail to that of the urban landscape.

The politics of interpretation

In his efforts to revitalise Prague Castle as an historic construct, Plečnik dissolved Theresian surface continuities with great precision in order to posit a new reality. Suspending those elements that once embodied a unified concept of power, he introduced pauses, silences, intervals, suspensions. Although his strategy of providing

139

22 Jože Plečnik, bastion overlooking Stag Moat and Prague Castle (1922–1924). (Photograph Caroline Constant)

new access to the past by opening historic sites up to reinterpretation and thereby giving them new life in the present was concordant with the most progressive reconstruction theories of the day, the risks involved in such an approach were considerable. If the resulting experience is analogous to the visual simultaneity of an archaeological plan, it also relies on historic memory, which the Communists sought to eradicate during their occupation of the Czech lands between 1968 and 1989. Both the association of Plečnik's contribution with the democratic period and the castle's heightened openness and visual accessibility countered Soviet aims.

Whereas the Soviet *apparatchiks* viewed Plečnik's work as a threat to their totalitarian aims, many of his Czech contemporaries looked upon his contribution with equal disdain. Pavel Janák, a devoted admirer who succeeded Plečnik as Castle Architect, summed up the differences between Plečnik's architectural approach and that espoused by his functionalist counterparts:

> Down below, the struggle for a way of thinking and building, the search for a single, universally valid conception that can be imposed and defended against all other possibilities, that would be applicable everywhere, that would be beyond questioning. Up here [in Prague Castle] an artist who simply builds, as if he had not the slightest doubt as to what he was doing ... Down below they are interested only in necessity and in justification ... Here we have an art full of modesty and devotion.[51]

Although the effectiveness of Plečnik's piecemeal interventions in Prague Castle derives in large part from his understanding of their broader urban implications, he encountered virulent opposition to his proposals for creating a monumental approach from the north. Local architects branded Plečnik a 'barbarian', condemning his lack of sympathy for the city's history in his plans for restructuring the ascent to Prague Castle. Sparked by opposition to his proposals to demolish components of the city's historic districts, they attacked Masaryk as Plečnik's sponsor. While the reasons for such opposition are complex, two factors stand out: a reaction against Alfred Hartig's late 19th-century modifications to Prague's Old Town, which impeded subsequent urban reorganisation efforts throughout the city, and conflicts in values with Antonín Engel, planner for the district of Dejvice to the north, who prioritised traffic requirements over issues of state symbolism and ceremony.[52] Complaints from the Society of Friends of Old Prague – whose approach to designing in an historic context was consistent with that of both Plečnik and his successor[53] – ultimately prompted the Slovenian to resign from his position.[54] The argument published in the society's newsletter conveys professional jealousy as well as ethnic prejudice:

> We have so many excellent Czech architects who would lovingly and patriotically take charge of the necessary adaptations without harming the monument left to us by our ancestors. We are now allowing a foreign architect, using a foreign style, and with neither love nor sensitivity for our historical monuments, to do what the former hostile government did not do. The women of the Czech Republic beg of you: Save our Castle.[55]

We are faced here with a paradox of conflicting interpretations. Whereas Plečnik's affiliation with Masaryk's democratic administration led the Communists to censure his contributions to Prague Castle (and the resulting lack of access hindered local architects from appreciating his work), the idiosyncratic nature of his forms blinded many of his contemporaries to their ideological implications. While the restoration efforts undertaken by President Václav Havel have enhanced awareness of Plečnik's remarkable contribution to Prague Castle, comprehension of its historic relevance will undoubtedly continue to elude the castle's record numbers of visitors. This is because Plečnik favoured the profundity of the unspoken to the clarity of the spoken. Although such repudiation of the conclusive is customarily associated with abstraction, Plečnik belied this conventional wisdom through the figurative essence of his forms. That their meaning should remain open and elusive, yet simultaneously historically grounded, constitutes the essence of his democratic approach.[56]

Acknowledgments

Research for this paper was supported in part by grants from the Graham Foundation for Advanced Study in the Fine Arts and the College of Architecture, University of Florida; translation from the Czech was supported by the Division of Sponsored Research, University of Florida. I am indebted to Peter Krečič and Damjan Prelovšek, who assisted me with my research in Ljubljana, and to Zdeněk Lukeš, Jiří Hrůza, and Ivan Plicka, who arranged for my numerous visits to Prague Castle and the castle archives. In addition to her able services as translator from the Czech, Kateřina Finková offered valuable historic commentary on the primary source material, while Christopher Long and Paul Kariouk provided insightful criticism of earlier drafts.

Notes

1 Architectural Museum Correspondence 63, cited in Richard Basset, 'The Work of Josef Plečnik in Ljubljana', *AA Files* 1, no. 2 (July 1982): 43, note 17.

2 After Otto Wagner recommended Plečnik to succeed him as Professor at the Vienna Academy in 1912, the Ministry of Education and Religion rejected his candidacy three successive times; Plečnik believed that Francis Ferdinand intervened with this appointment on nationalistic grounds.

3 Plečnik was invited to come to Prague by Jan Kotěra, a fellow student of Otto Wagner, who headed the Czech Association of Architects and was also a Professor in Prague's School of Applied Arts. Of two schools of architecture in Prague at the time, the School of Applied Arts (commonly called the School of Decorative Architecture) was the more artistically oriented; it educated individualists such as Kotěra, Pavel Janák and Josef Gočár), whereas Prague Polytechnic prepared the ground for the coming generation of functionalists. Soon after his appointment, Plečnik declined both a chair in architectural composition at Prague Academy and an offer to shape the new Yugoslav culture by forming a School of Applied Arts in Belgrade.

4 See *Styl*, vol. 7, no. 3 (1922–1923), special issue on Plečnik's work of 1901–1922. His competition submission for the Žižka monument in Prague of 1913 was Plečnik's largest public project of this period.

5 Records of Chancellor Šámal, cited in Vera Malá, 'The Castle Architect and the management of the Prague Castle building project' in *Josip Plečnik – An Architect of Prague Castle* (Prague: Prague Castle, 1996), p. 127.

6 Rothmayer was responsible for most of the construction documents for Plečnik's designs in the Prague Castle archive. After Plečnik resigned from his position as Castle Architect in 1936, Rothmayer stamped those drawings that he considered to be Plečnik's; his daughter retained many of the sketches Plečnik made to communicate his ideas to her father. I am indebted to Damjan Prelovšek for this information. Rothmayer continued working at Prague Castle under Plečnik's successor Pavel Janák, developing an independent approach that was sympathetic to the contribution of his illustrious predecessor. Rothmayer served in this capacity until December 1956 and Janák retired in February of the following year, a few months before his death.

7 For a discussion of various means for achieving a democratic architecture in the theoretical literature of the era, see Rostislav Švácha, 'Czech Architecture in Plečnik's Time and the Ideal of Democracy', in *Josip Plečnik – An Architect of Prague Castle* (1996), pp. 27–37.

8 Masaryk letter to Plečnik, 10 April 1925, Plečnik archive, Museum of Architecture, Ljubljana; cited in *Josip Plečnik: Architecture for the New Democracy*, prospectus for exhibition held in Prague Castle, 1996. For an alternative translation of this passage, see Peter Krečič, *Plečnik: The Complete Works* (New York: Whitney Library of Design, 1993), p. 55

9 T. G. Masaryk, *Svetová revoluce* (Prague, 1925), p. 563; cited in Damjan Prelovšek, 'Ideological substratum in Plečnik's Work', in *Josip Plečnik – An Architect of Prague Castle* (1996), p. 89.

10 See Wolfgang Kemp, 'Context as a Field of Reference and as a Process: One Thousand Years of Building and Rebuilding Prague Castle', in *Josip Plečnik – An Architect of Prague Castle* (1996), p. 216.

11 Tomáš Masaryk lecture of 7 March 1920, trans. in Damjan Prelovšek, *Jože Plečnik 1872–1957: Architectura Perennis* (New Haven and London: Yale University Press, 1997), p. 123. I am grateful to Professor Jiří Hrůza for first calling my attention to this document.

12 Charles Bridge is one of Prague's most distinguished landmarks; it was commissioned by Emperor Charles IV and designed by architect Peter Parléř of Gmünd.

13 Plečnik's restoration of the Habsburg coat-of-arms over the first court's entry gate was consistent with his modifications to the castle's Habsburg elements, which were primarily spatial in character. See Damjan Prelovšek, 'Ideological Substratum in Plečnik's Work', in *Josip Plečnik – An Architect of Prague Castle* (1996), p. 100.

14 During the Nazi occupation of Prague Castle, from 15 March 1939 to 8 March 1945, deputy reichsprotektor Reinhard Heydrich ordered the original flagstaffs destroyed, as their form made the German swastika appear to be hanging at half staff. Reconstructed in 1962, the present flagstaffs are more economically built of slim wooden strips. The Reich Chancellery opposed Plečnik's castle modifications and sought to reassert the German qualities of the complex, but to little other effect. See Vera Malá, 'The Castle Architect' (1996), pp. 136–137.

15 Damjan Prelovšek cites the poles in the Piazza San Marco, Venice, as a source for Plečnik's flagstaffs, while Tomás Valena argues for their roots in the pylons of Egyptian temple complexes. See Prelovšek, 'Ideological Substratum' (1996), p. 102; Tomás Valena, 'Courtyards and Gardens: Plečnik's interventions in the context of Prague Castle', in *ibid.*, p. 273.

16 In support of his transformed entry sequence, Plečnik sited a large State insignia

(never realised) on axis with the Matthias Gate at the point where the paving pattern splits. He also created a cross axis through the first court by cutting a passage through its southern wing that aligns with the northern passage to the New Bastion Garden.

17 Plečnik terminated the Columned Hall in a set of semicircular stairs surmounted by a balcony. He planned to build a stair to the piano nobile in the adjoining volume, but this idea was only carried out in 1954 by his colleague Otto Rothmayer, who transformed the remaining sequence of rooms leading to the Spanish Hall. In 1973–1975 the Communist regime aggrandised this processional route by enlarging Plečnik's entry door and inserting a monumental stair in the Columned Hall. They closed in the openings that led to the first and second courts, reducing the hall's function to a seldom-used ceremonial entry, and built an enormous coat room in the volume that previously housed Rothmayer's stair.

18 Objections from the Society for the Preservation of Old Prague (1929) prevented Plečnik's proposal for the Matthias Gate from being carried out.

19 Cited by Anna Masaryková, 'Masaryk a kontinuita Pražského Hradu' (Masaryk and the Historical Continuity of Prague Castle), *Masarykův sborník VIII, T.G.M. a naše současnost* (Masaryk Memorial Volume VII, T.G.M. and our time) (Prague: Academic Praha, 1992), p. 11.

20 The fountain of St. George originally stood by the southern wing of the Royal Palace, but was transferred during the mid-18th century to the wall that demarcated the boundary between the courtyard's two levels. In an early proposal for the third court, Plečnik planned to move the St. George fountain to a new platform between the Golden Portal and the foundations of the earlier basilica, positioning the obelisk on axis with the Royal Palace entry, where it would simultaneously frame the Golden Portal. Because it imposed a new hierarchy on the complex, placing primary emphasis on the Royal Palace and St. Vitus Cathedral while diminishing the role of the entry to the presidential offices, this scheme was inconsistent with the symbolic equilibrium that Masaryk sought among embodiments of church, state and early Czech history.

21 While these modifications amplified the court's ceremonial value, they also remained controversial. Plečnik's unified ground plane countered the desire of the Society for the Completion of St. Vitus Cathedral to maintain the court's existing level in the vicinity of the cathedral, while the Mánes Society of Artists deplored the prospect of 'a uniform and lifeless expanse of paving'. Tomás Valena, 'Courtyards and Gardens' (1976) p. 276. The attendant changes to the Royal Palace entry, which involved removing part of Pacassi's portal, prompted some of the most virulent criticism. See 'The Castle and its Surroundings. We were asked by conservation specialists to publish this essay', *Národni politika*, 28 April 1935; this essay, published anonymously, may have been written by J. R. Marek. See note 22.

22 The granite paving in the third courtyard has a multi-coloured appearance, owing to a variety of materials obtained from quarries throughout the republic; this material diversity reflects the new nation's cultural diversity while simultaneously fulfilling the practical requirement to complete the work in a brief span of time. Plečnik's level changes modified the appearance of the third court to such an extent that many critics thought he moved the Saint George fountain to a new site, but such was not the case. J. R. Marek claimed that 'St. George couldn't recognise the place to which he was returned after adaptation of the courtyard. Some clubs and civic associations were activated to protest the affair, for example the Club for the Protection of Old Prague or the Club of the Friends of the Lesser Town. The Club for the Protection of Old Prague rejected the ruthless levelling of the third courtyard. They declared that Plečnik didn't retain the historic character of the place and didn't respect its piety.' J. R. Marek, 'Quo usque tandem...?' in *Národní listy* (5 December 1935): 131; Marek first made his argument about the statue of St. George in *Lidové noviny* (1929).

23 The first attempt to obtain a block of granite for the obelisk in 1922 yielded a 34-metre block, which was deemed too long for safe delivery to Prague. The second block, 18 metres in length, was damaged in transport. The third and final attempt to obtain a 19-metre block resulted in a 3-metre segment breaking off in 1924. See Vera Malá, 'History of the Obelisk', in *Josip Plečnik – An Architect of Prague Castle* (1996), pp. 291–295. Plečnik used the obelisk's broken remnant for the Eagle Fountain at the Royal Palace entry. He rejected any further attempt to obtain a monolith, and Masaryk encouraged him to proceed with a design for the remaining fragment, sending him a postcard from Cairo on 6/4/27 depicting an Egyptian obelisk; Plečnik archive, Museum of Architecture, Ljubljana.

24 Masaryk originally wanted to place a Tomb of the Unknown Soldier in the base. Plečnik's numerous proposals for completing the obelisk included a crystal pyramidion and a gilded one; a version of the latter idea was carried out in 1996.

25 Malá, 'History of the Obelisk' (1996), note 12, p. 295.

26 On this issue Damjan Prelovšek cites Plečnik: 'Monuments that are set up like a *point de vue* – Paris – have a deadening effect on me. I prefer the surprises in Italian cities.' Prelovšek's source for this quotation is Vinko Lenarčič, *Spomini na Plečnika* [manuscript dating from the 1960s]; Damjan Prelovšek, *Jože Plečnik 1872–1957: Architectura perennis* (New Haven and London: Yale University Press, 1997), p. 134.

27 This tower is visible in the Royal Palace entry hall.

28 Archaeologists now believe that Vyšehrad was settled after Hradčany; the first Přemyslid ruler Bořivoj created the region's first Christian sanctuary at Levý Hradec, further north along the Vltava.

29 According to tradition, during coronation ceremonies of the high middle ages the stool of the farmer Přemysl was placed somewhere between the cathedral's Golden Portal and the present site of Plečnik's bull stair; the Přemysl's shoes were exhibited on it while the Czech king was sworn in. This ritual was abandoned during the Renaissance, when the coronation ceremony was relocated to Vladislav Hall, built in c. 1493–1502 to the design of Benedikt Ried. I am indebted to Katařina Finková for this information.

30 Smetana's patriotic opera *Libuše* (1881) and Alois Jirásek's *Old Czech Legends*, first published in 1894, were popular sources for these legends.

31 Prelovšek cites Plečnik's photograph of the gateway to a Slovak farm near Zvolen that is surmounted by a pair of oxen and a postcard depicting a bull atop a pillar. The latter is a funerary monument from Kerameikos Cemetery, near the Athenian acropolis, that he sent to Otto Rothmayer in May 1927, which he inscribed: 'Prague Castle – as an Acropolis'. Damjan Prelovšek, 'Ideological Substratum' (1996), pp. 95–96.

32 Tomás Valena, 'Plečnik's gardens at Hradčany: in search of the modern architectonic gardens of the 20th century', *ab* (arhitektov bilten/architect's bulletin) XXI, vol. 107/108 (May 1991): 41. Despite the optimism of this gesture, opposition to the Bohemian Estates forced Matthias to move to Vienna in the same year, and by 1618 Bohemia was engulfed in the Thirty Years' War; as a result, Prague Castle lost its status as a royal residence and became a provincial seat of the Habsburgs. Following the Theresian reconstructions, the Renaissance garden became known as the Garden of Paradise to distinguish it from the Southern Ramparts Garden to the west, built atop the debris from a fire that devastated the castle in 1541.

33 Working with the competition organising committee, Plečnik developed several proposals for the Paradise Garden. In the spirit of the historic garden, his initial designs were semi-private enclaves that terminated the linear garden on the castle's southern bastions, providing access to the official reception suite from an upper level. After the existing garden wall was partially demolished to move the granite basin into the Paradise Garden, Plečnik created a gate that opened to the New Castle Steps (1924).

Although the Paradise Garden was intended as a private enclave for the president, his family and guests, the gate established a route through it, and its iron grill diminished privacy within the garden, implying broader accessibility. During the 1930s Masaryk opened the garden to the public several times a year; public access was increased to once a week under the Communist regime; under the new democratic system the gardens are open daily.

34 Foundations for the obelisk can be seen in the vaulted 'crypt' that Plečnik built under the stair, where he intended to place an altar, creating a private chapel for Masaryk. This proposal was never completed, and the space is now used for temporary exhibits.

35 Plečnik moved the baroque fountain that previously occupied this site to the beginning of the Rampart Garden. According to Peter Krečič, Plečnik based his basin on the example in the Mausoleum of Theoderic in Ravenna; Krečič, *Plečnik* (1993), p. 58. Damjan Prelovšek argues that Plečnik derived the idea of linking the obelisk and granite basin from Bernini's fountain in Rome's Piazza di Spagna and the form of the basin itself from the bowl in front of Schinkel's Altes Museum in Berlin; Damjan Prelovšek, 'Plečnik au château Hradčany', *L'Architecture d'Aujourd'hui* no. 305 (June 1996): 58. Unlike Schinkel, who provided steps so that visitors could view into his basin and see their reflections in its polished underside, Plečnik precluded any means of approach.

36 Peter Krečič argues that the Good Shepherd is part of a standard iconography associated with monarchs or rulers. Krečič, *Plečnik* (1993), p. 61. Alvois Kalvoda's statue of Masaryk as the Good Shepherd is presently sited immediately below the Paradise Garden, on the parapet to the blind alley leading to the Matthias pavilion; this was the model for a larger statue originally intended for the Paradise Garden. Although Plečnik disapproved of Kalvoda's statue because it lacked a classical sensibility, a smaller version adorns the entry to the presidential apartment. See Damjan Prelovšek, 'Plečnik and Semper' in *Josip Plečnik – An Architect of Prague Castle* (1997), p. 211.

37 Plečnik never drew trees, indicating only their placement on his plans. His design entailed considerable modification of contours and adding of fill, and the bastion walls required substantial rebuilding to support the attendant loads. During the 1980s many of the specimens he preserved were destroyed when the communist regime built a series of service tunnels under the Southern Ramparts Garden.

38 Although the citizens of Prague gained the right to self-government in the revolution of 1848, the Germans prevailed in the elections of 1850 and maintained power until 1861, when the Czechs finally obtained a majority.

39 In keeping with Plečnik's intentions, Rothmayer subsequently lowered the Theresian wing that adjoined the medieval bastion and capped the remaining remnants of Pacassi's walls with terraces to facilitate views both to and from Vladislav Hall. During the 1980s the communists replaced Plečnik's aviary with a semicircular transformer.

40 The communist government reconfigured this bastion, removing the winter garden and shifting the position of the stairs that descend to a lower level.

41 Zdena Průchová, 'Josef Plečnik a Praha,' *Uměni*, vol. 20, no. 4 (1972): 445.

42 A similar sculpted head crowns the portal in the third courtyard leading to the presidential elevator; Damian Pešan sculpted both of these figures, as well as those on the beams of the 'bull' staircase.

43 Plečnik reiterated this theme in Ljubljana in both his Zois monument (1927) and transformation of the Roman wall into a park (1934–1937) that he created to mark the site of that city's medieval fortifications.

44 As the son of a Slovak groom and coachman and a Moravian mother educated in German, Masaryk had a personal interest in the political union of Czechs and Slovaks.

45 Damjan Prelovšek, 'Ideological Substratum' (1996), p. 92.

46 Prelovšek, *Jože Plečnik* (1997), p. 125.

47 Cited by Vladimir Slapeta, 'Jože Plečnik and Prague', in François Burkhardt, Claude Eveno and Boris Podrecca, eds., *Jože Plečnik Architect: 1872–1957*, trans. Carol Volk (Cambridge, MA and London: MIT Press, 1989), p. 92; the source Slapeta cites for this quotation is incorrect.

48 Plečnik's proposals for restructuring the ascent to Prague Castle, dating from 1921, 1922 and 1928, were published in: *Styl*, vol. 3, no. 7 (1921–1922): 23; *Styl*, vol. 3, no 8 (1922–1923): 43, 84; *Umĕni 5* (1922): 445. For further elaboration of these proposals and their negative response, see Jörg Stabenow and Jindrich Vybíral, 'Projects for Prague: Urban Projects for the Surroundings of Prague Castle by Josip Plečnik', in *Josip Plečnik – An Architect of Prague Castle* (1996), pp. 430–443, and Andrew Herscher, 'Prague and Ljubljana: Producing the Capital City', *ibid.*, pp. 445–454.

49 In his letter of resignation to President Edvard Beneš, who succeeded Masaryk in 1935, Plečnik argued: 'I wish that someone else may succeed better, and I also wish for my loving, last but one work – the path from Powder Bridge, above the Stag Moat, along the Ball Game Hall to the Belvedere to be completed as soon as possible.' Plečnik letter of 14 May 1936, Prague Castle Archives; cited by Prelovšek, 'Ideological Substratum' (1996), p. 104. The Royal Gardens and their historic buildings were restored in a conservative manner after 1945 by Pavel Janák, who succeeded Plečnik as Castle Architect in 1936. Janák also restored the Riding School, creating a new garage under its garden terrace.

50 Architectural Museum Correspondence 63, cited in Basset (1982): 43; see note 1.

51 Pavel Janák, 'Josef Plečnik v Praze', *Volné Smery* vol. 26 (1928–1929): 97; trans. in Vladimir Slapeta, 'Jože Plečnik and Prague' (1989), p. 91. Janák succeeded Plečnik as both professor at Prague's School of Applied Arts (from 1921) and Castle Architect (from 1936).

52 See Jörg Stabenow and Jindrich Vybíral, 'Projects for Prague' (1996), p. 440. In addition, Plečnik's urban proposals for Prague were sketchy and lacked three-dimensional resolution. Such opposition reached a decisive phase in May 1935, when the State Regulatory Commission rejected Plečnik's urban reorganisation proposal. I am indebted to Dr. Jiří Hrůza for this information.

53 For a contemporary discussion of Plečnik's approach to historic preservation in relation to that of his Czech colleagues, see Karel Guth, *Lidové noviny* (24 December 1929); cited by Zdeněk Luke š, 'Plečnikův Hrad v dobových ohlasech', *Pražský Hrad: Jiný pohled* (Prague Castle: Another View) (Prague [1995]), p. 72. Guth was in charge of the archaeological survey of Prague Castle undertaken at Masaryk's request.

54 Plečnik resigned from his post as Castle Architect in May 1936, although his last official visit to Prague was in November 1934. After Masaryk resigned due to ill health, the new Czech president Edvard Beneš sought to persuade Plečnik to continue in his position; when he declined, Beneš appointed Pavel Janák as his successor. See note 49.

55 *Za starou Prahu, Vĕstnik pro ochranu památek*, vol. 19, no. 3/4 (Prague, 1935): cited in Slapeta, 'Jože Plečnik and Prague' (1989), p. 92.

56 In 1994 Czech president Václav Havel appointed Professor Bořek Šípek of the School of Decorative Arts to serve as Castle Architect. While his work emulates Plečnik's, it lacks the ideological force of his illustrious predecessor.

Augustin Berque

Tokyo as emblem of
a postmodern paradigm

Fantasy and urbanology

Considering the production and audience of bestselling non-fiction books in Japan, if the sixties and especially the seventies were the decades of nippologies (*nihonjinron*), the eighties were those of tokyologies (*tôkyorôn*), including 'edotics' (*edogaku*). In the sarne eighties, the Japanese proved also very fond of writings about postmodernity, including the theme of the 'new paradigm' which seems to be preferably used in the present decade.

My hypothesis is that there exists a relationship between these three phenomena (the vogue of nippology, that of tokyology and that of postmodernology), and that this relationship reveals the emergence of a collective fantasy (*kyôdô gensô*) in the sense of Yoshimoto Ryûmei Yoshimoto employed this expression, notably, in regard to the emergence of the state. I shall use it in regard to the not uncommon idea that the XXIst century might be that of a Japanese hegemony, superseding the hegemony of the United States during the XXth century. In this sense, the problem is whether and how Japan can produce a paradigm of its own, and how tokyology can be related to this possibility.

As seen from Japan, postmodernity can only be synonymous with post-westernity, since modernity was equated with the Occident. In this respect, the much talked about 'bigemony' (a hegemonic duo of the United States and Japan) is a mere diplomatic euphemism. Indeed, a quarter of a century has already elapsed since the Japanese have begun to feel that they had caught up (*oitsuki*) with the West, and in the dynamics of this movement, they have had plenty of time to digest, quite logically, the idea that they have overpassed (*oikoshi*) it by now. Correlatively, the fashion of nippologies can be interpreted as expressing a newly recovered confidence in the identity of the nation, as well as a questioning of the validity of the Western model. The subsequent fad for tokyologies and edotics went further: the Japanese started to find in their capital city some virtues which were not only foreign to Western canons, but which might short-cut modernity and connect directly the Edo era (1603–1867) to postmodernity/post-westernity. In such a juncture, the thematics of postmodernity – though it stemmed from European thought rather than from Japan – has been tapped in order to nourish both tokyology in particular and nippology in general, in a semantic spiral from which the Japanese capital has emerged as already embodying the next century.

I shall consider this process as the beginnings of a possible hegemony, understanding this phenomenon as a collective fantasy which extends its aura not only among the Japanese, but also to some degree among the Westerners and the rest of the world. I assume that such a process is that of the making of sense, and that the essence of hegemony is precisely to make others feel as natural a sense which is in fact imposed upon them through various means, e.g. economic domination. Hegemony ends as soon as this sense is felt as unnatural, and this – unless it is countered by oppression – necessarily leads to a rejection of the means which had brought it forth.

For the time being, the greater part of the world feels as natural a sense of things – these range from a taste for Coca-Cola to commending the crusade against Saddam Hussein – which has its source in the United States. In collective fantasies, any one thing participates symbolically in the whole system, through a set of relations which one does not perceive as such. Should one feel these relations, then the whole set of meaning would start crumbling down. The reverse – the construction of meaning – is also true. For instance, the collective fantasy of the present hegemonic system works inasmuch as one does not perceive that liking Coca-Cola is related with hating Saddam.

In order to show these semantic relationships in the case of a virtual Japanese hegemony, I shall compare four books, which one can consider as representative on account of their fame (first case), or that of their author (first, second and fourth case), or simply their relevance to the above problematics (all four cases). My method is grossly that of the search for structural homologies within sets of analogies, as an author like, for instance, Panofsky has made use of when he showed the symbolic affinity of Gothic architecture and scholastic discourse.

Inasmuch as my task, here, will be to stress the semantic relationship which exists between nippologies, tokyologies and postmodernologies, it may perhaps be deemed a de-*sym*bolic, i.e. *dia*bolic endeavour to undermine the rise of the aforesaid collective fantasy. So, let me emphasise that this endeavour has nothing to do with Japan bashing, though, of course, it is only human and in its turn embedded within the semantic set of another collctive fantasy, the nature of which will be left as a pending question to the reader's perspicacity.

Ashihara's amoebic city

It was in 1986, at the height of the tokyologic wave, that Ashihara Yoshinobu published *Kakureta chitsujo* (the Hidden order). The book is basically about the spatial order of Tokyo, although it is presented in the more general frame of Japanese spatiality. The subtitle is devoid of ambiguity: *Nijuisseiki no toshi e mukatte* (Towards the city of the XXIst century) implies that what we shall learn about present-day Tokyo will reveal to us the reality of our cities of tomorrow.

Ashihara starts from an analysis of the relation between inside and outside. On account of mainly structural reasons (the wall supports the roof), European urbanity gave much importance to façades. See for instance Renaissance churches in Italy.

Correlatively, the external shape of buildings is determining. It bears consequently a high status; such is the case in Paris, the 'city of form' (*keishiki no machi*, p. 45). On the contrary, in a tradition like that of Japan or of the Tonga Islands, it is the pillars which support the roof; thus, the external envelope (our walls and façades) is not much significant. Hence a relative disinterest for the outline and decoration of this envelope. This opportunely accounts for the visual disorder of present Japanese cities: in such an urbanity, indeed, managing the aesthetics of the street should not make much sense.

Then Ashihara opposes an architecture – that of Europe – to be seen from a distance and an architecture – that of Japan – to be seen (or rather felt) close to. The Parthenon is to be seen from a distance, in the harmony of its form under the sky of Greece; when close to, it is only a mass of stones. On the contrary, Japanese architecture is to be appreciated close to, in its shadowy light, the fragance of its wood, the smoothness of its tatamis under a bare foot…

What holds for architecture holds also for the city. Europeans and the Chinese as well have been concerned in wholes (*zentai no keikaku*, p. 69), whereas the Japanese have cared about partial accomplishments (*bubun no kansei*, p. 69). Not only did they not show much interest for the grand symmetries which they had learnt from China, and gave them up soon after having imitated them in their first capital cities, but they made incompleteness and asymmetry the leading values of their aesthetics. Although, in the course of their history, the Japanese cities have borrowed much from China and the West, that was in fact in a completely different mind than that of these models.

In Japan, thus, it is the part and not the whole which counts. Now, isn't that precisely the tendency of postmodernity, which is gradually imposing itself on the world? In such a world, thinking on the basis of the part, without a definite principle at the start nor for the whole, is due to become an advantage (*yûi ni naru*, p. 79).

Tokyo is the very example of this spatiality in which, taking the part (the place of a given function) as a starting point, one increases it and thus progressively realises a form. Finalising beforehand the outlines of a whole form would quell the life and functions of architecture inside this outline. European urbanity, which favours style, is on the contrary imprisoned within its pre-established forms; giving greater place to the contents, Japanese urbanity smoothly adapts its forms to the evolution of the needs. By so doing, one eventually produces very complex forms, the outlines of which pertain to fractal geometry. There is indeed an order here, but it is an order hidden under the appearance of chaos.

Contrary to European spatiality, where one fixes the forms by starting from their external outline in a centripetal and substractive way (see Le Corbusier's Unité d'habitation in Marseilles), the order of Japanese forms is brought forth from the inside, in a centrifugal and additive way (see Katsura detached palace, in Kyoto). To each stage of this accretion correspond forms which are never but the sub-wholes of future forms. They are holons, each one endowed with autonomy at its own level, yet all bearing an affinity with each other, and the growth of which is an organic one, like that of living beings. Hence the infinite smoothness of the fabric which it produces: with its changing and ever adapting forms, the Japanese city, and Tokyo in particular, is an amoebic city (*amêba toshi*).

Nakane's mollusc society

In 1978, about a dozen years after *Tate shakai no ningen kankei* (Human relations in a vertical society), Nakane Chie gave a sequel to this famous longseller. That was *Tate shakai no rikigaku* (Dynamics of the vertical society).

While taking again the image of verticality in its title – *succès oblige* – the book in fact operates a radical shift. Nakane focuses here on a characteristic of the Japanese society which she had indeed already pointed out in *Tate shakai no ningen kankei*, but which did not satisfactorily match the idea of hierarchy implied by verticality: that propensity of the Japanese to organise themselves in relatively autonomous small groups.

The dynamics in question is that of these little groups (*shô shûdan*), which Nakane gauges around half a dozen members. According to her, they are in Japan more determining than the individual on the one hand, and the whole society in the other hand. The latter is not governed by principles, but through the interplay of these little groups, which influence one another at short range. Hence a great stability of the whole; because, in social movements, it is never the order of the whole which is questioned.

Nakane goes as far as to credit these little groups with characteristics comparable to those of the Western individual (*Oubei no kojin to onnaji yô na seishitsu*, p. 38), notably in respect of decision-making and leisure. Where the Western individual would decide alone in all conscience, where again he would prefer interindividual privacy, in Japan it is the little group which prevails.

One thing leading to the other, the proximity of these group interplays would explain that Japan alone among all the great societies of this planet presents some traits of unicity (*tan'itsusei*) which one usually notices only in much smaller societies, such as ethnic groups of a few hundred thousand persons.

Whatever the reality of the Japanese society and that of its 'Western' foil, what shall interest us here in Nakane's vision is the image which sustains it. She compares indeed the dynamics of Japanese groups to the movements of a starfish. The limbs of this echinoderm possess a relative autonomy, because its nervous system is not much centralised. It is through proximity, each one influencing its neighbour, that they eventually trigger off a movement of the whole asteroid. There is at work here neither a previously given direction nor any order emanating from a centre. This movement is thus aleatory for a while, but once it is launched it becomes unitary and compels all the limbs, which from thereon are caught within a general dynamics. Nakane finds nothing comparable in Western societies, which function like vertebrates, with a centralised nervous system: there, it is the centre/brain which emits an order and makes the whole society/body execute it – at the risk that some members rebel against the centre and thus deregulate the whole organisation. Such a risk does not exist in the Japanese society, which possesses both the advantages and disadvantages of a mollusc (*nantai dôbutsu*).

Imada's acentralism

Radically differing from the above two books, Imada Takatoshi's *Modân no datsu-kôchiku* (The deconstruction of modernity) does not deal with Japanese identity but with a general question, and he does this in terms of universality. This work is in itself a good synthesis, made essentially from a sociological point of view, of the motifs which agitate contemporary thought in the quest for a new paradigm. One reads thus successively about the turmoils of industrial society, the paradoxes of self-reference, the dissipative structures of our new sociality, to end with the advent of a jiseijin or 'Homo reflect' (*sic*, which in Japanese becomes *homo rihurekuto*), constitutive of a 'self reflexive society' (*jisei shakai*, p. 187).

Sociological as the point of view may be, what is there in common between Prigogine (dissipative structures), Varela (autopoïesis), Gödel (self-reference) and other leading postmodern motifs on the one hand, and on the other hand what concerns us here?

The link is that Imada is Japanese, that he writes in the national language, and that he is read by his compatriots. One shall not deem immaterial that the Japanese reader thus learns that beyond modernity (connote: beyond the Occident) will reign an order proceeding not from pre-set directive principles but from the coexistence of parts, which will co-adapt themselves in semi-aleatory wise into emerging macro-structures, endowed eventually with a unitary movement, but not manageable beforehand because devoid of a centre.

If this does somewhat matter, it is because one can see here rising to universality a figure which, besides, is already firmly rooted in nippology about Japaneseness itself. While deconstructing modernity in general, Imada constructs in its place something curiously analogous to that which Nakane had already shown about the Japanese society, and Ashihara about Tokyo; that is, a topological, proxemic, acentred, holonic, an-archic (in the sense of an absence of a pre-set ordering principle, archê) organisation.

To be sure, Imada's thesis is not consciously intended as a nippology, so much the less as a tokyology. His purpose lies elsewhere, and it shall only be right to mention that he also evokes of a lot of other themes than those I selected here; but it is precisely because this purpose lies elsewhere, and because it is situated on a universal plane, that it brings forth that very epistemological scheme which nippologies and tokyologies needed so badly in order to attain – emerging out of the solitary status which they had themselves elaborated – the dimension of a virtually universal paradigm. But, seen from the outside, this leaves indeed a pending question: why should this paradigm be of Japanese breed rather than simply human, or contemporary?

The acme of humanity

And what if the amoebic city and its mollusc society, short-cutting Western modernity, were in fact the extreme head of human evolution?

This is at least virtually the inference that the intellectual juncture of nippology allows a collective book to draw. It was recently published in bilingual (Japanese/English) edition, in the explicit aim of letting the world know better the nature of Japanese organisations: *Nihon-gata shisutemu/Japanese systems*. To be sure, the Japanese subtitle, *Jinrui bunmei no hiotsu no kata* (A form of human civilisation) is quite neutral, and the English one, *An alternative civilisation?*, is provided with a very temperate

151

1 Ikebukuro, Tokyo, 1997.
(Photograph Junko Fuura)

interrogation mark; but if one reads the contents while bearing in mind some reference to paradigms, then the matter, without doubt, is to be understood as *A feature of civilisation*.

This work was edited by a sociologist, Hamaguchi Eshun, to whom one is indebted for some well-known nippological achievements, mainly for having forged a new concept in order to distinguish *Hono japonensis* from the rest of humankind: *kanjin*, which is the reverse (in sinogrammatic guise) of *ningen*, the ordinary term for saying 'human being'. By dint of this trope, Hamaguehi intends to insist on the idea that the Japanese are contextualists, contrary to the Westemers, who are individualists (let us incidentally note that, in nippology, differing from 'the Occident' in some trait or other is enough to be unique).

The Japanese society is thus presented here as a 'network society' (*nettowâku shakai*), composed of 'contextuals' (*kanjin*). A contextual is not a colleetivist; it is his own well managed personal interest which makes him dedicate himself to the group, following three principles: mutual dependence, mutual confidence, and the relation to others posed as an end in itself, not as a means.

How this can work, the book details in about ten chapters, the less interesting of which is not the second one: 'The natural foundations of Japanese systems'. One learns here that the aforesaid systems belong to the 'hierarchical/autonomous distributed type' (*kaisô gata jiritsu bunsan shisutemu*), that is, multiplex groupings, the components of which at each level are holons, thus endowed with a strong autonomy and mutually adapting at each level as well as between different levels. As for Western societies, they belong to the 'tree' type, that is, centralised structures in which, at any level, the parts totally depend on the centre.

As could be expected, it is the starfish which affords our authors an illustration of these natural foundations of the Japanese systems. It is assisted in this semantic mission by the company of fish shoals, bioconvection, oscillatory phenomena, and rhythmical movements.

One shall not be surprised to discover that, however, the most accomplished incarnation of such hierarchical/autonomous distributed systems is no other than the human brain in person, with its modular structures which enable it to choose, according to the needs, between the advantages of centralisation (which gives rapidity in general action) and those of decentralisation (which gives flexibility in adapting to the context).

The reader is thus confronted with the necessity to infer (the book, to be sure, does not go as far as to conclude explicitly so) that Japanese society is the most human achievement on Earth, since it (needless to add, is the only one which) is organised like the human brain itself. The absolute singularity of the Japanese contextual, *ipso facto*, is turned over into perfect universality.

This anthropological mechanism, of course, is nothing new under the sun (we know that many societies have explicitly conceived of themselves as the only humans), but it is here instructive on two planes: first, because it uses to do so the latest conceptual devices of systemics, biology and physics, which proves that metaphors transcend science and technology; and second, because its leading motifs are identical

154

or at least homologous to those which haunt tokyology, which proves that cities are integrated through sets of metaphors (i.e. collective fantasies), no less than they are so through physical networks.

Conclusion: capital cities as fountains of meaning

The figure of the starfish (or its homologue the amoeba, etc.), differing from Aphrodite, did not unexpectedly come into being from the foam of the nippological wave. The essential motifs of this fantasy owe in fact much to Buddhism and Taoism. It is, for instance, at least to Nagarjuna (IInd–IIIrd century AD) that one can trace back the motif of an absence of centre; it is but another expression of a constant theme, that of the void or absence of foundation (*sunyata*), which travelled down the whole Mahayana tradition. In the same way, the semi-aleatory and co-adaptive movement of the starfish, and the correlated tokyological motifs of chaos, progressive anarchy and the like, are but new metaphors of the old Taoist theme of *wuwei ziran*; and so on.

Needless to say, such metaphors have a long history in nippology itself. For example, the analogy which Nakane draws between the Japanese small group and the Western individual was already drawn, in another metaphor, by Watsuji Tetsurô when he paralleled Japanese familial space (the house) with European individual space (the room). Hamaguchi's contextual also descends from Watsuji's ethics, though clad in postmodern garment (Arthur Koestler's holon, etc.).

Without delving further into the analysis of these metaphors, which belong to some classical anthropological processes of constructing of a collective identity (the starfish has something to do with totemism, for instance), I shall focus my conclusion on a point more explicitly akin to the question of capital cities.

A capital is not a mere material entity; it is also necessarily an emblem, a fountain of meaning which gives authority to a given power. Depending on the degree of this centralness in various fields, its semantic aura stretches to more or less distant horizons. Its vectors are symbols of diverse kinds. A determining question is whether these symbols transcend, or not, the limits of a given ethnic or national community. The centralness of New York, for instance, is notably sustained by the diffusion of the English language throughout the world. This is not the case with Tokyo. Yet language – and related domains like literature, theatre etc. – is but one semantic system among those which are at work in the making of the centralness of a capital. Architecture, or more generally said spatial organisation, is at least as powerful a semantic tool in that respect. It has been consciously used for example by the popes in the XVIth century against Reformation, in order to reassert the centralness of Rome. It is presently used, in quite similar purposes, by President Mitterrand in Paris, as well as by generations of presidents, emperors and kings before him, by Tokugawa Ieyasu in Edo, etc. The new Tochô in Shinjuku relates evidently to the same kind of symbolicity.

Yet an imposing spatial order is not all. If it were so, then Nicolai Ceausescu's Bucarest might have become a fountain of meaning for Eastern Europe; which seems not to have been the case. In order to make sense and thus nourish its centralness, the spatial order of a capital must symbolise the motifs of a semantic system which transcends its material forms and actual power. This is typically the case of such figures as, concerning Tokyo, I have pointed out in this paper. Speaking of a hidden order, of progressive anarchy etc. makes sense, but this is not because Tokyo would be materially chaotic or anarchic. Tokyo is in fact an obviously rational and functional entity, inasmuch as one considers the actual motivations of its main actors (e.g. transporting masses or workers, maximising real estate values, etc.). Yet veiling this rationality with images like that of a creative chaos or a starfish is not a purely ideological delusion. It would not make sense, and thus would not arouse a collective fantasy, if it had not some ground in the Japanese tradition of spatial organisation on the one hand, and in the present state of our civilisation on the other hand.

As for the first aspect, let it suffice here to bear in mind the image of a path in a garden like, for instance, Koishikawa Kôrakuen. As for the second one, I shall just mention that when Roland Barthes wrote, in *L'Empire des signes*, that Tokyo had a 'centre ville, centre vide', he related this to the question of the subject. By so doing, however allusively, he pointed out one of those symbolical links which work in the making of a collective fantasy. Barthes, for sure, was neither a japanologist nor an urbanist; but for that very reason, the formula which he coined, by connecting the image of Tokyo with the most fundamental and general question of postmodernity (the debasement of the modern subject), all the more efficiently participated in making Tokyo an emblem of postrnodemity.

This sole example is enough to show that the horizon of the semantic aura, the centre of which is embodied by Tokyo, already stretches widely beyond Japan and even Japanese matters. Correlatively, things from Tokyo have begun to bear something of the universal, like things from Paris or Vienna did in the Belle Epoque, or those from New York later in this century. In that sense, it is not absurd to imagine that Tokyo, in the coming century, might become the emblem of a certain hegemony. Aren't its holonic paths, amoebas and contextuals corroborated by the power of the yen, just like the franc corroborated the Haussmannian order of Belle Epoque Paris?

Be it as it may, if any form of Japanese hegemony is to take place, it will not do so without Tokyo as its emblem. There has never been any hegemony in human history that was not sustained by the image of a capital city, like Babylon, Baghdad, Chang'an or London; and such cities have always worked as sources of meaning, or foci of collective fantasies, not only as the central places of an actual power.

Now, whether postmodernity can be equated with post-westernity is a question of another dimension, which transcends the pros and the cons of the above argument. There are more paradigms in the skies, and more cities on Earth, than are dreamt of in all my japanology…

Ashihara, Yoshinobu (1986) *Kakureta chitsujo. Nijuisseiki no toshi e mukatte.* Tokyo: Chuokoronsha. Translated into English and French.

Barthes, Roland (1970) *L'Empire des signes.* Geneve: Skira. Translated into Japanese, English etc.

Berque, Augustin (1976) *Le Japon, gestion de l'espace et changement social.* Paris: Flammarion.

– (1982) *Vivre l'espace au Japon.* Paris: PUF. Translated into Japanese.

– (1993) *Toshi no kosumorojî. Nichi Bei Ô no toshi hikaku.* Tokyo: Kodansha.

– (1993) *Du geste à la cité. Formes urbaines et lien social au Japon.* Paris: Gallimard. Japanese translation forthcoming.

Hamaguchi, Eshun (ed., 1992) *Nihon gata shisutemu. Jinrui bunmei no hitotsu no kata / Japanese systems. An alternative civilisation?* Yokohama: SEKOTAC.

Imada, Takatoshi (1987) *Modân no datsu-kôchiku. Sangyô shakai no yukue.* Tokyo: Chuokoronsha.

Nakane, Chie (1967) *Tate shakai no ningen kankei.* Tokyo: Kodansha. Translated into English, French etc.

- (1978) *Tate shakai no rikigaku.* Tokyo: Kodansha.

Watsuji, Tetsurô (1935) *Fûdo. Ningengakuteki kôsatsu.* Tokyo: Iwanami Shoten. Translated into English.

Yoshimoto, Ryûmei (1968) *Kyôdô gensô ron.* Tokyo: Kawade Shobo.

157

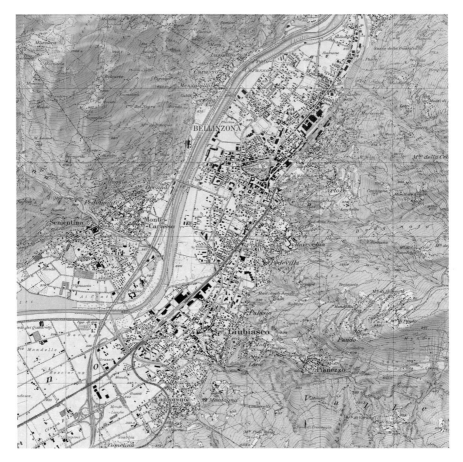

1 Map of Ticino valley. Note the existing urban settlement on the edge of the valley, the expansion area on the flood plain, and the suburban development on the lower slopes of the hillsides. The *autostrada* follows the west bank of the Ticino river past Bellinzoua and Monte Carasso.
(Drawing courtesy of Eidgenössischen Landestopographie)

Thomas Deckker

The re-invention
of the site

A new type of site has emerged as a focus of concerns among certain contemporary European architects. These sites are generally on the peripheries of cities, rather than in their historic centres, many of which are, in any case, post-war reconstructions: railway yards, the suburbs, and the suburbanised countryside. These architects have evolved a new attitude to the design of buildings as a response to these sites, which has informed their approach to other, more urban, contexts. Their work often appears exceptionally brutal: the design vocabulary is of strong and self-consciously basic geometrical form, of straightforward construction and materials, which derives its articulation as much from a response to its context as from its intrinsic concerns. Rather than celebrating, for example, construction or the logic of geometry, the main concern of this architecture seems to be the making of place, specifically urban place, on these marginal sites.

This attitude to the making of place challenges the conventional polarities of contemporary urban architecture: neither the rational anti-urban forms of much post-war architecture, nor the populist reaction against it.[1] In this work, the distinctions among the concerns of architecture, urbanism, and landscape design have been disregarded. Furthermore, the negation of representation – of looking like other buildings, implicit in populism, indicates a distrust of how and what architecture actually does reveal through its appearance. The intention of employing basic geometrical form and straightforward construction and materials is to emphasise personal experience: the critical appreciation of scale, form, material, light, view, and movement, for both architecture and site. It might be said that the site has been re-invented as part of architecture.

159

Such peripheral areas, and an architecture which responds to them and challenges them, may be seen in microcosm in the canton of Ticino in Switzerland and in work there of Luigi Snozzi (1932–) and Aurelio Galfetti (1936–). In the Ticino valley, there are three distinct settlement patterns, which helps to isolate the periphery as a distinct topographical entity (Fig. 1). Urban settlement originally took place on the edge of the valley floor, away from the flood plain, in compact and distinct centres. The flood plain, made safe for building after the construction of St. Gotthard autostrada in the 1960s, generally consists of large plain fields for the mechanised type of agriculture which replaced the earlier intensive farming on the hillsides, the lower stretches of which are now dominated by suburban development. The flood plain now contains the expansion areas of the adjacent towns and forms their peripheries.

2 Snozzi: Kalman house.
(Photograph Thomas Deckker)

3 Galfetti: elevator motor-room in
the Castelgrande.
(Photograph Thomas Deckker)

160

Snozzi identified the predicament of the simultaneous decline of the agricultural heritage and the new pattern of urban growth in Ticino:

> This big region, with all its historical and cultural heritage, is now threatened by two basic developments: on one hand, the exodus of population from the more remote and inaccessible areas, and on the other, the process of the agglomeration of villages on the peripheries of cities, which puts its entire culture heritage in serious danger.[2]

Snozzi and Galfetti seek to transform the destruction of the landscape in Ticino and the trivialisation of its heritage by engaging with the specifics of place. Snozzi's approach may be seen in the Kalman house (1974–76; Fig. 2) in Brione, a holiday house on a steep hillside overlooking Locarno. Ticino has gone directly, within a few years, from an agricultural region of absolute poverty to a favourite holiday resort of the German-speaking Swiss. The resultant indiscriminate building activity threatens to destroy the benefits its inhabitants are supposed to enjoy: these holiday houses, mostly in the representational styles found anywhere in Europe, relate neither to the topography of the hillsides nor to the established urban patterns of the towns.

Both the relation to its site and the appearance of the Kalman house are in marked contrast to the surrounding suburban development. The house is a concrete box with one open end, organised along a curved retaining wall which distorts the open end and extends out to form the side of a pergola overlooking Lago Maggiore. The curved retaining wall, running along the contours, represents and includes the landscape, in contrast to the rectilinear geometry of the house and pergola. The staircase runs through a three-storey-high light-filled void along this retaining wall (the entrance is at basement level), lit from above by a long window which re-establishes the horizon in the space – literally so, as the window is level with the side of the hill. The building has a material presence, but it is not dominated by its construction; there is no distinction between columns and walls – all surfaces, except the floor in red tiles, are in rendered concrete.

The Kalman house is one of several by Snozzi in Ticino which employ the same design vocabulary in the making of place at a domestic scale. The making of place at an urban scale may be seen in Bellinzona (pop. 17,000) and its suburb of Monte Carasso (pop. 1,700), where Galfetti and Snozzi were faced with the renovation of historic buildings and new urban buildings, as well as new works on the periphery. Their design intentions may be seen most clearly in the work on the peripheries of these towns, where the responses necessary to establish place in the large and vacant flood-plain have been refined and applied to other contexts. Although their basic aesthetic intentions were clearly present in their earlier work, the more extreme condition of the periphery has led to a more extreme response. Snozzi defined his objective in Monte Carasso as:

> The new interventions must simultaneously respect the existing architectonic and urban structure and establish a confrontation with it.[3]

It is this paradoxical respect and confrontation which makes the work of Galfetti and Snozzi so distinctive.

4 Galfetti: plan of Bellinzona, showing the Castelgrande and 'Murata' (1), post office (2), 'Bianco' and 'Nero' apartments (7), swimming pool (3), tennis club (4/5/6), and housing on the flood plain (10/11).
(Drawing by Aurelio Galfetti)

162

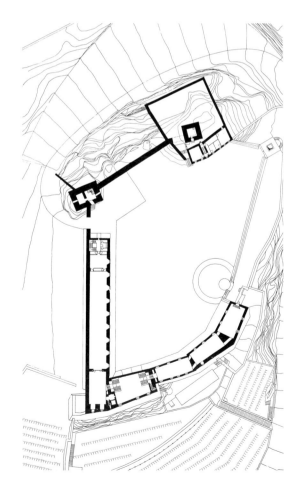

5 Galfetti: ground-floor plan of Castelgrande.
(Drawing by Aurelio Galfetti)

This simultaneous respect and confrontation may be seen in the work of Galfetti in the renovation of historic buildings as well as in new works (Fig. 4). The reconstruction of the Castelgrande in Bellinzona (1980–92) is probably his best-known work. It is truly a reconstruction, as the original castle had virtually disappeared under centuries of vegetation. Although the reconstruction is theoretically centred around a museum, its principal purpose seems to be to provide public spaces within and along the castle walls. It is a work in many ways comparable to Carlo Scarpa's reconstruction of the Castelvecchio (1956–73) in Verona: clear distinctions have been made between new and old, while both have served the creation of new uses and places. The Castelgrande is rather more modest historically and architecturally than the Castelvecchio, and the degree of dereliction much greater, and consequently the reconstruction has been less about uncovering the historical and architectural density than in the straightforward creation of new places within the fabric. This is the major divergence from Scarpa: Galfetti has reconstructed parts of the original fabric, and some of the site, to accentuate its spatial continuities.

The reconstruction of the site went so far as to include new landscaping outside the castle walls, as well as inside. New vineyards were laid along the contours to accentuate the form of the walls. New paving was laid around the courtyard; the white plastered walls of the castle buildings make it seem more like a piazza than a fortification. Although the walls were extensively reconstructed to appear original, in some places, such as the new terrace and the elevator motor-room, the new fabric is differentiated by material and geometry (Fig. 3). The most recognisably new elements are the new doors – black steel rectangles which do not follow exactly the shape of their openings; here respect and confrontation are most evident.

Although in the middle of town, the Castelgrande was virtually inaccessible from it (Fig. 5). Galfetti made two new links to the town, in addition to the original paths running along the contours. He incorporated the 'Murata' – the remains of the fifteenth-century town wall of the Sforza castle (Fig. 6), which juts out like a pier into the town. This contains two levels of walkway, the upper a conventional machicolated battlement, the lower a mural gallery. The 'Murata' was cut where it was later crossed by the Viale Portone, the main artery, which it now bridges over. Galfetti also extended the castle literally into the town by the extremely bold design of the elevator. This was excavated from the rock, with an entrance from the new Piazza del Sole like a big slot of light leading to the inner cave. Thus the spatial experience of the castle is transferred to the centre of the town, at a point previously inaccessible; the elevator is now merely a caesura.

From the castle walls, one can see Galfetti's other works in Bellinzona and, further afield, Snozzi's works in Monte Carasso. In the town centre is the Post Office (1981–85), while directly beneath the castle are the 'Bianco' and 'Nero' apartment buildings (1986-87).[4] Galfetti's most important contribution to Bellinzona, however, is the still-unfinished development plan for the flood-plain, in which structure was given to this amorphous area by robust concrete walls and geometrical plan shapes.

The Swimming Pool (1967–70) was the first of Galfetti's works on the flood-plain. It incorporated an elevated walkway, which, too, crosses the Viale Portone, to give access to the facilities.[5] The masterplan also included two housing projects (1983-85) –

6 Galfetti: 'Murata' showing new landscaping of castle and, in the distance, Monte Carasso. (Photograph Thomas Deckker)

7 Galfetti: Tennis Club. (Photograph Thomas Deckker)

164

unfortunately not built – and the Tennis Club (1982–85).[6] The Tennis Club (Fig. 7) is the most extreme of these designs – a two-storey high concrete spine wall, with an attached block containing, on the ground floor, cafés and communal facilities, and, above, changing rooms. The wall faces its car park in a single stretch of concrete, emphasised by horizontal ribs; the other is articulated by the large windows of the café and the cladding panels of the changing rooms. The wall controls the arrangement of the site on both sides, accentuated by rows of trees. From the car-park side, from where it is uncertain whether it is actually a building, it could be interpreted as just a wall, a landscape design or an adventurous work of 'land art'; it is not dissimilar to 'Shift' (1970) by Richard Serra – a series of steel plates set into a field. In any case, the major design statement is the creation of place in the landscape.

Across the Ticino river lies the suburb of Monte Carasso. The development of Monte Carasso has been completely dominated by Snozzi since 1978; every new building consistently expresses his preference for simple geometric forms and in situ concrete. The cantonal development plan envisaged it as a dormitory suburb of Bellinzona – a low-density centre-less agglomeration, but Snozzi, with the support of the municipality, proposed an alternative. Snozzi originally won a competition in 1978 for a school on the outskirts of the village, but from this extended his involvement into a plan for a definitive centre, with an increase in the density of the facilities and the fabric (Fig. 8). Snozzi believed that the cantonal development plan was not able to answer the problems of development in this type of site:

> I am convinced that one of the aspects which has determined the impotence of the development plan with respect to these problems, is its position of defence and its elaborate general regulations which do not take into account the specifics of place.[7]

To create a centre for Monte Carasso, Snozzi placed the school and mayoral offices within a former Augustine convent, which had been completely submerged beneath nineteenth-century developments, and created a piazza in the courtyard. Such is the success of the piazza that it is now used for summer festivals, a reversal of his renovation of the Piazza Grande (1989–90) in Locarno for the existing Film Festival. Other buildings were placed around the convent to reinforce its presence: the Palestra (1979–84) – a gymnasium, the so-called Casa del Sindaco (1984) – actually the Casa Guidotti, and the Banca Raiffeisen (1984) (Fig. 9). The gymnasium is a glorious light-filled basilica reminiscent of Kahn; here the municipality, to enable Snozzi's scheme to be realised, refused a subsidy on its construction costs from the army, who wanted to use it – with certain modifications – for military training.[8]

The convent in Monte Carasso has been restored in a manner reminiscent of Scarpa's reconstruction of the Castelvecchio or Galfetti's of the Castelgrande, with resolutely new elements juxtaposed against the old fabric. The homage to Scarpa may be seen explicitly in the gridded windows and doors of the school and Palestra. Like Galfetti at the Castelgrande, however, Snozzi has reconstructed some of the original

165

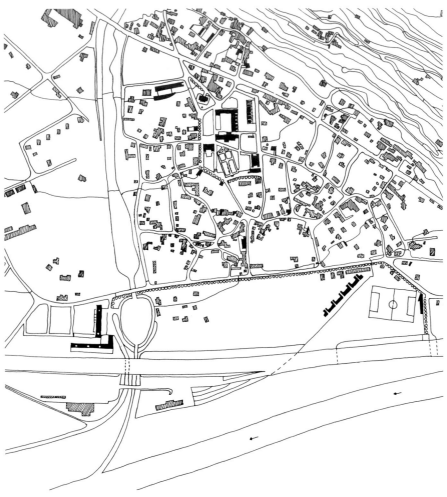

166

8 Snozzi: site plan of Monte
Carraso. Buildings in black are part
of Snozzi's new master plan.
(Drawing by Luigi Snozzi)

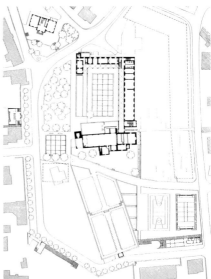

9 Snozzi: Monte Carasso plan.
Note the piazza (centre), Palestra
(bottom right) and Casa Guidotti
(top left).
(Drawing by Luigi Snozzi)

fabric to accentuate its spatial continuities.[9] The new fabric of the school, such as the enormous light-hoods over the classrooms, forms a new historical layer; the light-hoods act not only as a new, serial, form to be read against the existing fabric, but are inhabitable as separate study areas within each classroom (Fig. 10).[10]

The use of serial forms must be understood as a specifically contemporary form of composition, like the '15 Concrete Boxes' (1979) by Donald Judd at the Chinati Foundation in Marfa, as against the hierarchical and symmetrical form of the 17th-century convent. This is brought out clearly in drawings showing the original – axial – and reconstructed – serial – plans of the convent.[11] The gradual development of increasingly abstract and serial forms for the light-hoods and their increasing distinction from the existing fabric may also be seen in the various development stages.[12] Snozzi used serial forms in other projects on the flood-plain such as that for the Port in Brissago (1972); one of his contemporary aphorisms was 'variety is the prelude to monotony; to avoid it, repeat the basic unit'.[13]

The theme of respect and confrontation may also be seen in the planning of Monte Carasso. In place of the low-density residential development envisaged in the development plan, with houses set in the middle of their plots, Snozzi proposed to increase the density by 'filling in' between existing houses – such as the Casa Marisoli, and to reinforce the edge of the town – such as the Casa Briccola – a tower house – by Snozzi's pupil Ricardo Briccola. However, the material and geometry of these buildings are in sharp contrast to the existing – they are, like the Kalman house, concrete cubes. The street pattern takes the place of the contours of the hillside seen in the Kalman house: the Casa Guidotti, for example, is built up to the edge of the street, with the boundary walls, seemingly contiguous with the house, extending out to form a garage and entrance portico at the front and a pergola in the garden.

The edge of the town adjacent to the autostrada is further defined by a long wall of low-cost housing, the Quartière Morenal, currently under construction. The Quartière Morenal is analogous to Alvaro Siza's Quinta da Malagucira housing (1977; under construction) in Évora. As Snozzi says:

> It is exactly in this periphery that the first signs of the urban expansion of the neighbouring towns begin to show, and it is exactly here that new housing quarters of a more urban character are being inserted.[14]

The Quartière Morenal may be seen as the summation of Snozzi's work in Monte Carasso, in which he has addressed successfully the difficult problem of low-cost housing. Like Galfetti's Tennis Club, it asserts an extreme aesthetic position (Fig. 11).

The buildings of the Quartière Morenal consist of two long blocks, the lower of which runs parallel to the autostrada, the higher at right angles which separates the parking zone from a communal garden. They are cast totally in in-situ concrete, articulated only by the day-work joints of the floor slabs and vertical panel joints. The windows and aluminium shutters lie in the plane of the facade, which leads to a highly restrained surface. While this description may seem like that of many of the post-war

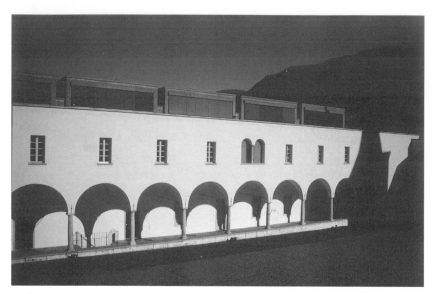

10 Snozzi: School. Note the serial
form of the light-hoods facing the
piazza.
(Photograph Thomas Deckker)

11 Quartière Morenal from the
garden facing the café terrace.
(Photograph Thomas Deckker)

slab-blocks which have, though the rationality of their use and construction, disfigured European cities, there are important differences. Firstly, the quality of construction is extremely high. Secondly, the restraint in the expression of this construction means that it may be articulated - by various sizes of openings, for example, to create specific places. Finally, the creation of specific places around the blocks – such as the shops and café on the terrace, and the workshop spaces next to the car-park, and the relation of the blocks to the town centre – such as the enclosure of communal garden (faced by all the balconies), reinforces a sense of urban presence. Thus, while it does not look like an historic city, it contains a set of recognisable urban spaces (Fig. 12).

The historic European city has become central to the discourse of contemporary architecture since – at least – the publication of Aldo Rossi's *The Architecture of the City* in 1966. There is surely no better illustration of Rossi's thesis of the political importance of architecture than the success of Snozzi's *piazza* as the focus of the re-urbanisation of Monte Carasso:

> There is something in the nature of urban artefacts that renders them very similar – and not only metaphorically – to a work of art. They are material constructions, but not withstanding the material, something different: although they are conditioned, they also condition.[15]

Rossi, on the other hand, claimed that the serial form and industrial materials of his Gallaratese housing (1969–73) in Milan were subconsciously inspired by the repetitive concrete bulwarks of the St. Gotthard autostrada, which he passed on his frequent journeys from Milan to Zurich in the 1970s.[16]

But the problems of the city changed radically in the 1970s; the periphery emerged as the site of a new urban form in European cities in response to enormous changes in urban life. If the 1960s was a period of revolt against capitalism in cultural history, it was also a period in economic history when the phase of 'late capitalism' is held to have come into being by historians such as Frederic Jameson, David Harvey, and Edward Soja.[17] According to Harvey, cities changed from places of production to places of consumption, a change symbolised by the publication in 1972 of Robert Venturi's *Learning from Las Vegas*, and so architecture too lost its rational imperatives.[18] Centres of cities became the site of the public display of consumption, while increased mobility meant their expansion.[19] If one result was the rise of 'post-modern' architecture which represented this power, with its crude spatial and material qualities, then another was the rise of a critical architectural culture.[20]

Although Rossi had reacted against the conditions of the modern city, his vision of pre-industrial archetypes could not be applied easily to the peculiar nature of the periphery. The generation of architects of Snozzi and Galfetti still maintain a relationship to architectural history, but tangentially rather than representationally. The 'inhabitable walls' of Galfetti's Swimming Pool and Tennis Club arguably have the same relationship to the 'Murata' – the remains of the fifteenth-century wall of the Sforza Castlegrande – as Siza's 'Quinta da Malagueira' housing does to the sixteenth-century 'Aguas da Prata' aqueduct in Évora.[21] In both there was a perfectly adequate functional explanation – in

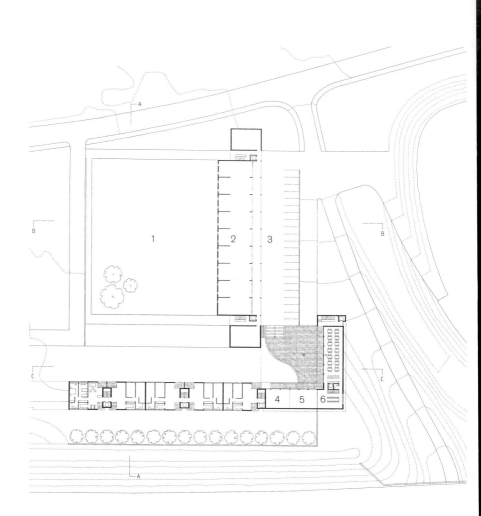

12 Snozzi: Site of Quartière
Morenal, Note the garden (1), the
workshop spaces facing the car
park (2/3), and the café and shops
(4/5/6).
(Drawing by Luigi Snozzi)

Bellinzona, crossing a busy road, and in Évora, providing a service infrastructure – but these are not adequate explanations. Nor does the appearance of the buildings – such as serial form and industrial materials – relate to the historical forms associated with European cities: it is a specifically contemporary aesthetic. While a contemporary aesthetic is not an indicator of quality or a guarantee of success, Snozzi and Galfetti show it can be valid.

The attitudes to aesthetics – and to politics – within this critical architectural culture may also be found among a group of – mainly American – artists – such as Donald Judd (1928–95) and Richard Serra (1939–). Judd and Serra also reacted against a particular contemporary urban landscape: the Meadowlands, New Jersey, the industrial hinterland of New York, during the 1960s. Their work is so provocative for architects because it is, in many important respects, indistinguishable from architecture; it too blurs the distinctions of sculpture, architecture, urbanism, and landscape design. Judd was directly involved in architecture, not only on the design of the buildings at the Chinati Foundation, Marfa, but also on the design of the Post Office Railway Station (1993) in Basle, on which he collaborated with its architect Hans Zwimpfer; the block planning invites one to read the city of Basle in the same way as the landscape in Marfa: as topography, devoid of historical association.[22] Serra's attitude to site is virtually indistinguishable from Snozzi's or Siza's:

> One of the basic problems posed by any context (landscape, urban, or architectural) is that of content... to be effective my work must disengage itself from the already existing content of the site. One method of adding to an existing context and thereby changing the content is through analysing and assimilating specific environmental components – boundaries, edges, buildings, paths, streets, the entire physiognomy of the site.[23]

This is, for Snozzi, the central issue of architecture: that the focus of interest in a work is the relations it enters into with its site, and not the work itself; it is a metaphor for the political relations of its inhabitants to the city.[24] There is a good reason to consider that the inclusion of site and the negation of representation in a work of architecture are overtly political. Guy Debord, in *The Society of the Spectacle*, linked representation with a particular political attitude:

> The entire life of those societies in which modern conditions of production prevail presents itself as an immense accumulation of spectacles. All that was once directly lived has become mere representation.[25]

This architecture is the architecture of resistance to the dominant myths of the consumer society. These architects seek to re-establish personal relations with collective urban life. They choose to do this in a progressive, rather than a regressive manner: a rejection of historicism in favour of the personal experience of scale, form, material, light, view, and movement. Their most extreme and successful work is exactly on the sites which this society has produced: the urban periphery.

1　These two categories are derived from Kenneth Frampton: *Modern Architecture, a critical history* (London: Thames & Hudson 1980; 2nd edn 1985) pp. 9–10. Frampton juxtaposed 'kitsch vernacular' with 'reductionism' in which 'the split between architecture and urban development has led to a situation in which the possibility of the former contributing to the latter and vice versa... has suddenly become extremely limited... [because of] the rationalisation of both building types and methods.'

2　Luigi Snozzi: 'Premessa per il progetto' in *Monte Carasso: die Wiedererfindung des Ortes / Monte Carasso: la reinvenzione del sito* (Basle: Birkhäuser 1995) p. 14.

3　Pierre-Alain Croset (ed.): *Luigi Snozzi a Monte Carasso 1978-1992* (Municipio di Monte Carasso c. 1993) p. 5.

4　Galfetti lives in 'Bianco'.

5　Access to closed facilities is denied by removing the floorboards from their entrance steps.

6　The development plan was changed to allow only sports on this site.

7　Luigi Snozzi: 'Premessa per il progetto' in *Monte Carasso: die Wiedererfindung des Ortes / Monte Carasso: la reinvenzione del sito* (Basle: Birkhäuser 1995) p. 14.

8　The reserve units of the Swiss army – in effect the entire adult male population – form local militias who usually train in community facilities which they subsidise. The modification in this case was the colour of the linoleum floor, which would have been required to be in olive drab instead of bright green.

9　Notice in particular the lowering of roof of the apse to accentuate the wall of the church in the *piazza*.

10 The light-hoods may also be derived from Le Corbusier's Venice Hospital project (1965).

11 Luigi Snozzi: *Monte Carasso: die Wiedererfindung des Ortes / Monte Carasso: la reinvenzione del sito* (Basle: Birkhäuser 1995) p. 28.

12 1979 project: pp.19–21; 1993 project: pp. 22–23. Luigi Snozzi: *Monte Carasso: die Wiedererfindung des Ortes / Monte Carasso: la reinvenzione del sito* (Basle: Birkhäuser 1995).

172

13 Peter Disch (ed.): *Luigi Snozzi: Costruzioni e progetti – Buildings and projects 1958–1993* (Lugano: ADV 1994) pp.103–104. Aphorism written while teaching at the Eidgenössische Technische Hochschule in Zürich 1973–75.

14 Luigi Snozzi: 'Il contesto' in *Monte Carasso: die Wiedererfindung des Ortes / Monte Carasso: la reinvenzione del sito* (Basle: Birkhäuser 1995) p. 12.

15 Aldo Rossi: *The Architecture of the City* (Padua 1966; Cambridge, Mass.: MIT 1982) p. 32

16 Aldo Rossi: 'Thoughts about my Recent Work' *A+U* May 1976 p. 74. Rossi was Professor of Planning at the Eidgenössische Technische Hochschule in Zürich from 1972 to 1975. The autostrada, designed by the architect Rino Tami, was known for its sensitive adaptation to the valley landscape. Tita Carloni: 'The Motorway as Architectural Landmark' *Modern Architecture Itineraries in Ticino* (Bellinzona: Ente ticinese per il turismo c. 1990). Snozzi worked briefly for Rino Tami in 1957.

17 Frederic Jameson: *Post-Modernism, or, The Cultural Logic of Late Capitalism* (New York and London: Verso 1991); David Harvey: *The Condition of Postmodernity* (Cambridge, Mass and Oxford: Blackwell 1990); Edward Soja: *Postmodern Geographies: The Reassertion of Space in Critical Theory* (New York & London: Verso 1989).

18 David Harvey: 'Flexible Accumulation through Urbanization' *Perspecta* 26 (1990) p. 253. Robert Venturi, Denise Scott-Brown, and Steve Izenour: *Learning from Las Vegas* (Cambridge, Mass. and London: MIT 1972; rev. edn 1977). The revised edition was subtitled 'The Forgotten Symbolism of Architectural Form'. The original publication in 1972 was before the transformation of Las Vegas by entertainment corporations.

19 See Margaret Crawford: 'The World in a Shopping Mall' in Michael Sorkin (ed.): *Variations on a Theme Park: The New American City and the End of Public Space* (New York: Hill and Wang 1992) pp. 3–30. Crawford describes shopping malls as places of disorientation and surveillance.

20 Donald Judd described AT&T, New York 1978–84, by Philip Johnson, as the paradigm of 'post-modern' architecture. 'A long discussion not about masterpieces but about why there are so few of them. Part 1' in Marianne Stockebrand (ed.): *Donald Judd: Architektur* pp. 179–83.

21 Both the 'Quartière Monrenal' housing in Monte Carasso and the 'Quinta da Malagueira' housing in Évora have won the Prince of Wales Prize in Urban Design, administered by Harvard University.

22 Immobiliengesellschaft Bahnhof Ost AG (ed.): *Bahnhof Ost Basel* (East Basle Railway Station) (Immobiliengesellschaft Bahnhof Ost AG Basle 1995).

23 Richard Serra: 'Notes from Sight Point Road' *Perspecta* 19 p. 157.

24 Snozzi is an 'autonomous socialist', not linked to the main Swiss socialist parties.

25 Guy Debord: *The Society of the Spectacle* (New York: Zone Books 1994; 1st publ. *La Société du Spectacle,* Paris: Buchet-Chastel 1967) p. 12.

Relating architecture to landscape through collaborations

Introduction

There is clearly an overlap between this section and the previous one since these articles discuss collaborations at different scales: from small private domestic projects through a public project with tremendous historical memory and international resonance (the landscaping up to the Acropolis), to a project in a large metropolis and finally to a project covering an entire Californian region. But these three articles therefore also cover four different types of collaborations: the collaboration between one architect and one landscape architect (Scharoun and Mattern), between a team of people (an EDAW project), and between a team of planners working on an entire region of California. And then the article about Pikionis discusses a collaboration which is often overlooked: the collaboration between the designer and the manual workers building the design. This is of course where a design can either come to grief or be actually enhanced by the enthusiasm, knowledge and skills of the manual workers themselves: they have the ability to improve a design, correct the designer's mistakes or sometimes wreck the design through misunderstanding, carelessness or deliberate hostility. There is here again overlap with Part Two: the Maeght Foundation involved near-perfect collaboration between patron, architect, artists, horticulturist and workmen.

177

Hans Scharoun, Schminke house, Löbau, Saxony 1932–33: garden by Herta Hammerbacher and Hermann Mattern.

1 Site plan, with owner's factory south of house. Angle change in house plan derives from site shape.
(Redrawn by author)

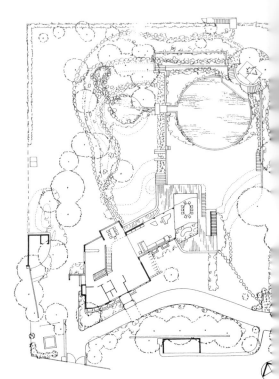

2 Garden plan including ground floor of house. Essential features, including round pond, predate house. (Redrawn by Laurence Pattacini after a reconstruction by Claudia Feltrop; see Risselada, 1997, p. 75).

178

3 Interior of solarium: garden enters house with south-facing winter garden.
(Scharoun Archive, Akademie der Künste)

4 House from North, showing projection over garden.
(Scharoun Archive, Akademie der Künste)

Peter Blundell Jones

Architect and
landscape architect
working together:
Scharoun and Mattern

Landscape architects all too often get a poor deal, called in too late when the important spatial decisions have already been made, expected to fill with unobtrusive low-maintenance planting the holes of unwanted space around the proud objects that architects have imposed. Even gardens for private houses are too often an afterthought:

> House and garden usually do not arise together and seldom at the same time. Mostly a house is built first and the garden made around it, but if there was a garden first, little of it remains undisturbed by the time the house is built. House-building is always a drastic intervention into an existing order, if only that of the biological society of weeds which covers and protects the earth. Garden-making is an extensive reordering set out according to new and inventive rules, yet always in sympathy with nature.
>
> The layout of the house requires a planner, that of the garden also. Often the representatives of these two entwined disciplines do not meet, or come together too late, when they can but tolerate each other. It would be better if they met to discuss and decide every detail before the first sod was broken. Best of all, the planning of 'house in its garden' should be a mutual undertaking.[1]

179

These reflections by the great German landscape architect Hermann Mattern towards the end of his career suggest that the kind of collaboration he wanted was too seldom achieved. Yet he did find a willing partner in one of the most famous architects with whom he worked, Hans Scharoun, and at the peak of their collaboration with the brilliant Kassel Theatre project of 1952 the two received equal billing. Their work there, as in earlier domestic projects, is seamless, for Scharoun always cared as deeply about the relationship between house and garden (or building and setting) as Mattern did about that between garden and house. They seem to have learned from each other, for if Mattern's wonderfully informal and almost Japanese feel for irregular paving was adopted by Scharoun, Scharoun's free design method undoubtedly influenced Mattern when, in the 1950s, he began to plan houses to go with his gardens. Because Scharoun was so much more widely known, his reputation has tended to overshadow that of Mattern, which is unfair to both. The unfairness to Mattern is obvious, but it is unfair to Scharoun too because it suggests an arrogance he did not possess, and undermines his lifelong and deeply held belief that architecture should be mutual work towards a common idea: a social product. As Alfred Schinz, who worked for him in the 1950s, has observed:

> Personally modest, Scharoun was quite direct and uncomplicated in his deep opposition to every kind of trumpeting design-publicity and marketing strategy. He considered the honours and public recognition that he gained as a shared thing serving the general well-being. That such honours were frequently given for talent and success which should single him out personally disturbed him considerably and led him to consider refusal; he wanted them only as a recognition that the idea, the spiritual standpoint which he felt bound him with others, had been understood. This was of the greatest importance for him and was the foundation of his work, to which he brought his artistic gift and creative fantasy as an additional factor, with joy but also with responsibility.[2]

Scharoun was born in Bremen in 1893 and went to study architecture in Berlin in 1912. His earliest projects show a concern with context, and a house design done as part of his entry portfolio to architectural school already shows a planned garden. The First World War took him to East Prussia, where in lieu of military duties he took part in the reconstruction programme, and there he stayed until 1925. Through sketches, correspondence and published competition designs he joined in Bruno Taut's Expressionist Movement and began to make a name for himself. In 1925 he took up a chair at the Breslau Kunstakademie, and soon began to work also in Berlin. His house at the Weissenhofsiedlung in Stuttgart of 1927, a hostel at the Breslau Werkbund Exhibition of 1929 and some ingenious blocks of flats in Berlin made his reputation as a rising if unorthodox star. The brilliant Schminke House in Löbau, Saxony of 1932–33 (Figs. 1–4) brought this productive period to a close, marking a plateau of maturity and establishing some of the most important characteristics of his later work, but because of the rise of Hitler it proved also to be his last piece of overtly modernist work for a couple of decades. The Schminke House also marked his first contact with Hermann Mattern, though it is Mattern's wife and working partner Herta Hammerbacher to whom the garden is credited.[3]

Born near Kassel in 1902, Mattern was nine years younger than Scharoun. His family could not afford to send him to architectural school so he trained as a gardener, completing the course in 1921. He went on to study garden planning at the Lehr-und Forschungsanstalt für Gartenbau at Berlin Dahlem, and then worked for a year in the gardens department for the city of Magdeburg. After a short period as assistant to the well-known landscape architect Leberecht Migge – the designer of gardens for Taut and Mendelsohn among others – he joined Karl Foerster at Bornim near Potsdam to specialise in garden design. Foerster was a leading landscape pioneer and plant breeder with an international reputation, who ran extensive nurseries in rural Bornim at the edge of the Berlin periphery. The firm employed some 300 gardeners and undertook hundreds of projects. Mattern and Hammerbacher worked for Foerster until 1935, and even after that the three continued to collaborate in a more egalitarian association. Mattern developed much of his plant vocabulary while working with Foerster, especially the use of perennials, for which the group was renowned in Germany.

It is evident from preliminary sketches that, in planning the Schminke house, a Modernist villa for a rich industrialist, Scharoun was deeply concerned from the start with the relationship between house and site. He considered different placings on the plot, and eventually resolved the conflict between the good northern views and sun from the factory side with a long thin plan (Fig. 1). There was a 26° angle shift between the site boundaries, which he adopted into the plan in a radical and dynamic way, and the falling level of the garden was used to make the house jut out dramatically over the lawn and pond. Just as the house projected itself into the landscape, becoming increasingly transparent towards its open east end, so the garden came back into the house (Fig. 3) in the form of a generous winter garden on the south side of its solarium, with a soil base and a miniature pool. The steps outside the house echoed those inside, and lines of movement flowed from house to garden, from garden to house. In short, everything possible was done to tie the house into the garden, to dramatise the difference between its various faces, to create series of outdoor rooms complementary to those within. In its essential relationship with its plot, the Schminke House was the complete opposite of Le Corbusier's free-standing Villa Savoye, which needed to treat the site as a *tabula rasa* to maintain its purity. The contrast shows the profound difference even at this early stage of Modernism between the organic integrative approach of Scharoun and the object-like monumentality of the International Style.

How much of this is Scharoun and how much Mattern and Hammerbacher? It is frustrating not to know, since the collaboration was evidently founded at this point. Scharoun's open attitude to creative collaboration was already evident in other aspects of the project, for he incorporated the brilliant lamp designs of Otto Rittweger and the fabrics of Otti Berger into the interior of the house in the same seamless way that he linked the house with the garden. He had a special gift for being able to include the ideas of others into his projects because of the open-mindedness of his approach and the breadth and inventiveness of his vocabulary.[4] Presumably he knew of Foerster's reputation and recommended the firm to his client Schminke, and at the crucial moment Hammerbacher was perhaps the designer free to undertake the long journeys to the site and take on the job. It must have been an enjoyable collaboration, because Mattern and Hammerbacher were soon commissioning Scharoun to build a house for themselves and their daughter, which was completed at Bornim the very next year.

The Mattern house (Figs. 5–9) is a little masterpiece, which stretched a tiny budget as far as possible.[5] With its low modest form, its garden walls running out to garage and summerhouse, its framing with low mounds and trees, it gets about as far as possible from being an object-building. Indeed, except from the air, it cannot be seen as a whole. The north-facing entrance side is quite cut off from the more generous and open garden side, where the Matterns created a number of linked outdoor rooms of varying orientation and intimacy, and where each transition between inside and out is

Hans Scharoun, Mattern house, Bornim, Potsdam 1932–4: garden by Hermann Mattern and Herta Hammerbacher.

5 View from garden. (Scharoun Archive, Akademie der Künste)

6 View from living room. (Scharoun Archive, Akademie der Künste)

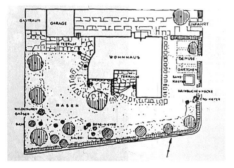

7 Site plan (from contemporary publication).

8 View from child's room across outdoor space into living room. (Scharoun Archive, Akademie der Künste)

182

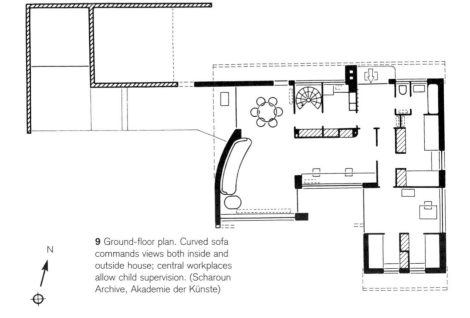

N

9 Ground-floor plan. Curved sofa commands views both inside and outside house; central workplaces allow child supervision. (Scharoun Archive, Akademie der Künste)

handled in a different way. In their organisation of the planting, with trees and shrubs to contain the less attractive distant views but small delicate plants near at hand, with subtle undulations of level and switches of ground surface from lawn to rockery to paving, Mattern and Hammerbacher developed their garden as the perfect foil for Scharoun's house, but this is hardly the right way to put it, for in this case the garden quite probably had the highest priority, even though the house was constructed first. However one looks at it, building and landscape are inseparable. The subtle shifts of scale and view occurring within the house just continue outside, showing a complete consistency of attitude. Architect and landscape architects shared the concept and merged their contributions in a wholly positive way.

Let us analyse the house and its setting more closely with the help of the plan. The house is approached via a country road, which runs in a north–south direction about 50 metres to the east of the plot. Its drive comes off this road at right angles and terminates in the garage to the north-west of the house having passed along the north side, where a projecting chimney and doorstep mark the entrance. The bedrooms, placed on the east side for the morning sun, look across a short garden space towards a hedge, which shields the view of the road. The living rooms of the house open up in various ways towards south and west, with selected views between trees to open country beyond.

A special requirement of the Matterns was that they be able to keep an eye on their baby daughter as they worked. She occupied the room projecting to the south-east, along with an au pair girl to look after her, each occupying one of the separate bed cubicles. The west-facing glass doors of their room open onto a small paved area, still under the roof, which could be used for outdoor play. Thanks to its position, this can be supervised either from the south-facing workplaces in the central study or from the built-in sofa of the living room. The same paved area also provides a way out into the garden eastwards from the living room. Immediately adjacent, adding to the sense of intimacy, were small-scale delicate plants and a miniature pond. Quite a different transition to the outside world is provided at the north-west corner of the house, where double glass doors lead from the dining area axially onto a wide strip of paving, which ends in a garden room. Here, sheltered from the north by the containing wall, larger-scale outdoor activities could take place, including dining and parties.

The most innovative area of Scharoun's plan is the part that lies between these two connections to the garden: the combination of curved wall, built-in sofa and great multi-pane window. The curved wall is the sole departure from the orthogonal that Scharoun allowed himself in this small house, but it is used to enormous effect. On the inside it contains and locates the curved sofa – the first of many to be found in Scharoun houses – and in so doing makes the furniture part of the architecture, even part of an internal landscape. The concave wall also makes the space expand towards window and outside world while shrinking towards the more intimate dining area. Convex on the outside, it sweeps the garden space invitingly towards the dining area doors, while the roofline continues to create a shaded and protected threshold. The great window partners the wall, void to its solid, defining the largest and most generously lit space, the

183

social focus of the house. Without the combination of these two elements the house is unthinkable. The multiple glazing bars are no accident: on the one hand they show protectively that there *is* a window, on the other they suggest three horizontal layers: top for daylight, middle for a standing view, bottom for a sitting one. The two opening lights set at the lowest level positively invite one to settle on the living room floor next to the radiator, to take view and air in intimate contact with the scented flowers in the raised bed immediately outside.

The curved sofa-wall is *the* key gesture: it transforms the plan. If north and east boundary walls can be regarded as a protective containment against the outside world, the sofa-wall is wholly within the house's most intimate territory, but differentiates the indoor from the outdoor rooms. A special innovation repeated in many later Scharoun/Mattern houses is the crumbly edge of the wall where it sinks into the garden, stressed with a battered corner where render gives way to rough stone. The passage from smooth to rough marks the transition from culture to nature. A hard edge would have detached the house starkly from the garden, but the opposite effect is wanted, so that one cannot decide where house ends and garden begins. So it disintegrates like a ruin, its base becoming lost in the planting. Was this Mattern's idea or Scharoun's? It parallels the random paving also used in this house, which Scharoun adopted at this time – perhaps again at Mattern's instigation. The point of random or, as we significantly call it, 'crazy' paving is that it sets up no geometric grid, no certain direction and no set axis: the stones are used as they naturally break (or that at least is the idea), instead of being cut into regular geometric shapes. Again, this organic form speaks of nature as opposed to culture, but it also fits in with Scharoun's increasing drive towards aperspectivity, towards irregular spaces that cannot be read geometrically and which vary in apparent scale.[6] In many of the later Scharoun/Mattern houses crazy paving is laid from the garden right into the living room and across to the hearth, just as the garden soil continues inside within the conservatory. Typically, the paving then changes into some more regular form of tiling or parquet for the more private areas of the house, while the most finely gridded geometric tiling is found in the purest, most private areas, where culture must exert control over nature: the kitchen and bathroom.

184

Planned from 1932, the Mattern House with its low-pitched roof just avoided the aesthetic restrictions imposed by the Nazis, but it already seems like an oasis of peace trying to turn its back on a troubled world, which was to be the pattern with Scharoun houses for the rest of the 1930s. Typically they had pitched roofs and small windows on the street side, giving them a modest, vernacular appearance, but could open up more generously towards their gardens with large windows and terraces. Restricted in his professional role to designing somewhat dull housing for others, Scharoun put all his creativity into this series of private houses, built mainly in the Berlin area. Perhaps in the development of his own natural sensibility he was becoming less interested in the architectural object and more interested in manipulating space, particularly with his experiments using curves and skewed angles in plan, but this tendency must have been exacerbated by the political conditions. To build an exuberantly modernist structure like the Schminke House was inconceivable: instead it was a question of how much one

Hans Scharoun, Baensch house, Berlin-
Spandau 1935: garden by Hermann Mattern.

10 Section showing terrain
between house and lake.

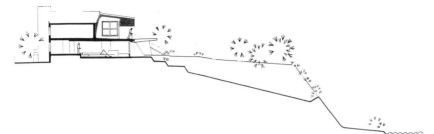

11 Garden plan including ground
floor of house.
(Redrawn by Peter Blundell Jones)

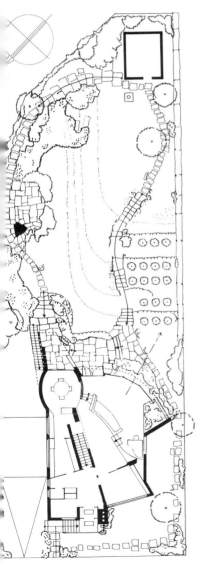

12 View of living room,
showing level change with
built-in seat and panoramic
window: dining room is to left.
(Photograph by Peter Blundell
Jones)

185

13 House from garden.
(Photograph by Peter Blundell
Jones)

14 House from approach side.
(Photograph by Peter Blundell
Jones)

could get away with. Houses had to appear conventional on the street, but it was possible to arrange an explosion of spatial delights within, and the surprise had a political meaning. For if the external conformity echoed the public persona that had to be adopted in the outside world, the secret interiors were havens where the unthinkable could be thought and the unsayable said.

Gardens were less ideologically charged, more politically ambiguous, and not inconsistent with Nazi rural myths. Thus Mattern's work continued, and despite his modernist connections he was able in 1936 to win the prestigious competition for the Reichsgartenschau in Stuttgart, which was to have taken place in 1939. Work started, but the show was cancelled by the war, and it finally took place as the Bundesgartenschau (Federal Garden Show) in 1950. This will be discussed later: meanwhile we continue the story of the collaboration. Scharoun built some 17 houses between 1933 and 1945, and planned seven more.[7] The most important ones all had gardens by Mattern, so the crucial collaboration continued, and there was every opportunity for exchange of ideas both ways. Lack of space prohibits describing all the projects here, so we will consider one as typical: the Baensch House of 1935.

It was through Mattern, already engaged for the garden, that Scharoun gained the commission for the Baensch house (Figs. 10–14). Another architect had planned a house that the lawyer client did not like, which perhaps also restricted the possibilities of the garden.[8] The site was a small plot at a place called Weinmeisterhöhe (literally wine-master-heights) in Berlin-Spandau, with a spectacular view over the Havel lakes. One of Mattern's great skills was to form the immediate garden in such a way that it seemed to echo the more distant landscape and take part in it.[9] Thus he made best use of the small plot by exploiting its spectacular south-facing view, which he framed with trees. The slope facing the lakes became a smoothly contoured lawn – Mattern loved a hill, for which he later gained the nickname Hügel Hermann – and terraces were created up the west side in memory of the former vineyard. An informal path led from the house around the east edge of the garden next to a curtain of trees, past a pond and shady sitting area and down to a small summer house at the lowest point. From there it rose again in a series of informal steps between the lawn and the vineyard terraces, arriving at a series of paved areas at the threshold to the house.

Scharoun set the house at the back of its plot to make the most of the garden, but also immediately engaged the conflict between the east-south-eastern alignment of the plot boundaries and the angle of view and sun to south. A series of plan sketches documents the build-up of ideas towards a very complex spatial arrangement, which makes the house seem to break out of its orthogonal shell and radiate out towards garden and view, while also picking up the terracing of the garden in its internal level changes.[10] It is a complex story, but here we need concern ourselves only with the relationship between house and garden, noticing the way in which every centimetre of that interface is exploited, and in a great variety of ways. Swinging round from east to west, we notice first the steps from the first-floor terrace, which itself radiates towards sun and view. This stair protects the edge of a roofed outdoor dining space placed immediately outside the indoor one. Moving on round and down three steps is another external sitting place, this time open to the sky, with double doors to the main living room. Next, maintaining the same level on the inside, comes a great bay window with a seat along its edge and low opening lights.[11] Outside, the ground drops away, the path is set back, and a bed of flowers for close contact is provided like that outside the big window of the Mattern house. At a larger scale, the big bay centres on the optimum view. The line of view relates it back to the built-in sofa in the level change and to the space behind; indeed the view is seen the moment one enters the room. Continuing our sequence westwards, the bay closes with a small winter garden or conservatory, with soil base and windows both to the house and to the outside. The end wall is exposed brick to show its outsideness. Apart from increasing the range of plants presented with exotic types that survive the winter, this also blocks the view of the neighbouring house. Beyond the conservatory, the round window next to the piano also faces west-south-west towards the neighbour, so it is glazed translucently.

Considering how each element develops on each side of the glass, the effect depends equally on the skills of Scharoun and Mattern, the former deploying furnishings, the latter groups of plants of varying scale and character, but within a shared understanding of the spatial intention. Their mutual understanding was profound and effortless, and their collaboration continued over the following years in several projects.

Scharoun and Mattern began their work together with the same commitment to informality. They shared an interest in the given orders of a landscape, and in the subtle interactions between the geometries set up at different times and for different reasons, each imbued with its own meaning. Just as Scharoun could relish the complex three-dimensional form of Prague with its endless historical layers as a rich example of Stadtlandschaft (city-landscape),[12] so Mattern relished the complex shapes, irregular boundaries and undulating ground of the old quarries at Killesberg in Stuttgart, which he rehabilitated as the first great postwar Bundesgartenschau (Fig. 15). The transformation of this apparently bleak landscape, which had been raped by industry, into the most beautiful of urban parks was a wonderful feat, all the more so because it finally seemed so natural. But every path had been laid, every tree planted, every group of plants carefully composed. If in such large projects Mattern could put into practice at much

187

15 Part of Hermann Mattern's garden at Killesberg Park, Stuttgart 1939, rehabilitation of a former quarry.
(Photograph by Peter Blundell Jones)

Peter Blundell Jones
Architect and landscape architect working
together: Scharoun and Mattern

larger scale design ideas he had pioneered in small gardens, Scharoun after the war applied the spatial ideas he had developed in the one-family houses to the realm of public buildings. Because he had been so completely confined to this small scale and private realm, in his case it had been for 12 years the only available design laboratory.

In 1946, thanks to a fortunate set of circumstances, Scharoun was for a short period made City Architect of Berlin. He was ousted before any significant plans could be realised, but he had the chance to get together a team of creative people who called themselves the Planungskollektiv,[13] to make a detailed analysis of the city and to propose a new order for its reconstruction. Their work was exhibited at the Berlin Schloss in the autumn of 1946 under the title *Berlin Plant*.[14] Analytical work included extensive research on the history of the city, whose forms and sequence of development could be understood in relation to political developments and changing deployments of military and

Historic plans of Kassel, north is top right.

16 River bottom left, medieval city right, and extensive fortifications where theatre will be.

17 Same area after Baroque expansion, with gridded Baroque new town left, medieval town right, and formal garden Friedrichsplatz in between. Baroque gardens are laid out on old river flood-plain.

188

18 Mattern's postwar plan for renovating the gardens: the theatre planned with Scharoun in 1952–53 is picked out in black. It is placed to mediate between Friedrichsplatz just above it and the steep slope down to the Fulda valley, and opens out westward onto a series of terraces.
(From Mattern, 1960)

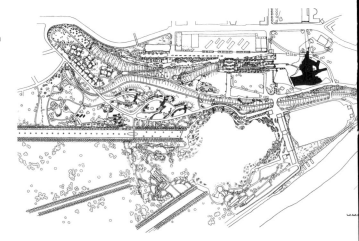

financial power. Radial medieval growth, for example, could be seen to be overtaken at a certain point by Baroque axes and grid planning. The studies undertaken on Berlin became the model for a whole series of what Scharoun called Strukturuntersuchungen – structural investigations, which decoded the history of every piece of urban context in which he was expecting to build. Quite typical was that for the city of Kassel, which held a major competition for its new theatre in 1952.

Mattern had moved to Kassel in 1948 to take part in the refounding of the Academy there, and in 1950 he gained the commission to replan the ruined gardens of the Karlsaue Park, which were completed for the Bundesgartenschau of 1955. The theatre site was on the edge of the valley and within the area being replanned by Mattern, so the competition proved an ideal opportunity for the two friends to work together again. The city lies on the north bank of the river Fulda, at a point where its flood-plain funnels in between two stretches of higher ground, linked by the main bridge. Karlsaue Park, laid out mainly in the eighteenth century, occupies a large area of flood-plain but also climbs the slope to north to link with the old city (Fig. 18). The theatre site lay on the edge of the slope, making an important transition between city and park. Kassel's fabric had been 80 per cent destroyed in the war, and its population reduced to a third. Its large nineteenth-century theatre had been gutted, along with most of the buildings in the park. To add insult to injury, mountains of debris from the destroyed city fabric had been dumped over the edge into the park. Mattern had to deal with its removal as part of his work in remaking the park, and with the restoration or stabilisation of the ruined buildings. He kept the main outline of the Baroque plan with its grand spaces and pavilions deployed along a central axis with canal-like side axes, but he did not attempt a faithful reconstruction of the Baroque garden. Instead he overlaid a new informal order of his own, recreating the old garden spaces in new ways, with new planting schemes, but also making new spaces. Particularly original was the addition of a series of teardrop-shaped plant beds around the edges of the central lawn: ungeometrical shapes at the centre of a powerful geometric scheme to provide a small-scale landscape within the large and to shift attention from the modestly restored pavilion. Mattern argued that a garden is never complete or static, for it is a changing panorama across the seasons; plants spread and plants die out, and the scale changes as trees grow. The Baroque scheme, built at another time for quite another social purpose, was never completed, and had been complemented by additions in the nineteenth century that were worth keeping. He argued further that earlier gardeners had a much narrower range of plants to choose from, some very labour intensive in terms of bedding out and overwintering, and the greater range of species now available also prompted reinterpretation. Thus he created for the show in 1955 a substantially new garden, which nonetheless absorbed, respected and showed off its earlier historical layers.[15] The design of the theatre envisaged a parallel kind of reinterpretation.

The old theatre, a free-standing monument in late nineteenth century Baroque, had occupied axially the south-east end of Friedrichsplatz, just where the square tips over the edge into the valley. Scharoun's Strukturuntersuchungen revealed that this square had a special role in the growth of the city, for it lay between the medieval heart to the

189

east and the grid-planned Baroque new town to the west, on ground that had once been part of the city wall (Figs. 16, 17). The square had lost this sense of in-between-ness in the nineteenth century, when it had been formalised as an extension of the Baroque grid plan, and the magnificent view out of it across the valley had been blocked by the building of the theatre. Given the chance to rebuild, Scharoun and Mattern wanted to return to the square some of its independence and special character, and to link it up once again visually with valley and park. They therefore devised an asymmetrical scheme, which pushed the bulk of the new theatre eastwards to open up the view, and they used the orthogonal and axially placed basement of the old theatre as a space to house the small experimental theatre, with an open public terrace on top. In relation to the park, the theatre became the end-stop for the terracing of the valley side, guiding the space of the valley up into the square. In the first version of the theatre design, a major road planned across the edge of the square was crossed by a pedestrian bridge, and Scharoun designed the first of his dynamic flowing foyers as a link between this bridge and the main theatre, making a virtue of the unusual downward progression that was prompted by the site. In its general layout the building showed articulated wings for offices, dressing rooms, workshops etc., with access for service and performers from the east, public areas on the west. The massing and profile of the building grew along with the planning process. Much of its bulk could be lost in the side of the hill, but the foyer emerged on top as a pavilion-like element, and the inevitable fly-tower was rounded in sympathy with the form of the hills beyond. As one might expect with Scharoun and Mattern working together, landform flowed into building form, and external spaces flowed into internal spaces. The transitions between foyer, external terrace and park would have been negotiated in a parallel way to those between house and garden discussed earlier.

The priority given to places and relationships, and the determination to acknowledge the many geometries of the site, meant that the building as physical object at first seemed somewhat amorphous, but after Scharoun and Mattern won the competition to great applause largely because of their design's contextual response, it was developed and worked through in detail. Work actually started on site, but some unknown foundations were discovered, and the delay was used by local opponents as an

19 Part of Mattern's gardens at Kassel, reworked for the Federal Garden Show of 1955.
(Akademie der Künste: Mattern catalogue)

22 Hermann Mattern: Mattern House Kassel, contemporary view: emphasis was naturally on the garden.
(Akademie der Künste: Mattern catalogue)

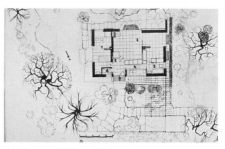

21 Hermann Mattern: Mattern house, Kassel 1950, ground-floor plan.
(Akademie der Künste: Mattern catalogue)

20 Scharoun and Mattern: Kassel theatre project 1953, model of revised version.
(Akademie der Künste)

excuse to drop the whole scheme. Paul Bode, a local architect whose competition entry had gone unnoticed, had been working secretly on an alternative version, and this was eventually built instead. Thus was lost the very best fruit of the Scharoun/Mattern collaboration and Scharoun's most important project prior to the Philharmonie. The fact that Scharoun always tried to engage context in his late work, yet failed to manage it as intended for one reason or another in nearly every case, shows not only the dominance of object-thinking in the culture of architects and planners, but also a more general lack of vision and commitment in city and landscape planning. Mattern continued to work with Scharoun, and produced a garden plan for the Philharmonie that was partly realised, but Berlin's Kulturforum has remained a torso, and every addition seems only to add to its sad incoherence.[16] The two remained friends until the death of Mattern in 1971, which was quickly followed by that of Scharoun in 1972. As late as 1968 they produced another house and garden, as architect and landscape architect respectively, for the Köpke family in Berlin.

191

That Scharoun and Mattern had arrived at the same approach is also borne out in Mattern's own building designs. He planned a few houses in the 1950s, including his own near Kassel, which echo Scharoun's in their free planning and modest form, and of course they show great attention to the inside/outside connections (Figs. 21, 22). Even at a much larger scale, when planning a pedestrian-based new town such as his project for Bad Westerhever of 1969 (Fig. 23), Mattern's vocabulary of high and low blocks

23 Hermann Mattern: Bad Westhever project 1969. (Akademie der Künste: Mattern catalogue)

interspersed with groups of courtyard houses, all laid out in an informal way, echoes the contemporary methods of Scharoun which had been established in Berlin with the Friedrichshain project of the late 1940s.

Like Scharoun, Mattern was an important teacher and the central figure for a whole school of landscape architects. He published a number of books, some specifically about garden design but others more general and philosophical. *Gras darf nicht mehr wachsen* (*Grass should not grow any more*), published in 1964, anticipates the green movement with its concern on the first page for the number of trees that will be cut to print the book. Its chapters, entitled The boat, The fence, The plough etc., discuss how we have treated the surface of the earth, and how every landscape is the record of human endeavour. The message that ugly, uncared-for landscapes reflect unsympathetic activities, and a lack of balance in our dealings with nature, is the constant refrain. Mattern preached that the provision of a healthy and beautiful environment is not just a matter of occasional parks and gardens, but of giving sympathetic form to all our activities and dealing sympathetically with the planet.

192

Bibliography

Akademie der Künste. *Hermann Mattern 1902–1971, Gärten, Gartenlandschaften, Häuser*. Berlin: Akademie der Künste 1982, Exhibition cat. no. 135.

Jones, Peter Blundell. *Hans Scharoun*. London: Phaidon 1995.

Mattern, Hermann. *Gärten und Gartenlandschaften*. Stuttgart: Gerd Hatje Verlag 1960.

Mattern, Hermann. *Gras darf nicht mehr wachsen*. Berlin/ Frankfurt/Vienna: Ullstein 1964.

Pfankuch, Peter, ed. *Hans Scharoun*. Berlin: Akademie der Künste 1993 (vol. 10 of Schriftenreihe, first published 1974).

Risselada, Max, ed. *Functionalisme 1927–61: Hans Scharoun versus de Opbouw*. Delft: Publicatiebureau Bouwkunde 1997.

Notes

1 The opening of 'Das Haus im Garten', in Mattern (1960), p. 92, my translation.

2 Alfred Schinz, 'Die Jahre mit Scharoun 1947–1955', *Baukultur* no. 3/4, 1993 pp. 30–33, my translation.

3 The garden is credited to Hammerbacher in the primary Scharoun source, Pfankuch (1974). Kürvers reports discussions with Mattern over the winter garden and also includes a reconstructed garden plan in his chapter of Risselada (1997).

4 The acoustician of the Philharmonie, Lothar Cremer, told me in 1978 that Scharoun was the most rewarding architect he had ever worked for because he could always somehow find a way to answer the acoustician's demands without compromising his own ideas.

5 According to Adolf Behne, writing in *Deutsche Bauzeitung* 16/1/35, vol. 3 p. 53, it cost 13000 Reichsmarks.

6 In the post-war years Scharoun and his co-workers saw the transition from perspective to 'aperspective' as part of a profound and far-reaching change of consciousness sweeping across society as a whole. The term was given definition in the book *Ursprung und Gegenwart* by Jean Gebser, which appeared in 1949 and was avidly read in German intellectual circles. A German philosopher who fled to Switzerland during the Nazi period, Gebser had been working on a general cultural theory since the 1920s, and finally put together the whole story in the 1940s. He explained the development of human culture in a series of phases, called archaic, magical, mythical, mental, and integral. The integral phase was supposed to mark the overthrow of dualistic thinking and the reincorporation of the mythical and magical along with the rationalism of the Enlightenment. The change from perspectivity to aperspectivity was very much the central idea of the book, the *Leitmotiv* that ran through everything. Aperspectivity was the characteristic of the integral phase, in contrast with the perspective, which arose with the Renaissance, or the unperspective that preceded it. It ushered in the new age, and Gebser attempted to show how it manifested itself not only in painting and architecture, but also in music, the sciences, and law. This is explored more extensively in my monograph on Scharoun (Jones 1995) and in the article 'From the Neoclassical axis to aperspective space' published in *The Architectural Review* March 1988.

7 According to the revised worklist in Pfankuch (1993).

8 Verbal information from Scharoun's assistant Chen Kuan Lee, from an interview of 1984.

9 This he achieved most spectacularly in his garden to the Peyron house at Glumslöv, Sweden of 1956.

10 For the full set of drawings see Jones (1995) p. 88.

11 The fine glazing was unfortunately destroyed in the war and replaced with larger panes, so is not seen in modern photographs.

12 For Scharoun's definition of *Stadtlandschaft* and his description of Prague see my *Hans Scharoun* (Jones 1995, pp. 109–111)

13 Its members were Wils Ebert, Peter Friedrich, Ludmilla Herzenstein, Reinhold Lingner, Scharoun, Louise Seitz, Selman Selmanagic, and Herbert Weinberger.

14 The *Berlin Plant* exhibition is best documented in Geist, Johann Friedrich, and Kürvers, Klaus. *Das Berlier Mietshaus 1945–89*. (3rd vol. of a series) Munich: Prestel Verlag, 1989.

15 See Mattern, 'Rekonstruktion historischer Gärten' in Mattern 1960, pp. 72–73.

16 For a more detailed version see my *Hans Scharoun* (Jones 1995, pp. 187–191, 222)

1 Road to Acropolis, sketch.
(Drawing by Dimitri Pikionis)

2 Construction of pavement in front
of St. Dimitrios church.
(Photograph Agni Pikionis)

3 The St. Dimitrios complex seen
from the opposite side of the road.
(Photograph Agni Pikionis)

Dimitri Pikionis in situ

4 Church wall at start of
Philopappus ascent.
(Drawing by Sasha Birksted)

There is a certain mystique surrounding the habits of Pikionis when working on site. Since every action of his was considered a matter of veneration by his disciples and an incomprehensible ritual at best by everyone else, there is comparatively limited evidence to support one's evaluation of exactly what happened on such occasions. Thus one has to piece together perhaps unsystematic yet revealing materials mostly dispersed in published reminiscences of his students in a collective edition in 1989. Even more difficult to obtain today is information never put to paper by those who actually met and worked with him. Finally some additional information is included in two reports of his addressed to the Ministry of Public Works, responsible for the Acropolis project, in 1955.

This probe is essential in understanding how Pikionis performed when faced not with ethereally theoretical matters but with the earthly demands of construction. He seems to be well aware of the difference when he dismissed a role for himself consisting of 'simply providing his platonic opinion in the course of the project'.[1] Pikionis the active architect will then emerge, perhaps to an unexpected degree, as a completely knowledgeable and

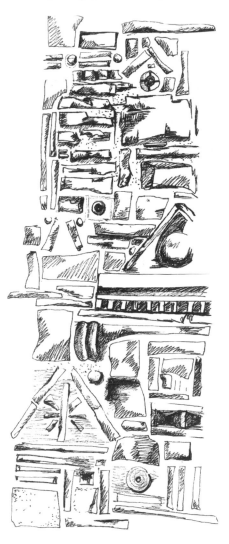

195

5 The walkway towards the
Acropolis.
(Photograph Agni Pikionis)

6 View of Philoppapus ascent.
(Drawing by Sasha Birksted)

experienced builder with a fair grip on the nature of materials,[2] their source and relative cost. According to an unusually extensive description by Pavlos Kalantzopoulos, he successfully managed to keep costs down while supervising the construction of a series of most unusual and demanding works. In performing this task he acted alone, without the help of a professional construction overseer.[3] The usual size of a construction team in his major projects would range from 20 to 30 workers.[4]

Two cases primarily represent Pikionis' behaviour when dealing with the landscape: the Acropolis site and the Filothei playground.[5] His presence on the site in both instances was continuous. When work stopped at noon for a two-hour break, he usually spent the time close at hand so he would again be present at 3 o'clock to resume his task. At a certain point his employers, worried about his frail health and old age, hired a taxi or a private car to drive him home for the noon recess. If the driver happened to be of a somewhat inquisitive nature he would be easily lured into a conversation by Pikionis on the project. Pikionis' motive, according to Kalantzopoulos, was never utilitarian: '... he wanted an [outsider's] eye to tell him what he saw, an eye far from the world of architects or artists'. On such occasions he would spend half an hour to an hour and a half discussing various aspects of the project with the driver while asking his opinion. He seemed 'like a personality out of a platonic dialogue'.[6]

Time seemed to be irrelevant in the case of Pikionis. He seemed never to be in a hurry while he went around performing his daily routines. He found time for everything he deemed worthy of his attention. At the close of the day's work, when people around him started to pack their tools and leave, Pikionis would still linger around on the site. He wanted to get a last impression of the work's daily progress, oblivious to the approach of darkness.[7]

197

7 Acropolis from the belvedere of Philopappou Hill.
(Photograph Agni Pikionis)

8 Road to Philopappou Hill with concrete infill.
(Photograph Agni Pikionis)

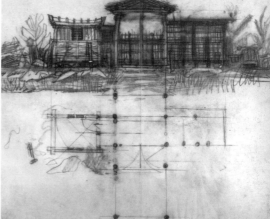

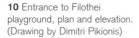

9 Entrance to Filothei playground.
(Photograph Agni Pikionis)

10 Entrance to Filothei
playground, plan and elevation.
(Drawing by Dimitri Pikionis)

It was a common secret that Pikionis prepared few if any working drawings related to a project under construction.[8] According to Alexandros Papageorgiou-Venetas, he 'consciously and consistently used a method of creative improvisation. He would spend endless hours on site, sitting on an old chair, in order to determine the basic tracing lines and to provide the experienced masons with relevant information. Drawings served only as reference points.'[9]

This fact is verified from various sources so it seems not to be an exaggeration. Pikionis himself provides another possible clue: he claims that the Acropolis project for one was started in such haste that he had no time to complete his proposal.[10] Yet almost in the same breath he justifiably claims that 'this project needs the broad exercise of an in situ self-activation, which would be impossible for any drawing to predict or contract to describe. In such cases a drawing or a set of specifications would be inadequate. The former is by no means meant to be implemented; it serves as an agent containing the general idea, which must then be interpreted.'[11]

A plausible interpretation of these conflicting statements is that the Acropolis project was admittedly started (and constructed) with utmost haste, primarily for political reasons, but the proverbial 'disorder' of Pikionis' mind played there a major role. Due to his keen understanding of the individuality of his proposal he was able to precisely foresee his role on the site even before actual work started. In his words: 'The architect himself should, with the help of his aides, become the interpreter of his work, I would rather say he would construct it himself, using the hands of the technicians. Only such an active supervision is capable of completing a sensitive and living form contrary to a typical and dead one.'[12]

201

11 Detail of the secondary path.
(Drawing by Sasha Birksted)

Who then could be his 'aides'? This term does not apply only to workers and technicians, professionally involved with manual tasks on the site. As mentioned above, even a taxi driver would be considered an aide, an advisor, by Pikionis. The fact that students were simultaneously called in to serve as 'aides', even as plain 'workers',[13] is an issue that should be discussed at some length. According to Papageorgiou-Venetas: 'A small group of dedicated students under his guidance was constantly occupied with setting the guidelines for the pavement's joints on the ground.'[14] Periklis Panteleakis adds to this a personal note; he describes his experience when he visited the Acropolis site while a student. He approaches the ever-present Pikionis who assigns to him the task of instructing a worker on how to build a certain ornament in brick: 'I showed the worker the way, being so proud that the Master had trusted me.' Then the worker reciprocates by asking his opinion about inserting a piece of broken pottery, which he had found lying somewhere, in the wall he was constructing. The student senses the 'deeper meaning of the words of the plain yet seemingly tender and dreaming worker', and marvels at Pikionis' ability to make his team members 'dream of the work'.[15]

A more detailed account is fortunately recorded by Nikolaos Moutsopoulos. He was a regular visitor to his teacher's sites and he notes that Pikionis consistently chose class assignments related to his projects:[16] 'Thus our experience was substantial in such matters and extended beyond theoretical research and selection of form sometimes to actual participation in the field, where select construction workers and masons instructed us how to build a wall.' This experience was unforgettable: 'We were not just alive then, we veritably flew in the clouds. In my memory Pikionis' figure sticks out as he knelt on the old worn marble slab, against the sun, caressing it. Around him lay the age-old demolition material... There we learnt the sacred marriage of marble ashlar stones with nameless Byzantine fragments in clay and all the ritual of fitting and closing joints.'[17]

He goes on to recount the master's behaviour: 'I remember Pikionis with a straw

12 Island paving.
(Drawing by Sasha Birksted)

hat, similar to the insular masons who worked next to him, wearing his spectacles with the thick lenses and a half-extinguished cigarette forgotten on his lips, murmuring something like a chant, like a heroic song... Then he suddenly got up and destroyed the arrangement we had admired a little time ago. Then he knelt down once more, asked for paper... with hands full of dust and the cigarette in his mouth and a pencil in hand he redrew the idea which stemmed from the new conditions and "necessity", again to be rejected after a while, if one of us were to fetch a new piece of rock, some white pebbles, a few old mosaic tesseras. So everything would start again from scratch, with a new drawing... Then he would look us in the face seriously, silent, trying to read a reaction in our eyes and we all nodded mesmerized that this was right...'[18]

Rare and unusual was such a communion indeed between Pikionis, workers and students joined together in this common endeavour, because it indicates no hierarchy of knowledge or authority. The 'wise', the 'plain' and the 'innocent' seemingly share those unequalled experiences on a strictly equal basis. The construction site actually reproduces a platonic society in miniature where conflicts have been completely removed. Pikionis reigns as the uncontested guide to knowledge and truth to which he arrives in an oblique, tortuous manner by constant trial and error. He keeps his power secret in an attempt to initiate his companions into the mystery of creation on their own. He knows that this is a 'work of art', a 'very wide, by its nature, complex' job, a project immersed 'in the spirit of historic propositions'.[19] He seems crushed by this responsibility so he needs the reassurance of a public consensus. Workers and students alike, the occasional taxi driver – practically anyone responsive to the issue – all are welcomed to join this mind's utopian feast.

No wonder the realisation of such a disorder sent tremours through the corridors of the Ministry of Public Works. Pikionis stood his ground and never succumbed to either pressures from above[20] or ridicule from his colleagues.

1 Letter to the Minister of Public Works, May 12, 1955, D. Pikioni Keimena (Texts by D. Pikionis), The Cultural Foundation of the National Bank, Athens 1985, p. 266.

2 There exists a detailed description of Pikionis' 'instructions on how to spread the concrete as it was poured in semi-liquid form' on the Acropolis site (A. Papageorgiou, 'Dimitris Pikionis. The landscaping of the archeological site around the Acropolis 1954–1957', *Pikionis*, folio 7, Athens: Bastas-Plessas, 1994, p. 23).

3 Since the Acropolis site project was initiated by a public agency (the Ministry of Public Works), Pikionis had to cope with various bureaucrats assigned as technical supervisors to him. The 'letter' quoted in note 1 was actually a complaint against their meddlesome activities on the site. See also A. Papageorgiou's account about the presence of 90 workers on the Acropolis site in the summer of 1956 (*op. cit.*, p.20).

4 P. Kalantzopoulos, 'Oi politimes ores' (The precious hours), *Dimitris Pikionis, Afieroma sta Ekato Chronia apo ti Gennisi tou* (Dimitris Pikionis, An Homage to a Hundred Years from his Birth), Athens: NTU of Athens, 1989, pp.71–74.

5 At least some suburban houses seem to have also claimed his attention, obviously to a lesser degree.

6 *Ibid.*, p.75.

7 *Ibid.*, p.76.

8 A. Papageorgiou mentions the existence of 'numerous preliminary drawings which Pikionis produced for St. Demetrius' at the Acropolis site (*op. cit.*, p. 26). Yet these were not meant to serve as working drawings but as a 'relatively detailed creative stimulus' (*ibid.*, p. 21).

9 A. Papageorgiou-Venetas, 'Dafni sti mnimi tou Daskalou mou' (A laurel in memory of my teacher), *Dimitris Pikionis*, *op. cit.*, p. 206. (He is not to be confused with Alexandros Papageorgiou, see notes 2, 3 ,8).

10 Letter to the Minister of Public Works, May 12, 1955, *op. cit.*, p. 267.

11 *Ibid.*, p. 268. His italics.

12 *Idem*.

13 According to G. Sarigiannis, at least in one instance a student from the School of Fine Arts was employed as a regular stone cutter (' "Ta erga ton peri tin Akropolin choron" . O Pikionis kai to elliniko dimosio' (Pikionis and Greek Public Services), *Dimitris Pikionis*, *op. cit.*, p. 250, note 67.

14 A. Papageorgiou-Venetas, *op. cit.*, p. 206.

15 P. Panteleakis, 'Pikionis, mia paga laleousa tis epochis mas' (Pikionis, an alive source of our times), *Dimitris Pikionis*, *op. cit.*, p. 162.

16 Class projects were not only 'related' to Pikionis' current projects but occasionally were downright proposals for specific items, where Pikionis appeared still hesitant. It is estimated that at least some of the drawings in the Pikionis archive were actually executed by his students who imitated his drawing style.

17 N.K. Moutsopoulos, "Mnimes apo ti zoi sto Polytechnio tin epochi tou Pikioni" (Remembrances from life at the Technical University at the time of Pikionis), *Dimitris Pikionis*, *op. cit.*, pp. 126, 129.

18 *Ibid.*, pp. 129–130.

19 Fragments of phrases included in Pikionis' letter to the Minister of Public Works (see note 1).

20 G. Sarigiannis, *op. cit.*

John Hopkins

Landscape architecture: ecology, community, art

Introduction

All professions dealing with the environment are concerned with the creation of Utopia. Landscape architects, architects, planners, engineers, ecologists, economists, sociologists, biologists – the list goes on – all respond to the basic human urge to create our own Garden of Eden. Creating landscapes within which we can work, play, live and learn – create the good life – is at the core of all we strive for. As D. W. Meinig in distilling the writings of J. B. Jackson on the American landscape wrote:

> In the broadest view, all landscapes are symbolic, every 'landscape is a reflection of the society which first brought it into being and continues to inhabit it', and, ultimately landscapes represent a striving to achieve a spiritual goal; they are 'expressions of a persistent desire to make the earth over in the image of some heaven'.[1]

As examples of 'the image of some heaven', Jackson himself cited the alternative Utopian views of Jefferson and Thoreau; the former agrarian and Classical, the latter middle-class, urban and Romantic. He argued that both these alternatives have now lost their philosophical justification, and in their place, 'The existentialist landscape, without absolutes, without prototypes, devoted to change and mobility and the free confrontation of men, is already taking form around us.' The reason, he concluded, is that we have lost the 'capacity – or the temerity – to contrive Utopias'.[2]

What history tells us, according to Jackson, is that '...a coherent, workable landscape evolves where there is a coherent definition not of man but of man's relation to the world and to his fellow men.'[3] At the end of the extraordinary twentieth century, we are coming close to having the knowledge, skills, ability – and imperatives – to have begun to outline a coherent definition of, more specifically and accurately, the relationship of humans to each other and to the environment and, therefore, to have the capacity (if not the temerity) to contrive our Utopia. The definition is succinctly encompassed in ideas of sustainability, which have grown directly out of *the* emergent discipline of the twentieth century: ecology.

Ecology and notions of sustainability are at the core of landscape architecture. The problem is that ecology is not enough. As our understanding of the human/nature relationship is clarified it is becoming apparent that landscape, in its broad definition as the place where humans and nature interact, is *the* important issue for our future. And landscape architecture, with its broad-ranging interests, skills and knowledge of human and natural systems is the best-placed profession to draw together emerging definitions of our future Utopia. Garrett Eckbo, one of the greatest writers and philosophers of landscape architecture, eloquently and consistently expressed his concerns for the *community* aspects of landscape architecture, for *art* as an integrated and essential component of landscape architecture, and for *ecology* as the underpinning rationale for landscape architecture and planning. What we now need to do is to combine *ecology*, *community* and *art* into a cohesive whole and, by using this triadic relationship as a framework, explore, examine and test the coherence of our definition of the human/nature relationship and our emerging Utopias.

John Dewey, the American philosopher, drew together the philosophic, scientific and aesthetic strands of early twentieth century thought to encompass ecology, community and art in his book *Art as Experience*.[4] For Dewey, ecological and community values derive directly from an understanding of the human/nature relationship and, indeed, that the formulation and understanding of this relationship is expressed in and through art: 'The sense of relation between nature and man in some form has always been the actuating spirit of art.'[5] He decried the separation of art from the realm of everyday existence which has '…weakened or destroyed the connection between works of art and the genius loci of which they were once an expression.'[6] Originally, art was an integral part of life, '…feathers, gaudy robes, domestic utensils, spears…,' etc., were a 'manifestation of the group or clan's worship, feasting and fasting, fighting and hunting and all the rhythmic crises that punctuate living'.[7] Art therefore draws the community together to share common experiences, that are not only 'commemorative', but also 'expectant, insinuating, premonitory'.[8]

During the twentieth century we have witnessed an increasing homogeneity of landscapes everywhere which is testimony to a philosophy of the human/nature relationship inspired by an abstract economics that militates against the expression of the genius loci. Dewey argues that this economic philosophy has also led to the isolation of art, and that this has caused the artist's role to become one of *self*-expression rather than the expression of the *collective identity*. The environmental and land artists of the seventies and eighties felt this acutely. Theirs was a reaction against 'gallery art' and also a desire to reconnect with nature. For Dewey, art that is widely appreciated is not only a sign of a unified society, but also a contributory factor in its creation. It is in this sense that Dewey considers art and morals indivisible – just as we need and are shaped by our physical environment, so it is with our moral environment. This reorientation of the role of art also applies to the role of the artist. The increasing separation of art from the realm of everyday experience has resulted in the exaggerated individuality of *self*-expression. However, the artist should be seen more as an interpreter for the community. Carl Steinitz, Alexander and Victoria Wiley Professor of Landscape Architecture and Planning at the Harvard Graduate School of Design, supported this view when he quoted from a 'commentary on Exodus XXXVI, the story of the design of the Tabernacle by Bezalel and Oholiab':

> The rabbis, too had a passionate love of beauty. They prescribed a special Benediction at the sight of a beautiful tree or animal, as well as on beholding the first blossoms of spring (Authorised Prayer Book, p. 291). Some of them conceived the whole of Creation as a process of unfolding beauty; and spoke of God as the Incomparable Artist. The highest artist, in the eyes of Jewish teachers of all generations is not the greatest master in self-expression, but in self-control; he who fashions himself into a sanctuary. …In this view, the artist is one who seeks wisdom, understanding and knowledge and who displays that understanding with artistic skill. The focus is on observing, feeling and interpreting rather than on self-expression.[9]

It is this role of the 'artist as interpreter' that necessitates as full an understanding as possible of the *genius loci*, of the 'spirit of place' which encompasses physical, historical, cultural and philosophical dimensions.

With such a philosophic background, a Utopia based on ecology, community and art becomes a possibility. And, if we accept landscape architecture as an art; accept art as the manifestation of the collective cultural, historical and philosophical identity of a community (the genius loci); and accept that art is not only a sign of a unified society, but also a contributory factor in its creation, then landscape architecture becomes truly significant. The following are offered as a palimpsest to this background.

207

Gray World, Green Heart

Robert Thayer, a landscape architect and professor at the University of California at Davies, defines the current state of thinking on sustainable community development and landscapes in his book *Gray World, Green Heart*.[10] In it he defines *sustainability* as 'a characteristic of a process or state that can be maintained indefinitely'; *sustainable development* as 'improving the quality of human life while living within the carrying capacity of supporting eco-systems'; and *sustainable* landscape as 'a physical place where human communities, resource uses, and the carrying capacities of surrounding eco-systems can all be perpetually maintained'.[11] Thayer acknowledges that the political and socio-economic mechanisms and changes necessary to achieve sustainable landscapes and communities remain inadequate, but does take heart from the fact that biodiversity and sustainability are now global political aims and that United States vice-president Albert Gore's excellent book *Earth in Balance* can only bode well for the future.[12]

Thayer argues that technology – both our love of and fear of (technophobia and technophilia) in a quintessentially dichotomous relationship – has led to the current environmental crisis and that we must begin to be the master of technology not the slave. He contends that we need to make transparent and visible the natural processes by which we survive and, in so doing, identifies one of the fundamental problems of contemporary society. Through the use of technology, we have been able to hide from ourselves the natural processes upon which we are dependent. We have become disconnected and dissociated from nature.

We can see this in our everyday lives whereby most of us plug in our computers, turn on the tap, flush the toilet, etc., and have no real conception or understanding of where the power and the water comes from or the waste goes. Similarly, our economy is becoming one of increasing abstraction – credit cards, direct transfers, share dealings, all become groundless electronic transactions with a subsequent loss of connection between work, pay, play and the environment upon which the economy is ultimately based.

Thayer argues that we must develop new *communities* and protect and develop existing communities based on the sustainable principles of utilising renewable energy sources; maximising recycling of resources and minimising waste; maintaining biodiversity; and using appropriate technology that supports these goals. In arguing for the development of sustainable communities Thayer cites examples such as Laguna West near Sacramento, California where Peter Calthorpe has designed a 3,000 plus housing unit community providing employment, schools and shops all linked by pedestrian/cycle greenways and linked to other communities by a public transportation system. Judged a worthy effort by Thayer, he admits that the political and economic realities defeated many of the original laudable proposals, but recognises the importance of developing prototypes as a means of educating politicians, developers and the public.

On a smaller scale, Thayer describes a cluster community of 220 homes on a 70 acre development called Village Homes in Davis, California. He knows it well – it is where he and his family have lived for more than 20 years. Roads are narrow and use of the car discouraged. Each house (built to maximise solar power) is built on a small lot in clusters of eight with a common area adjacent. A larger communally owned open area, which houses a community centre and swimming pool, is accessible by footpaths within an open space system that links all the houses. The open space is used to collect rainwater via a system of small dams and allow it to percolate back into the underlying aquifer and for children's play. There is a common orchard and vineyard and community garden plots or allotments which can be used free of charge. Ownership boundaries are not clearly defined and opaque fences discouraged. Maintenance of common areas is funded through a management charge and based on organic principles. Picking of fruit and cropping is arranged through a community run agricultural board. Here we have the nascent example of what a sustainable living community could be like. It is not fully sustainable but points us in the right direction. It is clear that the art of this community is enmeshed within its natural and native processes. Thayer's contribution to defining a future Utopia is clear, consistent and concise. It is thoroughly rooted in the indelible ecological relationship between humans and nature. His descriptions of community models are encouraging. However, the motivating and binding philosophy that draws ecology, community and art together is missing.

Camp Pendleton

The current state of the art of landscape planning at the regional scale, and of the possibilities afforded by our understanding of ecology and development needs, are illustrated in an exemplary study of *Alternative Futures for the Region of Camp Pendleton, California*.[13] The study exploits the impressive technological capabilities of Geographic Information Systems (GIS) with which complex databases of information can be created and then presented and analysed in a variety of visual ways. Computer-based geographic information systems were a direct development of Ian McHarg's original manual overlay techniques described in his seminal text *Design with Nature*.[14]

The study explicitly addresses the conflicts of differing patterns of development and offers stark choices as to how we might need to live in order to maintain acceptable levels of biodiversity. It was a collaborative effort between Harvard University Graduate School of Design (led by Carl Steinitz), Utah State University, the National Biological Service, the USDA Forest Service, the Nature Conservancy and the Biodiversity Research Consortium with the co-operation of the two relevant regional agencies, the San Diego Association of Governments, and the Southern California Association of Governments, and Marine Corps Base Camp Pendleton.

The study covers a region 80 by 134 kilometres between Los Angeles and San Diego straddling political and military boundaries. An initial GIS database was established predominantly from information already in the public domain but uncollated. This information covered such diverse topics as soils and agricultural productivity; hydrological models for each river watershed including up to 25 year flooding heights, soil moisture content and stability; fire models both for protection of development and for maintaining vegetation and habitat types; and visual models covering why people are attracted to move into the area. Biodiversity was measured through species richness models, single-species habitats, and landscape ecological patterns.

Following the collation of necessary data and conversion into graphic overlays, it was possible to model future development scenarios and test them against the primary goal of sustaining biodiversity whilst accommodating predicted population growth. Six development scenarios were modelled and analysed, first to the year 2010 and then to full development or 'build-out'. The first was a baseline study based on approved plans (Fig. 1); the second projected the development of the traditional United States pattern of low-density predominantly single-family dwellings (Fig. 2); the third followed a similar development pattern but introduced a conservation plan at 2010 (Fig. 3); the fourth

Water   Mixed Forest 96610 ha 3%   Grassland 82780 ha 2%   Single Family Res 304038 ha 9%   Military Impact 49981 ha 1%

Riparian Vegetation 11453 ha 0%   Orchards 3887 ha 0%   Altered Land 67463 ha 2%   Multi Family Residential 110903 ha 3%   Commercial Industrial 155939 ha 4%

Oak Woodland 56713 ha 2%   Sage, Chaparral 1080648 ha 30%   Rural Residential 906378 ha 25%   Military Maneuvers 116374 ha 3%   Trans-portation 165638 ha 0%

0 1 3 5 kilometers
0 1 3 5 miles

1 Land cover: plans build-out.
(Figs 1–6 published with the kind
permission of Professor Carl Steinitz,
editor, *Alternative Futures for the
Region of Camp Pendleton*,
California; Harvard University Press,
1996)

Water   Mixed Forest 79437 ha 2%   Grassland 0 ha 0%   Single Fam. Residential 321903 ha 9%   Military Impact 40415 ha 1%

Riparian Vegetation 7466 ha 0%   Orchards 10244 ha 0%   Altered Land 129912 ha 4%   Multi Family Residential 110567 ha 3%   Commercial Industrial 155011 ha 1%

Oak Woodland 46420 ha 1%   Sage, Chaparral 895394 ha 25%   Rural Residential 1061250 ha 30%   Military Maneuver 125940 ha 4%   Transport 17084 ha 0%

0 1 3 5 kilometers
0 1 3 5 miles

2 Land cover: spread build-out.

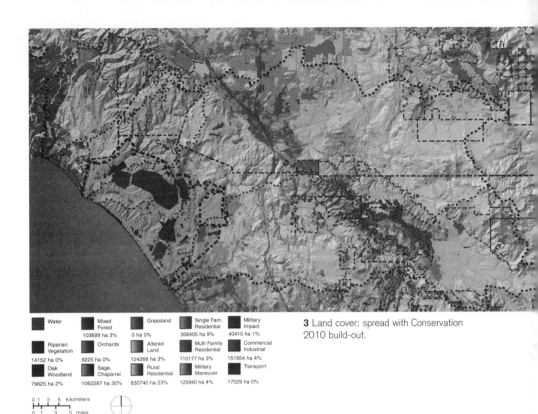

Water	Mixed Forest	Grassland	Single Fam. Residential	Military Impact
	103699 ha 3%	0 ha 0%	306405 ha 9%	40415 ha 1%
Riparian Vegetation	Orchards	Altered Land	Multi Family Residential	Commercial Industrial
14152 ha 0%	9225 ha 0%	124268 ha 3%	110177 ha 3%	151854 ha 4%
Oak Woodland	Sage, Chaparral	Rural Residential	Military Maneuver	Transport
79625 ha 2%	1062287 ha 30%	830740 ha 23%	125940 ha 4%	17029 ha 0%

3 Land cover: spread with Conservation 2010 build-out.

```
0 1   3    5  kilometers
0 1   3    5  miles
```

looked at 'private conservation' whereby large, contiguous conservation areas are incorporated within private, very low-density domains (Fig. 4); the fifth assessed multi-centre community developments (Fig. 5); and the sixth concentrated growth in a single, high-density new city (Fig. 6).

As this was a study and not a consultancy no recommendations were made. However, what became clear was that current, uncoordinated zoning, infrastructure, and development patterns would see a serious decline in biodiversity and also in visual quality of the landscape – one of the primary reasons for moving into the region! Also, the mission of Camp Pendleton – the training of the Marine Corps – depends on the diversity of landscape types and these would be severely curtailed without it becoming directly involved in and influencing the landscape planning and management of surrounding regional landscape. It also became clear that although the 'private conservation' model was attractive in terms of biodiversity, the 'multi-centre' and 'new city' models provided the best balance between human and conservation needs. It was also apparent that there was little time to act because the current development infrastructure was being planned ready for implementation.

Manchester city centre

If the Camp Pendleton study is exemplary in questioning development patterns at a regional scale, studies for the redevelopment of the city centre of Manchester, England are equally exemplary in questioning the nature of the city, its role and relationships. In

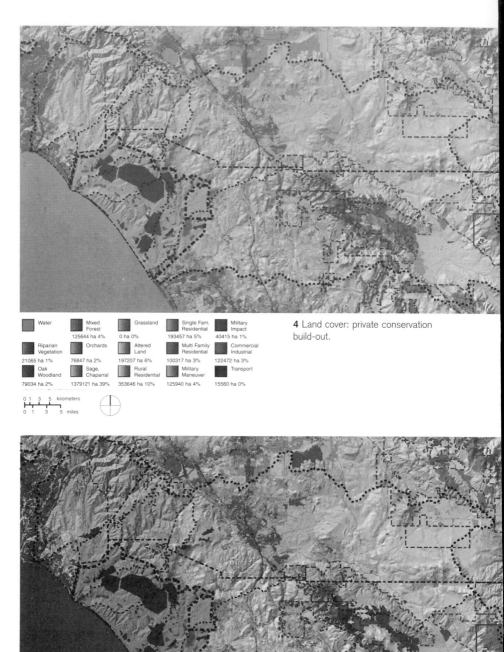

■ Water	■ Mixed Forest	■ Grassland	■ Single Fam. Residential	■ Military Impact	
125644 ha 4%	0 ha 0%	193457 ha 5%	40415 ha 1%		
■ Riparian Vegetation	■ Orchards	■ Altered Land	■ Multi Family Residential	■ Commercial Industrial	
21065 ha 1%	76847 ha 2%	197207 ha 6%	100317 ha 3%	122472 ha 3%	
■ Oak Woodland	■ Sage, Chaparral	■ Rural Residential	■ Military Maneuver	■ Transport	
79034 ha 2%	1379121 ha 39%	353646 ha 10%	125940 ha 4%	15560 ha 0%	

0 1 3 5 kilometers
0 1 3 5 miles

4 Land cover: private conservation build-out.

■ Water	■ Mixed Forest	■ Grassland	■ Single Fam. Residential	■ Military Impact	
98100 ha 3%	0 ha 0%	215932 ha 6%	40415 ha 1%		
■ Riparian Vegetation	■ Orchards	■ Altered Land	■ Multi Family Residential	■ Commercial Industrial	
11711 ha 0%	23236 ha 1%	91328 ha 3%	106913 ha 3%	125003 ha 4%	
■ Oak Woodland	■ Sage, Chaparral	■ Rural Residential	■ Military Maneuver	■ Transport	
62488 ha 2%	1177309 ha 39%	855777 ha 24%	125940 ha 4%	15326 ha 0%	

0 1 3 5 kilometers
0 1 3 5 miles

5 Land cover: multi-centres build-out.

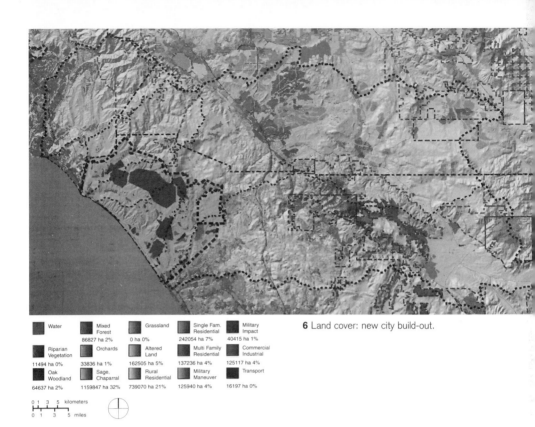

6 Land cover: new city build-out.

June 1996 a large terrorist bomb destroyed the city centre. Forty-nine thousand square metres of prime retail space and 57,000 square metres of office-based business activities were lost. No one was killed. A task force was immediately established – Manchester Millennium – bringing together public and private agencies to manage the recovery and reconstruction. An international urban design competition was won by a team led by EDAW (landscape architects and urban designers) comprising Simpson Associates (architects), Alan Baxter and Associates (consultant engineers), Benoy (architects specialising in retail developments), Johnson Urban Development Consultants (chartered surveyors) and Building Design Partnership (architects).

213

Manchester, along with many other great industrial cities, has been reconfiguring itself into a knowledge-based economy. The city centre was and will continue to be the focus of this exchange of ideas, information and culture. As the Camp Pendleton study concluded, higher-density city living is more sustainable than urban sprawl. It follows that our existing urban cores require revitalising – the urban landscape is where human nature dominates and acceptably so. In the ecology – community – art relationship community and art are pre-eminent in the city. That is not to say that ecology is ignored. The creation of parks, gardens, riverside walks etc. contributes to a sensibility of the human/nature relationship. The Manchester Masterplan explores and illustrates many contemporary notions in city living and these are encapsulated in the underlying principles of the Masterplan which were to create:

7 The Manchester City Centre Masterplan.
(© EDAW)

- a twenty-four-hour city centre by offering a diverse mix of retail, cultural, entertainment, residential and commercial uses
- central public spaces at both a grand and human scale
- pedestrian-dominant transport routes and nodes, and
- places, routes and views respecting the city's architectural heritage.

A comprehensive public consultation exercise was carried out including a MORI poll, a business survey and numerous focus groups. In addition, more than 3,000 people attended an exhibition of the proposals with more than 1,000 suggestion forms being completed. Public art is recognised as an essential component of the redevelopment and Grenville Davey – an artist who won the prestigious Turner Prize in 1992 – was appointed to the Masterplanning team at an early date to advise on opportunities, approaches and strategies.

New and redeveloped commercial, retail, residential and cultural space is proposed; however, the key to the Masterplan is the development of a series of high-quality, interconnected city streets, squares and parks. This has been made possible by formulating a transport strategy which provides excellent accessibility and convenient internal circulation for all users – a balanced, legible and sustainable transport network. The strategy seeks to achieve a 50/50 car/public transport share and to redirect the 30 per cent of traffic having no business in the city centre via an inner relief route. Bus routes are being rationalised and plans drawn up to improve reliability, quality and the image of bus services. Bus priority routes will be established and state-of-the-art low-emission and low-floor buses will have access to key pedestrian areas of the city. Zero emission, distinctive vehicles – the Metroshuttle – will be established on two city loops linking key locations and main transport interchanges. The existing tram system, Metrolink, will have a new station and will be extended. Park and ride schemes will be established at suburban railway stations to attract otherwise car-borne commuters. Cyclists will be encouraged by reducing the number of vehicles in the city centre; reducing the number of unnecessary journeys caused by inefficient bus routes, lack of legibility, poor parking signage, etc.; and the provision of bicycle parks in the city centre in the form of secure stands in public spaces and lockers on the ground floors of public car parks.

215

The significant public realm works comprise:

- New Cathedral Street/Exchange Square – one of the main elements of the Masterplan, it creates a direct visual and pedestrian link between St Ann's church, Exchange Square and the historic core around the Cathedral

- Exchange Square – a major new civic space at the heart of the redeveloped area. The focus will be a plaza which can be used for civic and cultural events. Cafés, restaurants and bars fronting the new square will be an attraction to the large numbers of people visiting the new retail and cultural facilities

8 Model of the proposals for Manchester
city centre.
(© EDAW)

- Corporation Street – designed to accommodate buses, taxis and pedestrians
  linking the main developments

- Millennium Quarter – a major reference point within the redeveloped city centre
  around which the Millennium Centre, Corn Exchange and leisure complex sit. It
  also includes the Cathedral Close, improvements to the River Irwell and the
  cultural gardens around the Millennium Centre

- Cathedral Close, Chetham's School of Music and the River Irwell – this area
  provides a major new urban park for the city centre comprising a lawn running
  between the Cathedral and Chetham's and along the river; improved access and
  viewing points along the river; pedestrian links from the park to the Ramada Hotel
  and a space in front of the Cathedral as a focus for ceremonial events. In addition,
  on the west bank of the River Irwell a park is proposed which relates to the
  transport interchange and new riverside pedestrian routes.

These public realm works will create the urban landscape settings for the development
projects:

- a large Marks and Spencer retail store focusing on a galleria that will provide new connections between streets

- the West Shambles mixed-use development comprising retail, residential (with internal private courtyard), commercial and a roof-terrace restaurant

- the Shambles Pubs – the Old Wellington Inn and Sinclair's Oyster Bar – to be moved and accommodated within the northern quarter of Exchange Square adjacent to the historic core of the city centre

- redevelopment of the Arndale Centre to include a new Winter Garden, new entrances and facades and new residential, commercial and, possibly, hotel space

- the refurbishment of the impressive Corn Exchange which sits at the centre of the new retail, cultural and leisure facilities

- the redevelopment of the Ramada Hotel reorienting activities towards the River Irwell in order to improve facilities and image of the hotel and to enhance this section of the urban river

- a major new landmark building, the Millennium Centre, which will celebrate the Modern City including an extensive public foyer, a series of gallery spaces with the capacity for hi-tech exhibits and a theatre/auditorium. Integral to this development is the creation of the cultural gardens surrounding the building, which include public art

- a regional leisure and entertainment centre comprising multiplex cinema, hi-tech leisure uses and supporting retail space and restaurants

- a variety of residential developments to increase opportunities to live in the city centre

A three-phase strategy for the redevelopment of the city centre will see completion of the major infrastructure and public realm works by the Millennium. The costs are in the order of £83 million of public investment and £350 million in private sector investment. The city received European Community structural funding for the preparation and management of the Masterplan and business support, matched by private and public sector contributions including funds from English Partnerships (the Government's regeneration agency), the Government Office for the North West (the Government's regional agency), and further European Community regeneration funds. The European city is important.

Speke Garston

Liverpool, like Manchester, is an area of industrial decline. The Speke Garston area south of Liverpool is Merseyside's largest concentration of manufacturing activity and the engine room of the Liverpool economy. It is a centre for international companies including Ford Motor Company Europe, Evans Medical, and Glaxo-Wellcome, with many local companies operating successfully. It was developed primarily in the 1940s as part of Liverpool's southern expansion. Much of the infrastructure is now outmoded and there has been little investment in upgrading that infrastructure and the environment. In 1996, Liverpool City Council and English Partnerships formed the Speke Garston Development Company bringing together land resources and investment for physical and economic regeneration. The Speke Garston Partnership was formed at the same time charged with investing in housing and community facilities infrastructure. Investment of some £40 million from the public sector over the next 10 years is planned to attract between £150 and 180 million of private investment. EDAW were appointed to lead the design team supported by WSP Graham (consulting engineers), Walfords (quantity surveyors), King Sturge (chartered surveyors), Heritage Architecture (historic buildings consultants) and CEDA (community development advisors).

The study comprised the redevelopment of the abandoned Speke Airport and its historic terminal building and hangars into a high-quality commerce park; environmental and highway improvements to 15 kilometres of roads through the area; the regeneration of Speke and Edwards Lane Industrial Estates and the former Bryant & May match factory. The objectives for the highway improvements were to enhance the overall image and environmental quality, to enhance ecological and biodiversity; to provide vegetated corridors along roads and around the airfield down to the River Mersey estuary (a Site of Special Scientific Interest due to its value as a bird habitat); and to mark the city boundary and significant junctions with gateway and marker features.

An Environmental Report was prepared for the airfield site covering planning status, statutory controls and designations affecting the site, ecology, soils, climate, topography, geology, hydrology, archaeology, visual assessment, and an assessment of environmental impact due to the proposed development and proposed amelioration measures. Principal issues that influenced the form of the development framework were the Old Terminal building (which is listed Grade II by English Heritage, the Government agency responsible for the protection of historic buildings), the flat nature of the site, its exposure to strong south-westerly winds, excellent views to the estuary and the Welsh hills beyond, and the adjacent Grade I listed Speke Hall and grounds.

218

The development concept is to create a new working community as an integral part of the regeneration of the existing business and residential communities. The plan comprises an infrastructure of roads and essential services within a public realm landscape framework around the perimeter of the airfield and adjacent to the roads. The design makes reference to the essential elements that characterise the estuarine landscape. The design language was developed to reflect and emphasise the subtle planar quality of the site in the layout and treatment of each element of the scheme. A refined palette of high-quality materials and finishes is consistently used in a simple, highly rational manner throughout the scheme. Choice and treatment of plant material utilises and enhances the properties of the estuarine ecology. Individual elements sit within an infrastructure carefully located within the landscape to allow views to the estuary and the Welsh hills beyond.

The core concepts for the initial Development Framework were as follows:

- In the context of the wider area, to provide continuous 'green' links of vegetation along the road corridors through and from the industrial estates, around the perimeter of the airfield, down to the estuary with fingers of vegetation into the commerce park. This is ecologically sound and sustainable

- This links in to the idea of 'emparkment', i.e. enclosing, defining and marking the commerce park as a special place. This is done with a perimeter railing design – based on the existing art-deco railings associated with the Terminal building – and a 15-metre wide strip of native woodland vegetation

- To ensure maximum flexibility in plot development

- To create a high-quality hard and soft landscape infrastructure which provides an attractive landscape experience on arrival at the commerce park and approach through it to the plot developments

- To identify what is special about the location – the *genius loci*, the local distinctiveness:

    i)   Openness, large scale, sense of space
    ii)   Views to the estuary and Welsh Hills
    iii) Prevailing south-westerlies from the estuary and the need to ameliorate views of the built development from the estuary
    iv)   The estuary landscape: water/edge/vegetation   219

- The response to this local distinctiveness is incorporated within the initial Development Framework as follows:

    i)   A long vista from the main entrance roundabout along the primary access road corridor towards the Estuary – splayed to enhance false perspective and openness and emphasise the view to the estuary and Welsh Hills beyond
    ii)   Concentration of the public landscape infrastructure adjacent to roads to enhance sense of space and openness
    iii) Slightly curved east–west roads to enhance sense of distance and openness
    iv)   Provision of secondary 'open space' routes as view corridors down to the

9 Plans from top to bottom showing the Phase I and
Phase II layouts; general arrangement for the east-
west access road; and the layout for Phase I.
(Drawing © EDAW. Published with the kind permission
of Speke Garston Development Company)

estuary between plot developments – these also allow for hiding of security
fences within flanking willow/poplar woodland and screen plot
developments from each other

v) The planting of 'closed' woodland on the southern edges of the east – west
roads which will:

   a)   protect the site from south-westerlies, and

   b)   screen the larger plot developments from the road

vi) Create a 'trees in grass' parkland landscape character on the northern
edges of the road as a foreground for better-quality building frontages

vii) Introduce the qualities of the estuary landscape through water bodies and
aquatic vegetation and key them into public landscape infrastructure as
linear canal/waterways focused on the estuary either side of the main
access road and to the south of the first-phase access road

viii) incorporate art as part of the landscape design rather than as stand-alone
set pieces

The Development Framework is a flexible plan; it is being changed as newly defined
needs and priorities emerge. However, the commitment and sensitivity to the community
and the environment mark this regeneration strategy. Community, industry, business,
employment, education, art and the environment are seen as an interlinked totality. Public

10 Axonometric of the plot entrance to the south of
the east–west road combining signage/markers, the
canal and woodland.
(Drawing © EDAW. Published with the kind
permission of Speke Garston Development Company)

investment in infrastructure is recognised as a means to an end. The triadic relationship
of ecology, community and art here is balanced.

Newcastle Drawdock

At a much smaller scale, the Newcastle Drawdock project raises issues of ecology,
community and the nature of the artist/landscape architect collaboration. The London
Docklands Development Corporation's 'Isle of Dogs Development Framework' published
in January 1994 defines a strategy for the overall improvement and enhancement of the
external environment of the Isle of Dogs.[15] Newcastle Drawdock at the south-eastern tip
of the Isle of Dogs on the River Thames was one of those schemes scheduled for
improvement during 1996–97. The Corporation appointed Tate | Hopkins as consultant
landscape architects for the project in August 1995 with Maunsell as consultant
engineers and Parker & Browne as consultant quantity surveyors. During 1996 Tate |
Hopkins merged their practice with EDAW and, with the agreement of the Corporation,
transferred the project to them.

The Corporation has a policy of promoting, encouraging and commissioning public
art, and identified Newcastle Drawdock as an appropriate scheme for the inclusion of an
artist as part of the design team. The Corporation commissioned the Public Art
Development Trust to recommend artists and, subsequently, to manage the artistic
commission. The brief issued by the Corporation and accompanied by a sketch design

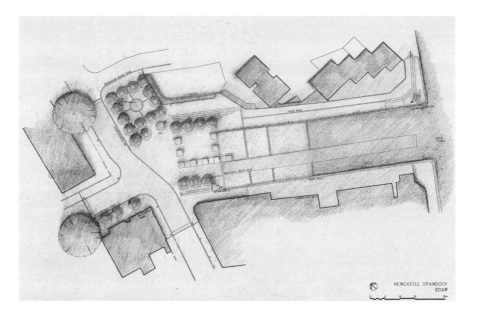

11 Newcastle Drawdock Masterplan.
(Drawing © Tate Hopkins)

was to unify the Drawdock with the surrounding elements of the site and to take advantage of its riverside location. The budget and final cost was approximately £275,000.

The project comprises the renewal of pedestrian and highway areas including the river walkway and lookout/sitting areas adjacent to the dock; the incorporation of an under-utilised neighbourhood park on the site of a chapel destroyed by bombs during the Second World War; and the creation of a seating area outside the Waterman's Arms public house. All areas are accessible to the disabled by the incorporation of ramps into the scheme. Flood defence levels had to be maintained, as did access to the river via the public slipway.

The Drawdock itself dates from c. 1850 and is listed Grade II by English Heritage along with the nearby Church of Christ and St. John and its Vicarage, the Waterman's Arms and the remaining cannon bollards. The magnificent views to and from the Royal Naval College, the Maritime Museum and the Cutty Sark at Greenwich are also mentioned in the listing. The whole scheme is within a designated Conservation Area. The design process included presentations and consultations with local residents and with several statutory consultees including English Heritage, the Environment Agency, the Port of London Authority and the Ministry of Agriculture, Fisheries and Food.

Visual surveys of the site and its environs were carried out and initial responses and reactions to the problems, possibilities and potentials of the site documented. These were presented to the Public Art Development Trust who subsequently selected six artists who they felt could conceptually contribute to the project. The Public Art

Development Trust in turn presented previous works of the artists and described their background, approach and rationale for selection to Tate Hopkins and officers of the London Docklands Development Corporation. Two artists were shortlisted and met the landscape architect on site to discuss mutual feelings about the site, the project and working methods. Grenville Davey – who won the prestigious Turner Prize in 1992 – was chosen and appointed before any design work was done. The project also won a Royal Society for the Arts 'Art for Architecture' award in 1995 which contributed funds towards the artist's fee.

The scheme draws together the physical, cultural and spiritual history of the site. However, at the same time it creates a contemporary context for daily use and enjoyment by local inhabitants, visitors and tourists alike. The scheme also reconnects the disparate elements into a cohesive whole, and attempts to create a work of landscape art that has meaning. Two public consultation meetings were held: the first to present sketch ideas and gauge public reaction; the second to present developed designs and to seek public approval and comment, which was largely favourable. In purely physical terms, the river, the walkway, the Drawdock and the adjacent park are opened up to create a single entity that includes Saundersness and Glenaffric Roads, the Waterman's Arms and Church of Christ and St. John. The design revolves around a reconfigured Button – a circular sculpture created by Davey as a gallery piece in 1988.

The new Button – One – is industrial grade, manufactured from galvanised spun steel and dressed with checkerplate, eyelets and oak. Four pieces – Four Thirds – each representing a third of One are inverted and planted as objects at critical points within the site – these, and One, also act as seats. Thus, Four Thirds act as reference points – static markers in a dynamic world. One is the hub around which the scheme revolves. Also, One and Four Thirds are each accompanied by one of the original cannon bollards – past, present and future combine.

The first critical point marked by the first piece of Four Thirds is on the site of the old chapel where a bosque of flowering cherry trees surround a circular paving feature which collects rainwater from the four cruciformed, 'rivers of life' – an Edenesque baptismal.

The second critical point is at the Drawdock head. Here, two lines of alder trees extend the line of the dock walls and mark the dock head when viewed from Glenaffric Avenue. Granite steps take up changes in level, and smoothed gravel paving flows up and down and in and out of the large, white, textured concrete plinths. A line of plinths march up the slipway and breach the flood defence threshold; these are covered in electro-plated stainless checkerplate steel – a cut above the rough and tough Durbar checkerplate of One and Four Thirds. A levelled area protected at the back and side by a galvanised steel railing act as a setting for the second piece of Four Thirds. Boats will be launched and landed at the slipway; people will walk up and down the slipway to meet the tide; people will sit and play on the plinths; the tide will roll in and out – it is a living, working place. The proposal to introduce intertidal reeds within the dock (a reference to what would have existed in this location prior to any development) was defeated by English Heritage, who insisted that this was not in keeping with the industrial history of

223

12 Plinths rising up to and marking
the flood defence threshold.
(Photograph © Martin Jones
Photography)

13 One of Davey's sculptural seats
– *Four Thirds* – and adjacent
cannon bollard; the bosque of
cherry trees around the cruciform
and circular paving feature which
collects water; large seating stones
which remain from the Chapel
which was originally in this location.
(Photograph © Martin Jones
Photography)

14 Looking down the dockside walk towards the River Thames with Davey's reconfigured Button – *One* – in the foreground. (Photograph © Martin Jones Photography)

15 Another of Davey's sculptural seats – *Four Thirds* – overlooking the River Thames towards the Naval College and Cutty Sark at Greenwich. (Photograph © Martin Jones Photography)

the site – a decision which questions which past one chooses to celebrate.

The third critical point is the lookout at the corner of the river walk and the Drawdock. The third and fourth pieces of Four Thirds are located here, back to back. One faces the magnificent maritime architecture of Greenwich and the equally magnificent industrial riverscape; the other looks down and along the river walkway. The Thames flows inexorably with the tide filling and emptying, filling and emptying, filling and emptying in an endless cycle – a timeless world.

Conclusion

The philosophic justification for a paradigm of landscape architecture based on ecology, community and art; for readings of the *genius loci* based on physical, historical, and cultural dimensions of place; for art as the motivating force behind the expressions of the human/nature relationship; and for the landscape architect/artist to act as interpreter for the community, underlies each of these projects and studies. Ecology, community and art are enmeshed in each to varying degrees. Robert Thayer argues for an essentially romantic vision of sustainable community design; the Camp Pendleton study offers stark choices as to how we might need to live in order to maintain acceptable levels of biodiversity; the Manchester Masterplan balances city economics, living and community needs; the Speke Garston Development Framework balances regenerative industrial and commercial economics, community development and environmental imperatives; Newcastle Drawdock raises questions of collaboration, community and history. Each attempts to intimate a better future in some way; none is perfect, all are challenging. The need to continue to develop our philosophies and to engage in debate about possible Utopias is critical to our future.

1 J. B. Jackson, quoted in D. W. Meinig, ed., *The Interpretation of Ordinary Landscapes* (New York: Oxford University Press, 1979) pp. 228–229.

2 J. B. Jackson, edited by Ervin H. Zube, *Landscapes, Selected Writings of J. B. Jackson* (University of Massachusetts Press, 1970) p. 9.

3 *Ibid.*, p. 9.

4 John Dewey, *Art as Experience* (New York: Milton Balch and Co, 1934).

5 *Ibid.*, p. 339.

6 *Ibid.*, p. 9.

7 *Ibid.*, p. 7.

8 *Ibid.*, p.192.

9 Carl Steinitz, Letter to the Editor, *Landscape Architecture*, May 1981, p. 442.

10 Robert Thayer, Gray World, *Green Heart: Technology, Nature, and the Sustainable Landscape* (New York: John Wiley & Sons, Inc., 1994).

11 *Ibid.*, p. 235.

12 Albert Gore, *Earth in Balance* (Boston: Houghton Mifflin, 1992).

13 Carl Steinitz, ed., *Alternative Futures for the Region of Camp Pendleton, California* (Harvard University, 1996).

14 Ian L. McHarg, *Design with Nature* (New York: Doubleday and Co., 1971).

15 *Isle of Dogs Development Framework* (London Docklands Development Corporation, 1994).

228

Introduction

Though some essays in previous sections cover contemporary cases, the emphasis in all the essays in this section is firmly on the contemporary. The four essays in this section deal with very contemporary environments, land use problems and political agendas, as well as spatial, temporal and material appropriateness. The work of Bernard Lassus addresses conditions such as the motorcar and roads. Derek Jarman's garden deals with the site of a nuclear reactor in an ecologically sensitive area. Jacqueline Osty's park deals with the complex contemporary problems of a site which has lost its ancient agricultural function, which is caught up in the problems of urban growth and suburban spread, and whose developer is a local government wanting to increase its status and its tourist revenues. Peter Salter's work also addresses contemporary issues such as the conflict of prefabricated building elements with local building techniques and skills, indeed the loss of local skills and techniques, and hence the loss of appropriateness of construction processes to the prevailing conditions. To avoid the nostalgic rejection of modern processes (of building, of fabrication, of production) while not either rejecting – or romanticising – traditional and ancient techniques and skills, Peter Salter refers to the landscape as a measure of appropriateness: landscape thus becomes a measure for architecture through the use of responsive materials, of suitable construction and of an adaptable geometry.

These four contemporary case studies therefore raise all the issues about materials, about temporal and spatial qualities, about geometry and form and scale, and about the issues of collaboration and professionalisation, that were discussed in the previous sections.

1 Bernard Lassus: Aire de Nîmes-Caissargues. (p. 232) (Photograph Jan Birksted)

Stephen Bann

The necessity of invention: Bernard Lassus's garden landscapes

The radical position which Bernard Lassus has come to occupy in the spectrum of contemporary landscape architecture can be summed up in a single phrase. Asked by Udo Weilacher in a recent published interview how he managed to 'reconcile the dichotomy between art and landscape architecture', he replied: 'It's quite simple. Art and landscape architecture are the same thing for me.'[1] But the implications of Lassus's statement need to be followed up in order for the full meaning to be grasped. It is not simply that he was originally trained as a painter, in Léger's studio, as Weilacher points out. The underlying issue is that garden artists of the past took it for granted that a creator of landscape would have a basis of instruction in the plastic arts; only in the present century has it become customary for a landscape architect to have little or no training in aesthetics. To defend the identity of art and landscape architecture is therefore a polemical stance, inevitably historicist in its recourse to earlier examples, but also impinging directly on the very concept of professional practice as it exists at present.

At this stage in his career, Lassus can justly claim to have shown how a reorientation of practice might take place. Appointed Professor of Architecture at the Ecole des Beaux-Arts, Paris, in 1968, he has more recently pioneered the first D.E.A. (Diploma of Advanced Studies) in Landscape to be founded in France, in a joint venture involving the Ecole des Hautes Etudes and the School of Architecture of La Villette. He also occupies the post of Visiting Professor in Landscape Architecture at the University of Pennsylvania, whose press will shortly be publishing a collected English edition of his theoretical writings, already sampled in two issues of the *Journal of Garden History*.[2] In this brief essay, I cannot hope to touch on more than a few examples of his practice. What I propose to do, therefore, is to approach two main issues. In the first place, I shall look at the general direction of his work from the 1960s onwards, emphasising the way in which he has combined sociological and historical study with a constant concern for the realisation of concrete effects in precise spatial conditions. In the second place, I shall look in more detail at the achievement of his recent work, in particular the Jardin des Retours (1982) and the Aire de Nîmes-Caissargues (1989–90).

Lassus's commitment to the artistic investment of the wider environment can be dated essentially to 1961, when he founded the Centre de Recherche d'Ambiance. At

Stephen Bann
The necessity of invention:
Bernard Lassus's garden landscapes

this point, his techniques closely paralleled those of the kinetic artists whose vogue in Paris, and throughout the West, reached its peak in the mid-1960s: he employed artificial light and movement in order to achieve intense presentations of colour and form, often on an environmental scale. However, his work was not gallery-bound: still less did he concern himself with retaining a modernist 'style' based on orthogonals and clear separation of colours. In fact, he never confused the need for clear analysis with the corresponding need to respect the phenomenal complexity of visual experience. In one project, he photographed the Gorges of the River Arodin, as a way of recording the experience of a walk along the river-bed; naturally, the verbal description of the need to balance one's weight exactly while picking one's way along the boulder-strewn surface was no less important than the visual record of placid depths and minor whirlpools. An exercise of this kind, one might say, was reflected in the turn which Lassus's plastic art was to take in the 1960s: towards what he called *brise-lumières*, or hanging structures displaying the infinite gradations of reflected and coloured light, and ambitious mosaic murals on a large scale, whose colour sequences were deliberately designed to 'blur' as the spectator moved in front of them.

In retrospect, it is possible to pick out in any number of examples from the early phases of Lassus's career the characteristic, and highly individual, blend of empirical study, rhetorical analysis, and artistic invention which has been maintained throughout his subsequent development. Empirical study has meant, for him, not only the poetic record of tracks along a river-bed, or in a pine forest, but also the quasi-anthropological survey of what he named the *habitants-paysagistes* (literally 'dweller-landscapers'): in general, retired workers who used their leisure to create imaginary worlds in the exiguous spaces available to them. Eschewing the recuperative strategies of the champions of *Art brut*, Lassus insisted that the place for these unique creations was not the gallery, but the specific locale in which they had been planted. It was not a question of creating detachable 'objects', but of opening up a space of invention in which colours, materials and often an identifiable iconography based in popular culture worked together to relieve the drab environment. As Lassus subsequently remarked of the statue of Snow White set up by M. Pecqueur at the edge of his small garden in the mining village of Ruitz: 'Only Snow White, who evokes a special relationship with the forest, is capable – as she reaches with her gaze for the horizon – of giving the little stretch of planted meadow the extent which was needed to become a measureless forest.'[3]

Lassus's survey of the *habitants-paysagistes*, which included numerous, anonymous examples of gardening practice as well as star cases such as M. Pecqueur's extensive work, taught him that such realisations were not merely aberrant protests against the uniformity of modern planning, but sophisticated manifestations of a rhetoric which could be understood and applied in other circumstances. For instance, he defined with the term 'retarded contrast' an effect which involved the 'carry-over of one of the characteristics of an element to the adjoining element at their common boundaries'.[4] Put in concrete terms, this might mean, for example, that the common element of red paint had been applied both to a gate-post, made of stone, and to a gate made of iron – with a certain shock effect, since the painting of the 'natural' stone would be unexpected.

Lassus realised that such devices were, in effect, strictly parallel on the rhetorical level to the time-honoured procedures of the *jardin à la française*, where the geometrical form of the topiary tree or hedge qualified it to be a medium term between the free form of the forest and the constructed form of the habitation.

The work which demonstrated most clearly Lassus's early conclusions about the 'classical' character of such systems of transition was his *Buissons artificiels* (artificial bushes), installed at a school in Guénange, Lorraine, under the 1% scheme for artistic contributions to an educational building. Just as he had insisted in previous commissions on extensive mosaic walls, rather than localised objects, so at Guénange Lassus saw the problem as one of establishing a medium term between the prefabricated modern school building and the surrounding woodland, rather than offering a 'sculpture' to stand freely within an alotted courtyard. Consequently, he arranged for a special colour range of enamel-coated balls to be mounted on parallel metal strips, which suggested the rhythmic rise and fall of bush and plant shapes. These colourful elements descended the lawn, setting up the same kind of spatial punctuation as a topiary hedge.

It is implicit in Lassus's development as a landscape and garden artist that no absolute privilege should be accorded to the 'natural' as opposed to the artificial; nor should the natural world be present in the token form of 'generic greenery' as in the schemes of many modernist architects. The point is that the scale between 'natural' and artificial or man-made is a continuous one, in which an individual element has its value simply because of its relative position in a series. The enamel ball in its coloured array becomes 'natural' in relation to the rigidity of the low-cost modern building, just as the topiary in the French garden appears 'artificial' beside the untreated tree. Indeed Lassus developed this intuition experimentally, with the aid of French government research funding, when he set up a project entitled *Les Verres et les bouteilles* (glasses and bottles). What happens to a uniform row of bottles when we fill one of them half-way full of wine, or if we place a full wine-glass in front of them? Or if we add a bunch of grapes to the series? In each case, the new element modifies the series by reconfiguring it not just in visual, but in semantic terms. And general conclusions can be drawn from this process, such as that 'heterogeneity is more welcoming than homogeneity'. Or to translate the abstract formula into more meaningful terms, 'only a landscape sub-stratum which is sufficiently heterogenous can accommodate original additions'.[4]

Research projects of this kind, together with the inventive 'games with the public' which Lassus continued into the 1970s, were always implicitly allegorics of the state of contemporary landscape, and the ways in which people might be empowered to make their own contribution towards its amelioration. But, whilst he was only too ready to signal the achievement of the retired miner, or the HLM-dweller who created an eruption of foliage in the constricted space of a concrete balcony, Lassus could not fail to be aware that it was the duty of the landscape artist to intervene on a larger scale, if only to palliate the deadening effects of mass low-cost housing. Most remarkable of all his achievements, in terms of sheer scale, was the immense project of 'coloration of facades' – to the extent of 20,000 individual lodgings – which he carried out in the 1970s/80s for the housing company set up to manage the extensive real estate owned

235

Stephen Bann
The necessity of invention:
Bernard Lassus's garden landscapes

2 Bernard Lassus: Belvedere, Aire
de Nîmes-Caissargues,
Autoroute A.54, 1993.
(Photograph Bernard Lassus)

236

by the declining iron and steel industries of Lorraine.

For this enterprise, Lassus devised the term *paysage critique* (critical landscape). There was no ideal solution to the problem of rehabilitating endless blocks of cheap apartments, in an area where declining population was inevitably following industrial decline. To that extent, any new scheme was bound to impinge 'critically' on the viewer, suggesting that no amount of ingenuity could camouflage the reality of the situation. Nevertheless Lassus's response to the challenge, facilitated by the housing company's courageous decision to demolish a significant number of buildings and so free a large amount of space, reached considerable heights of invention. People who earlier had no means of identifying their own apartment in the uniform grid of a concrete facade could now locate its refurbished substitute as nestling under an Alsace gable, or bordered by bulbous green trees. Lassus's skill in adjusting the range of colours used to the precise environmental conditions – developed as early as in the 1960s in his mosaic facades for the new town of Quétigny-lès-Dijon – was here exploited to create a new urban folklore, and a series of landscape vistas explicitly dedicated to the art of the classical garden. Here the passer-by could glimpse, in the newly cleared space, urns, belvederes and a distant horizon.[5]

I have used the word 'invention' more than once in commenting on the character of Lassus's approach to landscape. This should not be taken to mean that he plucks his ideas out of the air. On the contrary, as I have shown, he is distinctive for the extensive research – artistic, sociological and anthropological – which has come to support his basic concepts and procedures. But this in no way alters the fact that the creation of landscape, for him, is a poetic enterprise. Just as he resists the still potent modernist assumption that the natural environment is hardly more than a negative ground against which to place the heroic built form, so he castigates the contemporary fashion to collapse issues of landscape design into those of ecology. As he has explained on more than one occasion, ecological rectitude is a precondition of good landscape design, but it is by no means a sufficient condition. A place can be cleansed of pollution without in any way becoming a beautiful landscape.[6] Equally, the commitment to poetic invention means that a great deal can be achieved without necessarily involving enormous labour and expense. Faced with a project for rehabilitating a small island which was down-wind of a chocolate factory, Lassus made a proposal which comprised a simple notice-board with the announcement: *Par vent d'ouest, mousse au chocolat* (With the west wind, chocolate mousse). Anticipating the possibility that visitors would be troubled by the displaced odour, he gave it a new meaning by an expression which condensed two readings of the word 'mousse': an attractive chocolate dessert and 'moss' as a landscape feature.

This proposal typifies the approach which Lassus, in conjunction with the Swiss critic Lucius Burckhardt, termed 'minimal intervention'. However, Lassus's commitment to poetic strategies has not inhibited him from undertaking major construction works when the project required them. In the case of the Jardin des Retours at Rochefort-sur-Mer, for example, he insisted on rebuilding a massive stone wall which separated the area of the Corderie royale from the public gardens adjacent to the town centre, and on

3 & 4 Bernard Lassus: Nîmes-Caissargues,
Autoroute A.54, 1993.
(Photographs Bernard Lassus, Jan Birksted)

providing access through a large stone ramp. From his perspective, it was necessary to obtain a dissociation of the visual and the tactile point of view: in other words, visitors had to have a chance of taking in the overall vista of the garden from a level where they were barred from immediate access.[7] It is a mild irony that, in this case, the works in stone have quickly achieved the effect of seeming to have been in place for centuries! For Lassus, however, the point is certainly not to maximise the visible evidence of the designer's intervention. It is enough for him that the desired effects should be obtained.

In my concluding section, I want to look in more detail at two of the projects which demonstrate the special character of Lassus's landscape poetics. To do so is not to exhaust the range of his work, by any means. The sequence of coherent garden designs for specific places, produced from 1975 onwards, is a cornucopia of fertile ideas, even though none achieved realisation before the Jardin des Retours. Also, Lassus's current work includes a motorway rest-area (*aire d'autoroute*) at Crazannes in the Charente

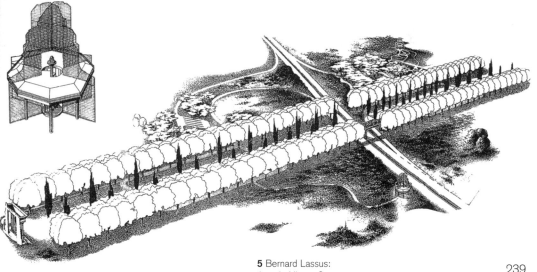

5 Bernard Lassus:
Aire de Nîmes-Caissargues,
Autoroute A.54.
(Drawing by Bernard Lassus)

239

which surpasses in audacity everything that he has done so far in this highly public and promising domain. But the two sides of Lassus's production can perhaps be most satisfactorily represented, at this moment, by the motorway rest area of Nîmes-Caissargues, carried out in 1989–90, and the *Jardin des Retours* at Rochefort, begun in 1982 and only now reaching completion.

Nîmes-Caissargues, in the first place, illustrates Lassus's innovative thinking about the new contemporary context in which the garden designer may be challenged to work. Why create a garden in a motorway rest area, in the first place? The obvious answer is that motorway passengers need distraction, and to the extent that the rest area establishes a contrast to the frenetic conditions on the motorway, it will have succeeded

6 Tontines with exotic plants in the Rigging Area, Jardin des retours, Rochefort-sur-Mer. (Photograph Bernard Lassus)

7 Le chemin de Charente, Jardin des retours, Rochefort-sur-Mer. (Photograph Bernard Lassus)

240

all the more. But there is a secondary point, well perceived by Lassus. As travel by motorway becomes more and more prevalent, it becomes more and more likely that car travel will almost completely avoid urban centres. For a city like Nîmes, then, the rest area has a function which could be called annunciatory. It offers not just a literal 'view' of the adjacent city, but a concrete expression of its 'Nîmeness'. Perhaps the odd traveller might be tempted to delay their journey, and spend time in the city itself?

The garden thus becomes, in the guise of a motorway rest area, a meeting point of different functions and expressions. Indeed, in his recent *Dictionnaire historique de l'Art des Jardins*, Michel Conan has cited Nîmes-Caissargues precisely as an example of a *jardin vertical* (literally, vertical garden), that is to say, one which brings out the 'heterogeneity of the elements which enter into a creation of a place'.[8] On the primary level, as it were, the need is to establish different types of vegetation: olive groves, to answer to a certain expectation of Provençal landscape, and a contrasting formal garden, cutting across the axis of the motorway, which puts the visitor in mind rather of the historical elements of landscape design. 'Nîmeness' is stressed partly through the construction of a metal belvedere, illuminated at night, in the shape of the well-known local Roman monument, the Tour Magne; from the spiral stairway leading up the viewing platform, the visitor can scan the horizon, eventually gaining a vista of the city which might well include the monument itself. But Lassus's most daring stroke is the incorporation of the entire neoclassical facade of the demolished theatre of Nîmes, which occupied a position adjacent to the Roman Maison carrée, and was removed to make room for Norman Foster's glistening glass Carré de l'Art. Placed as it was in the very centre of the city, opposite what is probably the most exquisite specimen of Roman architecture north of the Alps, this nineteenth-century colonnade could only have seemed

8 The Rigging Area, Le Jardin des Retours, 1982–1995. (Drawing by Bernard Lassus)

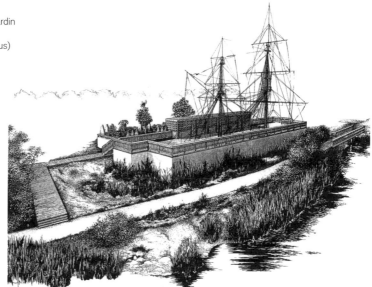

241

second-best, and it is easy to appreciate Foster's wish to remove it. But at Nîmes-Caissargues, its *comparative* authenticity can be reestablished. On a site where there is no authentic monument, it represents the point in the scale closest to the authentic (Figs 1, 3, and 4). Once again, Lassus seeks to show that such values are not pre-established, but depend on the specific spatial context in which the element occurs.

At first sight, the Jardin des Retours is much more similar to a traditional garden in its concept than the rest area of Nîmes-Caissargues. But this appearance could be deceptive. As noted before, Lassus undertook substantial preliminary work on the levels through which access is obtained, before engaging in the planting of the area. This was consistent with his strong view that the Corderie royale – a fine seventeenth-century building which originally served for the production of cordage for the French navy – should not be treated as a substitute *château*, with formal gardens in the French style

Stephen Bann
The necessity of invention:
Bernard Lassus's garden landscapes

being arranged symmetrically around it. Instead, he decided to emphasise the length of the building, but to ensure that, from the front giving onto the River Charente, the view would be broken up into a series of vistas obtained through dense riverside planting. Approached by boat along the river, the building therefore offers a series of different perspectives, rather as the ruins of Rievaulx Abbey in Yorkshire are displayed from the eighteenth-century viewing terrace constructed on the heights above. For the casual walker along the riverbank, who can take either a winding path (Fig. 7) or a more formal paved walkway, there is a similar pattern of concealment and disclosure, which punctuates the movement parallel to the facade.

It is appropriate to comment on how the walker perceives the central feature of the Jardin des Retours, since this emphasis perhaps brings out best the radical nature of Lassus's approach, and incidentally his unacceptability to the majority of landscape architects in France and elsewhere. Those who are looking for dramatic intervention, at Rochefort or in his other schemes, will not find it; indeed the common criticism seems to be a variant on the Emperor's New Clothes – that he has done little or nothing at all with the site. Even well-intentioned bureaucrats have misinterpreted his intentions by offering publicly commissioned sculpture to 'fill' the supposedly empty spaces! But Lassus's work is perceptible particularly in the nuances, such as his careful treatment of ground and paved surfaces: the level of the lawns, for example, is slightly raised *vis-à-vis* the cobbles surrounding the Corderie, so as to underline the point that the garden is a new one, and not a revival of an earlier scheme. The finesse of Lassus's treatment will probably not be perceived on a conscious level by the casual visitor, and it will certainly not be apparent from photographs. But the success of the scheme can be measured by the way in which people use the garden, and, in the case of the inhabitants of Rochefort, seem to behave as if it had always been there.

These points about the deceptive simplicity of the Jardin des Retours apply particularly to the side bordering the Charente. On the town side, the retaining wall and the ramp offer a different kind of vista, which is markedly exotic, and related to the important history of Rochefort as a port providing access to the New World, and receiving as a by-product of commercial and naval activity some of the first plants from far-away places that have become naturalised in Europe subsequently: the *Begonia* genus, for example, takes its name from Michel Bégon, Intendant of Rochefort, and his grandson, the Admiral de la Galissonière, gave his name in turn to the large-flowered magnolia, whose seeds he brought back from America in 1711. Entering the garden by the ramp, the visitor can already sense this exotic note, as the path is threaded between ranks of Virginian tulip trees, and a row of palms rises in the middle distance. It is Lassus's intention to stress this aspect of the garden as a place of 'returns' not only in the general planting, but also in the addition of specific facilities. The town of Rochefort has already purchased a *Begonia* collection which is due to be housed in a greenhouse on the site.

The Jardin des Retours is also provided with particular features, each of which merits a separate description: the Labyrinth of Naval Battles, only recently accessible because of the slow growth of its yew hedges; the Rigging Area, where the masts of a

242

pre-nineteenth century sailing ship have been recreated on the remains of a concrete blockhouse (Fig. 8), and the wooden deck carries 'tontines' modelled on the baskets used to repatriate tender plants from the tropics (Fig. 6); the stone jetty where the flags of the Admirals fly … All of these enrich the experience of a complex artistic creation which is, and could only be, a garden: that is to say, a meeting-place of aesthetic, historical and economic functions which does not betray the achievement of the great European gardens of the past.

Notes

1 See Udo Weilacher, *Between Landscape Architecture and Land Art* (Basel: Birkhauser, 1996), p. 109.

2 See 'The landscape approach of Bernard Lassus', in *Journal of Garden History*, 3 (1983), pp.79–107, and 'The landscape approach of Bernard Lassus: Part II', in *Journal of Garden History*, 15, 2 (1995), pp. 67–106: both sets of texts translated and introduced by Stephen Bann.

3 See Bernard Lassus, 'The garden landscape: a popular aesthetic', in John Dixon Hunt and Joachim Wolschke-Bulmahn (eds), *The Vernacular Garden* (Washington D.C.: Dumbarton Oaks, 1993), p. 151.

4 See *Bernard Lassus-XIVème Biennale de Sao-Paulo*, exhibition catalogue (Paris, undated).

5 See *Bernard Lassus, Villes-paysages couleurs en Lorraine* (Batigere, 1989), for an extensive documentation of the different schemes.

6 See Bernard Lassus, 'L'obligation de l'invention', in Augustin Berque (ed), *Cinq propositions pour une théorie du paysage* (Paris: Champ Vallon, 1994), pp. 81–106.

7 Lassus had already introduced this principle in his earliest garden scheme, *Le Jardin de l'Antérieur* (see *Journal of Garden History*, 3 (1983), p. 84).

8 See Michel Conan, *Dictionnaire historique des jardins* (Paris: Hazan, 1997), p. 136.

Jan Birksted
The prospect at Dungeness:
Derek Jarman's garden

1 Dungeness landscape with Prospect Cottage and the nuclear
reactor in the distance on the right.
(Drawing by Jan Birksted)

244

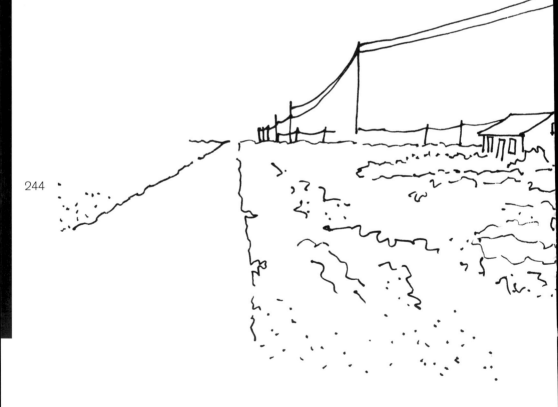

Jan Birksted

The prospect at Dungeness: Derek Jarman's garden

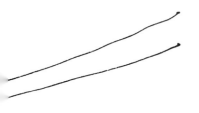

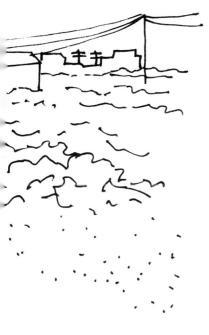

An asphalt road, bordered by tar-stained and weathered telegraph poles, stretches into the distance alongside sagging telephone wires. Shingle extends on both sides and, beyond muddy sand-flats, the sea is at low tide. Weather-boarded timber shacks and beached clinker boats are scattered on the shingle. Under the thin cloud-cover, the intense shadowless light bleaches everything. A seagull wings across the sky and screeches. A small propeller airplane hums into sight from across the sea. The sun breaks through and 'the wet shingle glistens like pearls of Vermeer light'.[1] Only slowly does one become aware of the many activities and sounds. A trail of smoke rises from the landscape and travels across the horizon, followed by the hissing of a steam-engine. Eerie sounds drift along on the wind: the ringing of bells, the muffled clanging of metal, even the high-pitched wail of sirens. Abruptly one notices beyond the sand dunes a remote and massive outline: Dungeness nuclear power station. Uncannily, the distant sounds of life emanating from the nuclear power station increase the silence: 'the slight hum and the occasional whistle deepens the sense that those who ran them have left long ago'[2] writes Derek Jarman. It is here at

245

Dungeness – where 'the nuclear power
station hums (chiming the hours like a
clock) and a steam locomotive passes'[3] –
that Derek Jarman[4] conceived a garden:

> ... the word paradise is derived from
> the ancient Persian – a 'green' place.
> Paradise haunts gardens, and some
> gardens are paradises. Mine is one of
> them.[5]

Derek Jarman's garden stands out in the
shingle landscape by its vivid colours:
Christopher Lloyd describes how he saw
'some brilliant flower colour ... in a flat
landscape... scattered with huts and
sporadic habitations, with pylons and
overhead cables and power lines'.[6] A green
paradise in the barren landscape of a
nuclear power station would naturally seem
to be inhabited by the themes of life and
death. Indeed, Derek Jarman's garden,
established during the last years of his life,
'merged with Derek's struggle with illness,
then contrasted with it, as the flowers
blossomed while Derek faded'.[7] And survival
lies at the very origins of how Derek Jarman
conceived and developed the garden since
it 'started accidentally: a sea-worn driftwood
staff topped with a knuckle of
beachcombed bone was used to stake a
transplanted dog rose, and an elongated
lowtide flint protected a seedling seakale
from careless feet. Over the coming year
more beachcombed treasures were added.'[8]
The plants in Derek Jarman's garden are
thus locally found plants, such as gorse,
broom and blackthorn blossom, adapted to
the (salt saturated) soil and climate: 'Sea
kale (*Crambe maritima*) is the dominant
plant, more abundant here than anywhere
else in the British Isles. It is the first
coloniser above the tideline, with tap roots

2 A green paradise.
(Photograph Jan Birksted)

3 Foxgloves.
(Drawing by Jan Birksted)

that delve in search of moisture. Jarman quoted twenty foot as a root length, measured on a plant that had become exposed after a storm.[9] But Derek Jarman also transplanted to his garden local plants that were growing in other parts of Dungeness. He thus tells the story of how 'once, when I was transplanting a small seedling to the garden, I was assaulted by an ecological puritan from Canterbury.'[10] One must remember that Dungeness is an 'SSSI', a 'Site of Special Scientific Interest', therefore with strict restrictions on what can be grown. In addition to these native plants already around the cottage or transplanted from the roadside or from the shingle beach, Jarman included plants that, though not native, have been introduced long ago and now grew wild, such as Rest-harrow (*Ononis repens*), Valerian (*Centrathus ruber*), foxglove, horned poppy (*Claucium flavum*) and dog rose (*Rosa canina*).[11] There are also vanished native plants that have been brought back such as 'fennel and the stinking hawksbeard that has been reintroduced by the ecology department of Sussex University'.[12] In addition, Jarman purchased plants in nurseries on the drive to Dungeness from London. Jarman also introduced a raised herb and vegetable garden with 'thyme and oregano, hyssop, lavender, rue, fennel and rosemary, caraway, artemisia, pinks, a few sweet peas, night-scented stock, rows of lamb's tongue, purslane, peas, radish, onion, lettuce, spinach and purple rocket'.[13] Graded topsoil was brought in for these vegetables and herbs, as well as manure, dug down under the shingle, for the other plants. A bee-hive was introduced between the raised beds of vegetables and herbs. Jarman used selective pest-killers: 'Oh, those pesky browntail moths are munching again. I'm

247

Jan Birksted
The prospect at Dungeness:
Derek Jarman's garden

going to go to war. I expect they're highly protected but I'm going to shut my eyes to the slaughter. They're killing the prostrate blackthorn which is rarer than they are in these parts.'[14] In this respect, Derek Jarman writes that 'my garden is ecologically sound, though work of any kind disrupts the existing terrain.'[15] Derek Jarman's statement about Dungeness agrees with Peter Youngman's analysis that 'prized species-rich vegetation is a man-made phenomenon and needs management to maintain it; that ecological disturbance does not necessarily involve ecological destruction.'[16] Yet nuclear power stations also attract new forms of life. The nuclear power station at Sizewell, for example,'is providing nesting places and food supplies for a large variety of birds: kestrels and black redstarts, as well as the more common and to be expected species, nesting in the buildings; cormorants on the offshore cooling water structures; twenty different species feeding at and around the sewage works; and many others feeding and nesting in the natural vegetation that has grown up during the past ten years on the extensive areas excavated and filled'.[17] Similarly, Derek Jarman's garden treads a cautious path between management, disturbance, destruction and conservation: by (artificially) controlling certain features to prevent the inevitable (natural) destruction of others. Derek Jarman's garden is ecological precisely because it creates a 'prized species-rich vegetation'.[18] But, simultaneously, it goes against purist ecological principles by using chemicals as well as introducing non-native species and even non-native soils. This garden plays on the ambiguities, complexities and inherent contradictions of the ecological position. Jarman, for example, bought one plant in a nursery – thrift – that already grows wild on the other side of Dungeness, and this plant is now growing so well that it is seeding itself this side of Dungeness.

We find identical complexities, ambiguities and contradictions when it comes to the architecture of the cottage which the garden surrounds. Prospect Cottage is a fisherman's clapboard cottage, painted with black pitch, similar to all the other cottages that line the road along Dungeness. It is not only a vernacular building, but a vernacular building of the most ordinary kind. The roof is corrugated metal. This is not spectacular, memorable or heroic vernacular architecture, but vernacular architecture defined as the cheapest form of DIY. It has all the qualities of a found object. And yet, already in its cheap found DIY form, it had one unusual feature: bright yellow door-frames and window-frames. This feature has been retained: 'The windows are painted the cheery yellow that they were when we found it.'[19] Following tradition, the house regularly gets re-tarred to withstand the weather. In some ways, the original condition of the house has been restored since 'stripping carpets and plasterboard revealed the wooden rooms'.[20] But in many other ways, the house has been altered by the building of an extension behind and by the replacement of the front-door and of the windows by 'old-fashioned windows'[21] with small window-panes, so called 'Georgian' windows, available in DIY supermarkets. So, like its surrounding garden, Prospect Cottage is a blend of native features, of found non-native features and of designer features. Like the ambiguities, complexities and contradictions of the ecological garden which blends natural with artificial, Prospect Cottage too blends original vernacular, naturalised vernacular and architectural design. The very symbol of this is the yellow door-frames and window-

248

frames. At Sizewell nuclear station, a similar proposal was made to use yellow paint: '…
the main colour to be used [at Sizewell] is blue… There also remains a curious proposal
to paint the permanent beach gantry a vivid yellow, an unfortunate little sneer at Suffolk's
gentle hues.'[22] So the yellow colour of Prospect Cottage is both natural (since it was
found there) and unnatural (since it goes against the landscape hues of southern
England), both a feature of a found vernacular building and of a 'designer' object. Even
the very 'finding' of Prospect Cottage is built on ambiguity, complexity and contradiction.
Prospect Cottage was found by Derek Jarman who already knew that it was there to be
found:

> I had noticed the little fisherman's cottage, with its black varnish and yellow
> windows, before, when I was in Dungeness making two images in The Last of
> England. I had been struck by the area's otherworldly atmosphere – unlike any
> other place I had ever seen – and the extraordinary light.[23]

Not only are the 'designer' aspects of Prospect Cottage and its surrounding garden built
on paradoxical contrasts, but confronting the multitude of found objects – 'rusty metal,
corkscrew clumps, anchors from the beach, twisted metal, an old table-top with a hole

4 Prospect Cottage.
(Photograph Jan Birksted)

Jan Birksted
The prospect at Dungeness:
Derek Jarman's garden

for an umbrella, an old window, chains which form circles round the plants'[24] – are scholarly references such as John Donne's poem 'The Sunne Rising', which is inscribed on the south side of the cottage:

> Busie old foole, unruly Sunne,
> Why dost thou thus,
> Through windowes, and through curtaines call on us?
> Must to thy motions lovers' seasons run?
> Sawcy pedantique wretch, goe chide
> Late schoole boyes and sowre prentices,
> Goe tell Court-huntsmen, that the King will ride,
> Call countrey ants to harvest offices;
> Love, all alike, no season knowes, nor clyme,
> Nor houres, dayes, moneths, which are the rags of time…
> Thou sunne art halfe as happy as wee,
> In that the world's contracted thus.
> Thine age askes ease, and since thy duties bee
> To warme the world, that's done in warming us.
> Shine here to us, and thou art every where;
> This bed thy centre is, these walls they spheare.

5 John Donne's poem on the side
of the house.
(Photograph Jan Birksted)

John Donne's poem makes 'the connections between gardening and the early Elizabethan period'.[25] What so interested Derek Jarman was the writings of the Renaissance herbalists Culpepper and Gerard, who made explicit links between the physical and the spiritual through herbalism: Derek Jarman saw his garden as 'a therapy and a pharmacopoeia'.[26] These Elizabethan references are also associated with the seashore, and feature in Derek Jarman's film *The Last of England*:

> Elizabeth: All my heart rejoiceth at the roar of the surf on the shingles marvellous sweet music it is to my ears – what joy there is in the embrace of water and earth.
> Dee: Yea – a great elixir is the seashore. Here one can dream of lands far distant, and the earth's treasure.
> Elizabeth: The sea remindeth me of youth...[27]

In addition to these complex references to the Elizabethan age – intertwining with the themes of life and death – we find direct references to other gardening traditions: Japanese Zen gardens in the raked shingle, Italianate gardens in the luxuriant use of statuary, French formal gardens in the symmetry and geometry of the front garden.[28] Derek Jarman also explicitly mentions the work of Gertrude Jekyll whose 'observations about the use of colour in gardens are nowhere more apposite than here.'[29]

In the complex criss-crossing and overlapping of 'high culture' – historical

6 Statuary in the garden.
(Photograph Jan Birksted)

Jan Birksted
The prospect at Dungeness:
Derek Jarman's garden

gardening traditions – and 'low culture' – found objects – significant is the method of joining them in simple juxtapositions through *assemblage*. This is a garden of assemblage. And it is in this respect that Derek Jarman's garden is often categorised as 'an artist's garden', that is, a garden whose purpose is to display individual art-elements – sculptures, flowers – rather than to offer an organised overall spatial experience. And this would seem quite accurate when one considers the garden at Prospect Cottage as an assemblage of native plants – such as sea kale – and of imported plants – such as paeonies – and of decorative items – driftwood and beachcombings. This profusion of plants and objects is reminiscent of the nineteenth century romantic ideal of the British Cottage garden 'rich with a medley of herbs, vegetables, fruit and flowers (usually "old-fashioned")'[30] with 'bees humming'.[31] As such, it is a 'delicious rural study'[32] and 'a repository of rustic values and rural simplicity'.[33]

But Derek Jarman's cottage garden, in total contrast to the traditional cottage garden which is seen as standing in opposition to industrial urban society, highlights the industrial context – Dungeness nuclear power station – which looms so menacingly in the distant landscape. Thus the landscape beyond the garden plays a crucial role. Not only does the nuclear power station appear as a literal sign of power but it resonates with metaphoric meanings since 'at night it looks like a great liner or a small Manhattan ablaze with a thousand lights of different colours.'[34]

And this relationship of the landscape to the garden is of course mediated through the boundary of the garden. But what is important here is precisely that there is no

7 The Japanese Zen garden.
(Drawing by Jan Birksted)

boundary: 'it has no fence or boundaries, so who can guess where it ends?'[135] This is of course the exact definition of the English landscape garden which is 'directed outwards towards the countryside [...] to allow the owner and visitors to look outwards – to the countryside and encircling "nature", without the visual impediment of a wall, hedge or railings'.[36]

We can now see how the very concept of Derek Jarman's garden, and the very quality of its spatial experience, is that of an *assemblage* of cottage garden and landscape garden. Jarman's garden is a conflation of the two traditional typologies of cottage garden and landscape garden. But how is this conflation of cottage garden and landscape garden produced?

Central to the English landscape garden is the relationship between garden and landscape whereby the landscape becomes the garden and vice versa – an equivalent and equivocal relationship. The ha-ha[37] is the boundary device, or 'frame', which performs this transformation of garden into landscape and landscape into garden. If we consider the argument that frames 'are shown to be not simply, as Kant intended to show, extrinsic, external, detachable from the work of art [...] but rather play a central, albeit clandestine and disguised role',[38] we can begin to distinguish the logistics of the ha-ha. The ha-ha does not only and simply provide the necessary spacing for the creation of the aesthetic object – he garden – within the world – the landscape. What is specific to the English landscape garden is precisely that the ha-ha transforms the garden into landscape and the landscape into garden: the frame thus reinvents the interior as exterior and the exterior as interior. The framing devices around the English Landscape garden are not boundaries providing a point of equilibrium to counter-balance the elements – garden and landscape – in order to preserve the garden as paradise within the landscape, but they are catalysts that metamorphose each element in the equation. Such metamorphosis takes place, for example, at the landscape garden at Rousham, where William Kent used both the ha-ha and an existing river to effect:

> ... you see from here five pretty Country Villages, and the Grant Triumphant Arch in Aston Field, together with the naturial turnings of the Hills, to let that charming River downe to butify our Gardens, and what stops our Long view is a very pretty Corn Mill, built in the Gothick manner but nothing sure can please the Eye like our Short View, their is a fine Meadow, cut off from the garden only by the River Charvell whereon is all sorts of Callle feeding, which looks the same as if they was feeding in the Garden.[39]

253

But, despite the subtle play between garden and landscape, between inside and outside, the spectator is not, at Rousham, invited to step out physically into the landscape and look back towards the garden.[40] The house retains at all times its focal role as viewing-point.[41] However, there is no physical boundary around the garden of Prospect Cottage, either visible or invisible. The boundary here is of a more elusive kind. The boundary is a feeling: the feeling of unease at not knowing where it is, at crossing over unwittingly, at walking around in a private garden, at trespassing on a domestic setting.[42] This unease

Jan Birksted
The prospect at Dungeness:
Derek Jarman's garden

increases proportionately as one approaches the cottage. Unlike a physical boundary constituted by a geographical line across the landscape, this subjective and elusive boundary is a function of distance.[43] And the visual corollary of distance is scale. It is scale which is so manifest and conspicuous at Dungeness which offers extreme situations from which to observe such conflicts of scale as 'from the top [of the old lighthouse where] you can see that the Ness is made of waves of shingle fanning out to the sea'.[44] Indeed, from the top of the lighthouse, Prospect Cottage is even difficult to spot in the immensity of the landscape where land and sea and sky extend to infinity. From Prospect Cottage, the towering lighthouse and the colossal nuclear power station appear diminutive in the limitless landscape. But then from the shingle beach, all proportions are unexpectedly reversed: Prospect Cottage is miniaturised under the sky while Dungeness power station appears immense on the distant horizon. The instability of these continuous shifts and reversals in scale, originating in the fluidity of viewpoints, stems from the very absence of boundaries. In that ceaseless instability of inversions and reversals of scale lies the source of the criss-crossing and overlapping between the two typologies, Cottage garden and Landscape garden.

And then, just as the traditional ha-ha reinvented the exterior as its opposite and the interior as its opposite, here the lack of boundary around the Cottage garden – since the industrial world, which the rural idyll of the cottage is meant to banish, is in full

8 View of Dungeness from the lighthouse.
(Photograph Jan Birksted)

view – highlights its opposite. And the landscape garden, built on the notion of a prospect out over the world which it dominates, is transformed into its opposite: a landscape of domination.

One place only exists where the incessant spatial instability comes to a standstill: from inside Prospect Cottage, the spaces of the landscape, framed by the yellow windows like paintings in their golden frames, remain firm, except for their appearance, which changes with the time of day, with the seasons, with the weather, with the natural conditions: 'the golden flowers [of gorse that] put the winter gloom to fright',[45] 'the velvet carpet [of the mosses] after rain'.[46] This spatial stability brings forth temporal instability. Time is the other critical theme in Derek Jarman's garden. The many elements of the landscape – 'the bees of infinity'[47] – become symbols of time. And the found objects in the garden – the Second World War anti-tank fencing used as plant climbing frames, the driftwood and beachcombings – become fragments of history. Everything here is imbued with history: the plants with historical folklore – 'elders keep witches at bay, and any old cottage garden that has not been modernised will have one growing alongside the house'[48] – or with personal history – 'I have always loved this plant. It clung to the old stone walls of the manor at Curry Mallet which my father rented in the early fifties.'[49] Memories and history cling to the plants and to the statuary. The house itself has memory built into it as in the 'attic which used to hold the nets and cork floats'.[50]

9 Changing scales at Dungeness.
(Photograph Jan Birksted)

Jan Birksted
The prospect at Dungeness:
Derek Jarman's garden

Prospect Cottage is part and parcel of the unfolding of time. Hence the importance of light:

> Twilight here is like no other. It lingers in a perfect calm. You feel as you stand here that tired time is having a snooze.[51]

And at night both cottage garden and landscape garden, hidden in darkness, merge into one space of darkness, the space of the universe:

> O Paradise, my garden dressed in light, you dissolve into the night.[52]

At night the different spaces, like during the day the framed spaces seen from within the yellow windows of Prospect Cottage, become fixed in darkness, invisible. Space melts into time. Space becomes time.

So in the garden of Prospect Cottage, process is everywhere: inversions, reversals and transformations between different landscape traditions, between different scales of space and time, and between time and space themselves. Everything here is process and instability. The references to the English cottage garden and landscape garden work through reversals and inversions. The eighteenth century landscape garden provides a panorama out over the surrounding countryside which implies control over that countryside; here the view is outwards towards a dominating, if not domineering, countryside. The Victorian version of the cottage garden implies self-sufficiency and innocence; it seems to do so here too, but paradoxically overlaid with the sense of loss of self-sufficiency and lack of innocence. The cottage garden itself does not remain the same: some species perish in the salty shingle conditions, others thrive, sometimes a flower will 'jump the boundary and seed itself all around like the fennel'.[53] What is central to the garden at Prospect Cottage is change and process. One returns to the garden at Prospect Cottage not to see it again, but to see how it has changed.[54] This garden takes instability to its limits. Change and activity – the light, the life of animals[55] and plants, gardening as an activity – lie at the cross-roads of space and time. Indeed the very word 'prospect' lies at the intersection of time and space. Paradise may haunt gardens, but time haunts paradise.

256

10 The lizards.
(Drawing by Jan Birksted)

11 Boats on the shingle.
(Photograph Jan Birksted)

Jan Birksted
The prospect at Dungeness:
Derek Jarman's garden

1 Derek Jarman, *Derek Jarman's Garden* (London: Thames & Hudson, 1995), p. 89.

2 Derek Jarman, *Kicking the Pricks* (London: Vintage, 1987), p. 240.

3 Derek Jarman, *The Exhibition of Derek Jarman, Luminous Darkness* (Tokyo: Uplink, 1990).

4 For an account of the life and work of Derek Jarman (1942–1994), artist, film-maker, writer and designer, see Michael O'Pray, *Derek Jarman, Dreams of England* (London: BFI Publishing, 1996) and Roger Wollen, *Derek Jarman: A Portrait* (London: Thames & Hudson, 1996).

5 Derek Jarman, *op. cit.*, 1995, p. 40.

6 Christopher Lloyd, 'The Jarman garden experience', in Roger Wollen, *op. cit.*, pp. 147–8.

7 Keith Collins, 'Preface', in Derek Jarman, *op. cit.*, 1995, p. 5. Derek Jarman died of an AIDS-related illness.

8 Keith Collins, *op. cit.*

9 Christopher Lloyd, 'The Jarman garden experience', in Roger Wollen, *op. cit.*, pp. 147–8.

10 Derek Jarman, *op. cit.*, 1995, p. 30.

11 Christopher Lloyd calls them 'feral': 'The wild, or introduced and feral, plants on the Ness are a significant feature.' (Lloyd, *op. cit.*, p.150.)

12 Derek Jarman, *op. cit.*, 1995, p. 28.

13 *Ibid.*, p. 57.

14 *Ibid.*, p. 45.

15 *Ibid.*, p. 30.

16 Peter Youngman, 'Sizewell Nuclear Power Stations, 1. The proposals', *Landscape Design, Journal of the Landscape Institute*, Number 154, April 1985, pp. 28–32, p. 32.

17 *Idem.*

18 *Idem.*

19 Derek Jarman, *op. cit.*, 1995, p. 69.

20 *Ibid.*, p. 65.

21 *Idem.*

22 Hal Moggridge, 'Sizewell Nuclear Power Stations, 3. Advice to The Suffolk Preservation Society', *Landscape Design, Journal of the Landscape Institute*, Number 154, April 1985, p. 35.

23 Derek Jarman, *op. cit.*, 1995, p. 64.

24 *Ibid.*, p. 109

25 Michael O'Pray, *op. cit.*, p. 38.

26 Derek Jarman, *op. cit.*, 1995, p. 12.

27 Derek Jarman, *Dancing Ledge* (London: Quartet Books, 1984), pp. 252-3.

28 Derek Jarman had once drawn a project for a garden for his sister: 'The result would have been in the 16th to 17th-century Franco-Italian tradition' with architectural features such as obelisks, a temple and statuary and including also 'an oriental tradition' (Roger Woollen, *op cit.*, 1996, pp.18–9).

29 Derek Jarman, *op. cit.*, 1995, p. 20.

30 Christopher Thacker, *The Genius of Gardening, The History of Gardens in Britain and Ireland* (London: Weidenfeld & Nicolson, 1994), p. 274.

31 Ouida, 'Gardens', in *Views and Opinions*, 1895, p. 48; quoted in Christopher Thacker, *op. cit.*, p. 275.

32 *Idem.*

33 Gillian Darly, 'The English cottage garden', in M. Mosser and G. Teyssot (eds.), *The History of Garden Design, The Western Tradition from the Renaissance to the Present Day* (London: Thames & Hudson, 1991), pp. 424–426; p. 424. Gillian Darly also writes that cottage gardens are often supported by those who are 'radically inclined' and that the 'English cottage garden has achieved a resonance few other approaches to gardening can claim.'

34 Derek Jarman, *op. cit.*, 1995, p. 67.

35 *Ibid.*, p. 63.

36 Christopher Thacker, *op. cit.*, pp.166–7.

37 '... an "invisible wall", in the form of a ditch, dug out carefully along the outer boundary of the garden, deep enough to prevent cattle from entering the garden and to allow the owner and visitors to look outwards – to the countryside and encircling "nature", without the visual impediment of a wall, hedge or railings' (Christopher Thacker, *op. cit.*, p. 167).

38 Irene E. Harvey, 'Derrida, Kant, and the performance of parergonality', in Hugh J. Silverman (ed.), *Derrida and Deconstruction* (London: Routledge, 1989), pp. 59–76, p. 63.

39 This contemporary description of Rousham by the head gardener can be found in John Dixon Hunt, *William Kent, Landscape garden designer, An Assessment and Catalogue of his Designs* (London: A. Zwemmer Limited, 1987), p. 83. This account is also reproduced *in toto* in Simon Pugh, *Garden – Nature – Language* (Manchester: Manchester University Press, 1988).

40 This is not to ignore (1) how one can look back towards the Praeneste Terrace across the river and across the external landscape from the far end of the garden, near the bridge, and (2) the way in which the Theatre plays a labyrinthine game with its human visitors who become – alternatively – statuesque spectators looking outwards towards the external landscape-as-stage, or human actors watched by the spectatorial statuary, or actor/spectators held in the (imaginary) gaze of the external landscape.

41 This is the very purpose of the landscape garden, in terms of their social and political context. See John Barrell, *The Dark Side of the Landscape, The Rural Poor in English Painting, 1730–1840* (Cambridge: Cambridge University Press, 1980) and Nigel Everett, *The Tory View of Landscape* (London and New Haven: Yale University Press, 1994).

42 Keith Collins, who now lives at Prospect Cottage, writes: 'Dungeness is a magical location. When you visit, tread softly, for many choose to live here for the solitude and silence that once attracted Derek, and now holds me' (Keith Collins, *op. cit.*, p. 5).

43 It is poignant to note that one neighbouring house presently has a notice indicating that planning permission is being sought to erect a fence around it (September 1997).

44 Derek Jarman, *op. cit.*, 1995, p. 126.

45 *Ibid.*, p. 23.

46 *Ibid.*, p. 33.

47 *Ibid.*, p. 55.

48 *Ibid.*, p. 27.

49 *Ibid.*, p. 53.

50 *Ibid.*, p. 69.

259

Jan Birksted
The prospect at Dungeness:
Derek Jarman's garden

51 *Ibid.*, p. 44.

52 *Ibid.*, p. 44.

53 *Ibid.*, p. 50.

54 Process can be captured in several forms such as the written diary, documentary photography and film. And Derek Jarman's garden is featured in two books – *Derek Jarman's Garden* (London: Thames & Hudson, 1995) and *Modern Nature* (London: Vintage, 1992) – and forms the setting of two films – *The Garden* and *The Last of England*. Derek Jarman's garden – as process – is thus inhabited by the written word, by photography and by film – it is inseparable from these art forms. In this way, Derek Jarman's garden is not really a garden at all, but a trope. Jarman himself writes about the importance of the garden to him as metaphor. Michael O'Pray has pointed out to me the multitude of other appearances of gardens in Jarman's work, such as the plastic garden in *Jubilee*, such as *Garden at Luxor*, such as the fact that 'he kept lots of plants in his flat (and outside) on Charing Cross Road'; and Michael O'Pray even suggests that perhaps 'the primary colour costumes and *mise-en-scene* of *Wittgenstein* against the black background is like his garden against the darkness of death, Dungeness, night, etc.' (personal communication).

55 '...the lizards that run hither and thither in the santolina and bask in the sun are out' (Derek Jerman, *op. cit.*, 1995, p. 44)

Peter Salter

Building in Nature

Much of contemporary architecture appears brittle in its ideas of 'accommodation' and use of materials. It is determined by value judgements, removed from the physical qualities of landscape and the material's inherent qualities and workmanship. We need to search for a wider basis for thinking about making architecture. As a teacher, I am interested in landscape, because the issues it raises for architecture are clear and demanding. It provides a grounding, a centre of gravity – an opportunity for a more accurate and generous architecture.

In working with Landform Geography we are working with what is physical and particular, where there is a clarity to the issues of site, territory-making, and inhabitation responsive to that site. This sets up an architecture that is sensitive to ageing and weathering, and to aspects of time in relation to the cycles of erosion and deposition. These processes become strategic tools for determining the spatial arrangement of enclosure and the displacement of light. Through looking at detail, we become sensitive, not only to the channelling of water and run-off but to the material working of the building, its wear corresponding in some way to the habitual use and pleasure of that building.

In the late 1980s I took my students to Inisheer, an island off the west coast of Ireland. We went to build a curragh, the traditional tarred fishing boat of that region, and the only means of transport for these island people before the arrival of the aeroplane and cargo ship. Our interest did not imply any sense of nostalgia for the vernacular or for the past, but rather a recognition of the boat as a tool and a catalyst of ideas from which to explore a range of architectural issues and structures. Before the building of the airstrip and the quayside, the curragh transported goods and technologies to the islands. If such imports could not be brought on this rowing-boat, the island people had to 'invent' different ways of living and particular technologies based on the island's geography. So the curragh became a measure of the place.

Four families inhabited this limestone sea-washed platform without soil or trees. They cleared the rock-strewn pavements to make dry-stone-walled enclosures. With layers of sand lain over seaweed from the seashore, they made fields for cattle and vegetable cultivation, finding an essential logic of accommodation and an aesthetic response to an economy of means. Springlines identified striations of different porosity in the rock, which became the terraces for inhabitation. The disposition of settlement in the wind shadow of such terracing was 'registered' in the three-room traditional dwelling, its two opposing doors reflecting the predominant onshore and offshore winds, its thatched roof held down with weighted nets against south-westerly gales.

In such circumstances, the curragh, the settlement and the field systems, were measures of the community, and tested the strength of every household and the fitness of its men. Today ambitions have changed. The Inisheer community now measures itself against the wider community of Eire and Europe. The eightseater aeroplane arriving twice daily and the weekly cargo ship bring new influences, new building materials and methods of construction. Together, such components and standard house plans challenge the island community to find a new vocabulary for living in such a place.

The boat as a carrier of ideas and a measure of values becomes a metaphor for a preoccupation with the tracing of territory, through its navigation markers and its material detail. It serves as a deck, on which commonly held ideas may become critical, providing a new centre of gravity which identifies aspects of the physical world. In circumstances where the observation of phenomena drives architectural ideas, the metaphor might be thought to sit uneasily; but when borrowed from the material world, the metaphor will return there, yielding only that which is physical and particular, a renewed sense of materiality. In the end, our prime concern as architects is the making, the creating and the adjustment of structure. We are working with what is technically understood in relation to perceptual notions, setting up a poetic for others to interpret.

In 1991 my students designed and constructed a building for a field in the Norfolk landscape. The building was critically sited on the boundary between a small parcel of land (designated as 'set-aside') and the larger agricultural landscape beyond. Access to the building was from a small overgrown and intimate country garden, the walk to the building gradually revealing the wide horizons and light quality so specific to North Norfolk. The building encapsulated and echoed this movement between the small-scale enclosure and large-scale territory. Supported on six legs, the cill of the building emphasised the view of the horizon. Its double-height interior space was hung with tools

1 The skeletal structure of the curragh on Inisheer, Aran Isles. (Photograph Peter Salter)

for working the field. The cabin trapped within this space was scaled as a piece of furniture, with an elevated window offering views over an ever larger territory, setting up a range of scales within a sequence of movement and space.

Building in such circumstances requires new rules and judgements of appropriateness to be made. The vernacular tradition has been evolved by craftsmen and is not to be copied by architects. We look at vernacular detail to 'train the eye', to look for similar tolerances and new thresholds, places of overlap, in order to gain new understandings and renewed groundings. The details of our Norfolk building were finely controlled, to emphasise or suppress its construction as an aesthetic of an economy of means.

I am interested in an architecture that has little need of reading to be understood, that relies instead on the accuracy of a developing sensibility and registration of context, to set up resonances within the building. Through its detail and material reflections one may determine the quietness of the room, revisiting such a room in every project, learning little by little to 'work' the calmness of the architecture. (I am not talking about traditions and techniques, but about the power of materials to hold space.)

Returning to Venice exposes once again the powerful physical presence of space. The agents of such spaces, weathering light and water, combine to scour, deepen and make brilliant the material surfaces through a process of erosion, redistributing material exfoliations and river silts through fluvial action. Such circumstances demand the accurate 'placing' of platform levels between sky and silt-laden waters. Judgements were made, accepting occasional seasonal flooding, in order to maintain levels for the disembarkation of people and goods from vessels on the canal. The tolerances between water surface and platform remain vital to the quality of reflected light for those that promenade along the arcades of the Doges' Palace and the Piazetta. On the piano nobile level of the Doges' Palace the rhythm of windows in the Council Chamber and the extent of the terrazzo floor reflect light deep into the section of the room. The colour and contour of the marble fragments, worked with linseed oil, match almost perfectly the reflections of the lagoon waters beyond. Terrazzo is perhaps the most ideal material for Venice. Its surface forms a polished crust, while the thickness of the compound remains

263

2 Side elevation of the black building, Norfolk, showing the overtness of certain details. (Photograph Peter Salter)

flexible enough to take up the limited movement of the building, due to the dynamics of the fluvial silts on which the building is founded.

The physical processes of sedimentation have been exploited by the Venetians, passed back and forth between usefulness and idea. It is as though strategies of layering become a preoccupation, and part of a vocabulary for building. The making of a platform on the 'hard backed' silts of the lagoon is resonant with the use of sedimentary materials in construction. Istrian stone is a modified sedimentary rock; because of its weight, it is used sparingly. Its pale delicate colour, together with its resistance to water and its ability to be 'worked', designates its use in window reveals and doorcases, where it repels water on two surfaces and reflects light back into the interior of the building. It is also used at water level, against the weathering effects of tidal range and the constant slop of canal waters churned and deflected by passing vessels. In such circumstances, its use as a damp-proof course is less important than the protection of surface. The face of the stone is always laid against the ingress of water and weathering, its bedding planes turned away from potential inundation, and the exfoliation of its surfaces protected from constant wet and dry and the freeze-thaw actions of weathering. The range of sedimentation and layering is found in the most delicate of artefacts, from the constant patching and rebuilding of the patina of the bronze lion to the build-up of the layers of lacquer on the surface of the gondola, to waterproof and protect it against wear.

The fluvial silts of the lagoon were once the debris and 'outpoor' of the River Po. This material was collected in suspension during the course of the river's journey across the North Italian plain. Trapped by sand spits, the silts are re-formed by the 'slop' of each lagoon tide. This continual redeposition of silts builds up precarious layers for inhabitation, territories of ever-increasing fineness, ranging from fields formed on the sand bars to the most delicate courtyards and rooms. Torcello, the earliest settlement of the Venetain archipelago, is built on such a sand bar, the lagoon water protecting it from invasion. Its cathedral lies so close to water level that the layers between the sand bar and its pavement are imperceptible, the fine tesselation of the pavement echoing the wave pattern of silt below. The shift in the pattern of these small tiles testifies to the gradual settlement of the building, like debris slewed across the top of a wave.

264

Osaka Folly

The Folly was designed in response to an invitation from Arata Isozaki to take part in the 1990 Garden and Greenery Exposition at Osaka. A new landscape was laid on the side of an artificial hill, made from the debris of the city. The first proposition set out a deeply creviced oya stone pavement which delineated the extent of territory for building. In an artificial landscape, that belied process and context, the oya stone provided a grounding, a place of weathering and wear. It was to be occupied by three small buildings, each one 'registering' different qualities of corrosion and decay. The first trapped light through plant growth in a Cor-ten steel chamber. The second used bimetallic corrosion, a process which would be increased through the gradual etching away of the sheet steel. The third building was constructed of lead, and offered itself as a measure of the deterioration and changing spatiality of the other two rooms. All three registered the humidity of the

3 Rear elevation of Oska Folly.
(Photograph Peter Salter)

climate through the staining of the oya stone pavement below.

This first proposition was unacceptable to the client. Through a series of revisions a new timber building emerged, in which the three separate constructions of the first proposals were transformed into a light-collecting snorkel. This was placed deep within a cage structure, supported on four columns at ground level. The territory of the building was defined and plotted with five massive earth walls. Within this powerful spatial arrangement the ground was excavated, providing a room at the heart of the building, which registered the light and a quiet sense of interior.

The rammed earth construction used layered inert clays of different colours together with earths from the site. Constructed in formwork, the rammed earth walls had a high water content. As a consequence, the rapid evaporation initially caused massive erosion of the surfaces. However, as the water content decreased, the walls became more stable and sprouted young green shoots of bamboo. This evaporation from the walls set up air currents within the building, transforming it into a cool retreat.

The realisation that building detail may be found within the architectural strategy, and correspondingly that strategy may be based on detail, is a recognition that a building

265

4 Oska Folly: detail of the rammed earth construction, showing the striations of clay. (Photograph Peter Salter)

may carry certain resonances of a wider context. This relationship between strategy and detail necessitates the making of rules for the design of the building and its construction. It allows us to trace connections, to adjust our groundings, to make judgements about appropriateness and accommodation. Using our intuition, we can take our experience of building and begin to make judgements about the overtness of the architectural enclosure. An example of this, I found on a trip to Russia with students in 1993.

After twelve hours driving through deep snow, down fire lanes cut through dense forest east of Arkhangel, we arrived at the remote eighteenth century village of Yedoma. Constructed from logs, the settlement is founded on land cut out of the forest, on the edge of a frozen river. The territory is divided between grazing land, stables, barns and wells, held in common for the village, as against private inhabitations, grain stores, bath-houses, outside toilets and dwellings. The church and bell tower, as public buildings, are located separately on a hillside bluff overlooking the river. This demarcation of land and buildings is also reflected in the domestic arrangement and occupation of the winter dwelling. The privacy of summer rooms is forgotten, as they are shut down against the winter weather. The room adjacent to the wood-burning stove becomes a common room, in which private lives are discretly played out.

Kamiichi Mountain Pavilion

Following the Osaka Folly Project, Toyama Prefecture Commissioned a mountain pavilion for the town of Kamiichi. The site is 2500 metres above sea level, in a national park, on a rocky spur called Bambajina at the edge of a melt water river. The building was to be left uninhabited for seven months of the year, except for roosting birds and small animals. The river-cut gorge, partly embanked, has twelve metres of snow in the winter, blowing up from the lower valleys in October.

The pavilion, formed ike a 'beached' boat high up in the mountain, is hydrodynamically shaped against the snow. The uniformly distributed snow loads are displaced by outer shells, creating an inner landscape. A room to look at the peaks of Mt Tatiyama is sheltered within these timber lattice structures, setting up a borrowed landscape to view the mountain side.

The building is seen in a sequence of views from a looping pathway between the mountain road and the river. This idea of viewing and movement is then repeated within the building itself. The north-facing shell has few windows, in order to restrict the ingress of bad spirits; it faces an exposed face of rock across the river. The south shell has a gutter over the entrance, with a seat providing a welcome resting place for climbers and walkers in the park. This gutter channels water through the entrance of the building like a small offshoot of the main river, guiding the visitor towards the interior rooms with their distant views.

The building is constructed on a concrete base above flood level. It is made in timber, using traditional Japanese carpentry techniques. Originally, the pavilion was to be skinned in Cor-ten steel. However, the water-laden environment of snow and mountain mist would have precluded a substantial protective layer of rust from forming.

5 North elevation of the Kamiichi Mountain Pavilion sitting on a plinth above the flood level at the edge of a melt water river. (Photograph Peter Salter)

6 Detail of the copper shell of the Kamiichi Mountain Pavilion, showing Bambajina beyond. (Photograph Peter Salter)

Consequently, the building was finished with copper tile and sheet. Each October the pavilion is prepared for the winter, and every spring the townspeople come and open it up again, allowing light into its dark interior.

Sandra Morris

Parc St. Pierre, Amiens

The slim gothic spire of Amiens cathedral pierces the blanket of low-lying fog that habitually clothes the early spring landscape of the Somme valley. In the Parc St. Pierre, shrouded in mist, it acts as a marker.

Amiens, the regional capital of Picardy, achieved fame in the sixteenth century for the manufacture of a particular satin cloth made with gold and silver thread; water mills situated on the many branches of the Somme have played an important part in its economy. Nowadays it is more readily associated with the First World War cemeteries scattered throughout the surrounding countryside. In 1990 the mayor and town council had the foresight and ambition for their town to launch an international competition for the design of an urban park which would be comparable to the contemporary parks of other regional towns such as Montpellier and Lyon.

The site and its culture

The existing site consisted of some twenty-two hectares, of which approximately sixteen already belonged to the municipality. Bordered by the River Somme to the south and west, the site included the Etang St. Pierre, a large pond formed in the lowlying marshland, popular with local fishermen. The rest of the area housed a series of tumbledown sheds, a youth hostel, an old-fashioned camping site, a tennis club, a football field, some uninhabited houses, and a collection of family allotments. Cut off from the town, it nevertheless constituted a public space that was important to local inhabitants.

269

Separated from the site by the raised embankment of the Boulevard de Beauvillé, a busy highway running north out of Amiens, lay another pond, the Etang Rivéry, and beyond this a unique river landscape known as the Hortillonnages. The origins of this man-made landscape are known to go back more than five hundred years, perhaps even to Roman times. Flowing slowly through the low-lying countryside, the River Somme, together with its tributary the Arve, has created over time a series of small tributaries and islands. The constant accumulation of silt prevented the water from flowing freely, while the extraction of peat as a source of fuel meant that it was no longer present in sufficient quantities to absorb flood waters. In the thirteenth century the Abbey of St. Acheul bought land in the Neuville area of Amiens and offered it to the peasants as vegetable gardens, or *hortillonnages*, from which the monks received tax revenue. The name is presumed to derive from the Latin *hortus*, a garden, and the men and women who made and maintained these gardens in the marshland were called *hortillons*. Until well into the present century the gardens covered a large area of Amiens on both banks of the Somme, including the communes of Rivéry, Camon, and Longueau. Today there are still 300 hectares of this landscape, although some of the plots have been allowed to revert to wilderness while others have been taken over as weekend homes. Whereas in 1906 there were still 950 *hortillons*, by 1960 their numbers had reduced to 110, and by 1975 there were no more than 15.[1] The gardens, known as *aires*, are reached by boat on canals dug and maintained by the community, known as *rieux*. They are separated from one another by privately owned ditches. The narrow strips adjacent to the river were called *jours*, in recognition of the amount of land that could be tilled in a day. It has always been possible to grow three crops a year on this rich peaty soil, but it dries out quickly and needs to be well watered and manured. Until the last fifty years, vegetables were transported to a special market in the St. Leu district of Amiens in flat-bottomed boats, known as *cornets*, wooden baskets piled high with stacks of carrots, radishes, salads, including vegetable varieties no longer grown that the *hortillons* generated from their own seed. It was a strenuous but rewarding life, as vegetables were scarce and of poor quality in other parts of Picardy. The women operated the market side of the

I Overview of the park from the slope
of the Boulevard Beauvillé.
(Photograph Sandra Morris)

business, and family tradition dictated that the gardens were passed down from one generation to the next, thereby forming a very enclosed community with their own version of the Picard dialect and their own costumes and tools for maintaining the banks and clearing away the water plants. This activity was and still is essential to the preservation of the local ecosystem. The silt dug out of the ditches is used to build up the banks, which in many cases are further protected with planks of wood secured with acacia poles.

In the Middle Ages the Abbey of St. Acheul, as the landowner, was able to insist that all canals were drained and the banks cleaned on a specific date. But by the mid-sixteenth century the *hortillons* came into conflict with the local millowners, who needed to raise the level of the water to ensure the constant operation of the mills, which in turn provided the Chapter of the Cathedral with taxes. Locks were set up across the river, raising the level of the water upstream and threatening to flood the *hortillonnages*. The monks enabled the *hortillons* to form a corporation to defend themselves against the millowners. The Revolution of 1789 gave them their independence, but they found it hard to survive on their own, and in 1859 they formed a Gardeners' Syndicate. Thirty years later Amiens local council took over responsibility for ensuring the drainage of the canals. Since 1975, however, the protection and maintenance of this important site has been managed by the Association pour la Protection et la Sauvegarde du Site et de l'Environnement, which also promotes an awareness of the environment. This means that

2 Vegetable garden in the Hortillonnages, showing detail of bank maintenance on the public 'rieu' and neglect on the side of the private ditch.
(Photograph Sandra Morris)

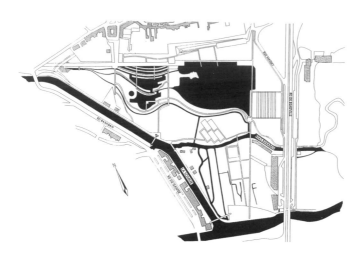

3 Plan of the Parc St. Pierre.
(Drawing by Jacqueline Osty)

although the growing of vegetables in the traditional way is no longer viable – they can now be transported into town from all over Europe in refrigerated containers – the landscape is recognised both for its cultural heritage and for its potential as a wildlife and botanical reservation.

The competition brief and its realisation

So how was this unique site to be incorporated into the programme for a new urban park? This was one of the most important objectives stipulated by the mayor and municipality in their competition brief. The park was seen as a means of revitalising the settlement, by evoking its rich natural culture, and by making connections between the different parts of the city, the town centre, the proposed new university campus at St. Leu, the northern suburbs at Rivéry, and the Hortillonnages. For the inhabitants, young and old, it was to provide a major public space, which would also attract tourists through its links with the cathedral and the Hortillonnages. The presence of water in a variety of forms, and of a rich indigenous vegetation, was seen as a way of reaffirming the town slogan 'Amiens ville verte Amiens ville bleue'.

Forty-eight teams entered the competition, from which seven were invited to submit to the second stage. Jacqueline Osty, a young landscape architect from Paris, trained under Michel Corajoud at the Ecole Nationale Supérieure du Paysage in Versailles, was the winner. Her scheme was chosen by the jury because it both respected the given programme and demonstrated a particular understanding of the site. Her use of water as the conceptual theme of the park was based on a simple but carefully studied hydraulic system. Unlike some of the other competitors, her scheme combined natural planting with a highly structured plan, providing direct access to the suburbs, and allowing for intimate private spaces as well as open areas for organised activities. The project was to be completed in two phases, the first dealing with property

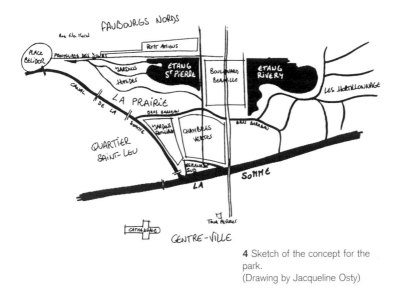

4 Sketch of the concept for the
park.
(Drawing by Jacqueline Osty)

already owned by the town, the second with property which had to be acquired. The estimated cost was 45 million francs.

The massive earthworks that had to be undertaken to create the east–west Promenade des Jours in the north, the main structural element of the park, together with the shaping of monumental steps on the slope to the east below the busy highway, caused some consternation among those who feared the disappearance of familiar landmarks. The banks of the Etang St. Pierre were also redesigned to form a lake, leaving the more natural edge with reeds and rushes to the south, and creating a more architectural feature to the north, where a hard edge meets the promenade, with two wooden jetties provided for local fishermen. Further ponds were excavated, to provide the lower marsh area, and a hydraulic system was put in place. Finally, the main axis was paved with reconstituted marble chippings laid in concrete, and the less important pathways were laid with a fine hoggin or covered with wooden decking. The park was opened to the public in July 1994.

The success of the project as an urban park is demonstrated by its constant use throughout the year, by people crossing from one part of the town to another, by youngsters bicycling, rollerskating, playing basketball, or just moving around in groups, and by families picnicking, or taking the dog for a walk. Nothing has been vandalised, and security at night is ensured by carefully designed lighting on all the main paths.

The design strategy

In February 1992 when construction work was about to begin, Jacqueline Osty described her idea for the park: 'Inscribed in the bed of the river, the Parc St. Pierre is indissolubly bound to the Somme, whose waters retain the memory and identity of place.'[2] Her strategy for the water system is the key to the park as a whole. The elegantly designed plan for the northern half of the park is called the *chevelure* – a

273

branch of the Somme provides the starting point for one of the three channels that form the strands; the other two emanate from the St. Pierre lake. The three flow almost imperceptibly westward, below the formal water lily gardens to the north and the lower marsh ponds below, to meet in a single channel that comes to a point within a symbolic labyrinth borrowed from the floor of the cathedral and used as a motif on the park furniture. Here, at the furthest westerly point of the park, below the main entrance from the Place Bélidor, the water seems to disappear, and is redirected back towards the St. Pierre pond.

Held within the arms of the three channels, the marsh ponds offer more intimate areas, enclosed by thick plantings of willow and alder, reminiscent of the banks of the narrow *rieux* and the wider spaces of the peat bogs with their willow hedges that can still be found among the Hortillonnages. References to this ancient landscape are more obviously readable in the southern half of the park defined by the Bras Baraban, where original ditches have been retained to drain the low-lying land and provide parcels or territories that recall their former usage. In the southwest, close to the Somme, allotment gardens have been reintroduced, accessible from the towpath but separated from the main body of the park by the traditional channels.

5 Water lily gardens on the southern side of the Promenade des Jours. Pergola designed by Maurer & Orgi, Architects. (Photograph Sandra Morris)

Formal structure of the park

In spite of these evocative references to marks already written into the landscape over generations, the formal structure of the park is undeniably contemporary and clearly defined. There are three main areas of the park: the Etang St. Pierre and the water system it generates; the southern section lying between the Bras Baraban and the Somme; and the Etang de Rivéry on the eastern side of the Boulevard de Beauvillé. The plan shows two main axes: the Promenade des Jours running from the western entrance at Place Bélidor to the foot of the slope below the highway, where it meets the north–south axis that takes the visitor over a series of bridges to meet the southern terrace (the most formal part of the design) at the edge of the Somme, which addresses the Cathedral and the town. Those wanting to reach the town from the northern suburbs move west over an elegant footbridge, sixty metres long, the Pont de Samarobrive (Samarobriva – bridge over the Somme – being the Roman name for Amiens).

The Promenade des Jours is, as its name suggests, a place for walking and being seen, in many ways a traditional French *allée*, emphasised by a line of newly planted plane trees. Close to the labyrinth and its access point from the Place Bélidor the walkway is covered by a metal arbour designed by the architects Maurer & Orsi, which,

6 Bridge over the Bras Baraban connecting the northern and southern parts of the park.
(Photograph Sandra Morris)

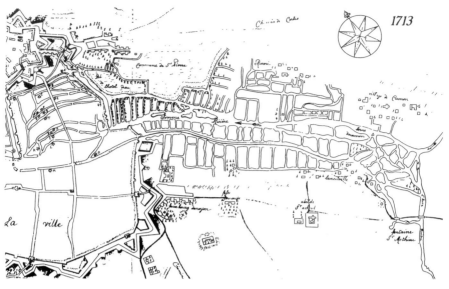

7 Map of the Somme River 1713 showing how it flows through *hortillonages* and divides into narrow canals on entering the town. Abbey of St. Acheul to the south-east.
(From Duthoit, *Le vieil Amiens,* also used in *The Vernacular Garden,* Dumbarton Oaks)

in the absence of any major building, serves as a threshold to other events encountered on the promenade. Here the boundaries between public and private space are barely defined, the gardens of the houses in the northern suburb of St. Rivéry reaching right up to the edge of the walkway. The presence of these houses is always felt. The gardens retreat away from the path to make room for a children's playground set behind a brightly painted blue wall, only to re-emerge in an abstract tracing of low hedges on the northern slope facing the Etang St. Pierre, which retains the memory of the garden plots.

The southern views from the promenade are very different, a landscape of water intersected at intervals by straight pathways in wooden decking offering constant glimpses of the cathedral spire. These pathways invite exploration of the wilder marshland area hidden within thick vegetation.

Arriving at the Etang St. Pierre, the walker is suddenly brought to a halt, confronted by the calm expanse of the lake before moving left onto a narrower section of the path. It is almost as if the plan has been adjusted at this point to allow the presence of the cathedral and its reflected image to be recognised in all its power. This relationship between cathedral and water evokes the early history of the Hortillonnages. A sculpture placed above one of the cathedral doors records the building of the great gothic church on the site of a field of artichokes, presented to the Church by two *hortillons* in 1220.[3] Back in the park, the association is symbolically represented in the engagement of the water in the labyrinth.

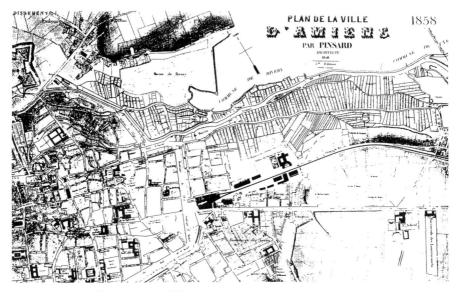

8 Plan of Amiens 1858 showing
the extent of the *hortillonnages*,
including the site of the present
park in the Marais de Rivéry area
top left.

At the end of the Etang St. Pierre the promenade comes to an abrupt end.
Instead of continuing into the distant landscape in the French Classical manner, it meets
the edge of the monumental slope carrying the urban highway. Here the walker is forced
to take a sharp turn to the right, joining the inhabitants of the northern suburbs as they
make their way south across a metal and wooden bridge that crosses the edge of the
Etang St. Pierre. Although never far from the nearby slope, this bridge nevertheless
focuses attention on the calm water and its wildlife, offering yet another view of the
cathedral.

The Boulevard de Beauvillé on its high embankment makes a powerful statement
that could not be ignored in the design of the park. With the reorganisation of the
planting, and the introduction of a grid of *Ginkgo biloba* beside the stepped terrace, the
slope has become a viewing platform for the northern area of the park. It does however
inevitably separate the Etang St. Paul from the Etang Rivéry and the Hortillonnages.
Jacqueline Osty made a conscious decision not to bridge this road. Instead, she decided
to make use of the existing tunnel that allows the Bras Baraban to pass from one area to
the other. By means of a minimal intervention, an elegant metal footbridge with wooden
decking suspended from one side of the tunnel, the visitor moves away from the
north–south route and passes effortlessly through to the world of the Hortillonnages,
close to the point where in summer the flat-bottomed boats leave on a tour of the
waterways. The Etang Rivéry, with its background of social housing, awaits further

277

development. This will always remain the least designed part of the park; it looks at its best in winter when the ice nudges into the nearby *rieux*.

Vegetation and planting

The choice of the *Ginkgo biloba* on the embankment among so much indigenous planting seems particularly pointed. The sole surviving representative of a family of trees that grew some 180 million years ago, it has never been found growing in the wild, even in its more familiar surroundings in China and Japan. With the possibility of growing to 30 metres, with almost vertical branches and leaves that turn gold in autumn, it will eventually be an important feature of the park. The only other exotic tree to have been introduced is the *Taxodium distichum* or Swamp Cypress, a native of the southern USA, which is planted close to the ponds to form a transitional wooded area between the more intimate marshland spaces and the large public space of open meadow to the west. Once again this is a tree of considerable stature, sometimes growing to 45 metres. It is one of very few deciduous conifers, its fern-like foliage turning a distinctive red-bronze in autumn.

The question of colour at different times of the year has been very carefully considered in the choice of vegetation, particularly in the enclosed marshland spaces. A notice posted on the Promenade des Jours indicates the range of moisture-loving plants to be found on the site. These include a wide range of alder, poplar, bird cherry and

9 Pathway over water gardens lined up on cathedral spire.
(Photograph Sandra Morris)

willow.[4] In winter the edges of the ponds and water channels in this western area are lined with startling red and gold stems of willow, whereas in summer the foliage is so dense that the winding paths become enclosed like the channels of the *rieux*, flowing spaces suddenly opening out to reveal an unexpected outdoor room. The lower marsh pond has one of the few built features of the park, a small belvedere structure reached from two directions by a wooden footbridge that passes through irises and bullrushes to offer a protected seat. The idea of 'green rooms', a tradition that recalls the *bosquets* of the French classical garden, is developed in the southern half of the park as a way of enclosing the various caged sports facilities, such as basket ball, roller-skate and hockey pitches.

An outstanding feature of the planting throughout the park is the way it blends with the mature existing trees, largely Lombardy poplar (*Populus nigra*), White poplar (*Populus alba*) and white willow (*Salix alba*), which lend a sense of scale and permanence to the park. They have been allowed to remain, even where they infringe on new plantations, as on the southern terrace with its grid of young plane trees (*Platanus x hispanica*), presenting a formal facade to the town. Generally, planting has been restricted to trees and shrubs, with the exception of the water-lilies (various species of *Nymphae*) in the water gardens south of the Promenade des Jours. In the allotment gardens to the southwest of the park keen amateurs produce a riot of colour among the vegetables, competing with the planted banks of the *hortillons* further upstream.

Issues raised

The Parc St. Pierre is both strategically and culturally a park grown out of the waters of the Somme: water as a regenerative force, water inviting the play of light and reflection, water as movement, flowing from east to west, incorporating the meander and the strictly controlled canal, borrowing its vocabulary from the river with its embankments of wooden planking and sluice gates and rejecting the cascades and fountains of the classical garden, and finally in the winter water frozen but never quite motionless. Like any public park designed within the last ten years, the Parc St. Pierre raises the question as to what an urban park might mean at the end of the twentieth century. Amiens is a small town, and its citizens are never far from the countryside. Riverwalks have always been well used. Nevertheless, they have recognised the value of an amenity that not only enhances their natural environment, but actually ensures its long-term survival.

Deliberately understated, the park is nonetheless carefully structured, controlling the daily movement of people from one part of town to another. Although provision is made for a variety of activities and sports, ensuring the engagement of both young and old, the Parc St. Pierre manages to avoid the limitations of the sports park, and the moral hectoring of the nineteenth century that sees parks as a way of improving social behaviour. Unlike many other contemporary parks, it is almost devoid of notices telling people what they should not do, or what route they should take.

What ensures its rôle as a park for the future is the flexibility of its open spaces. Who knows whether basketball or skateboarding will be the sports of tomorrow? The open meadowland along the towpath provides ample space for a new generation of university students to use as they please. Perhaps there could have been more intimate, enclosed spaces for those who prefer to enjoy the water landscape alone, but as the young trees mature new possibilities will arise.

Most importantly, the park serves as a hinge between the different parts of the town and the Hortillonnages. Looking at the sketch plan, it is clear that Jacqueline Osty envisaged this landscape divided by the Boulevard de Beauvillé as two sides of the same coin – on the eastern side, the vestiges of an historic culture, and on the western side its contemporary counterpart, more accessible and more consciously man-made. The ecological repercussions of this strategy are evident. The ecosystem of the river landscape is respected and preserved, encouraging the presence of rare plants and bird life. This has been achieved without nostalgia, without attempting to resurrect a way of life that can no longer be sustained. By a careful reading of the landscape, Jacqueline Osty has found a vocabulary with which to create a 'sense of place', a park for all seasons.

Bibliography

Michel Conan: 'The Hortillonnages: Reflections on a Vanishing Gardeners' Culture' in *The Vernacular Garden,* eds: John Dixon Hunt & Joachim Wolschke-Bulmahn (Dumbarton Oaks, 1993)

Jacqueline Osty: 'The park on the Somme at Amiens' *Topos*, 10 March 1995

'Les Hortillonnages – une tradition maraîchére' (Axio, in collaboration with L'Association pour la Protection et la Sauvegarde du Site et de l'Environnement des Hortillonnages 1991)

I should also like to thank Jacqueline Osty and the Mairie of Amiens (Cadre de Vie et Environnement) for being so generous with their time and documentation available.

280

Notes

1   Michel Conan, 'The Hortillonages: Reflections on a Vanishing Gardeners' Culture', in *The Vernacular Garden*, eds: John Dixon Hunt & Joachim Wolschke-Bulmahn (Washington DC: Dumbarton Oaks, 1993).

2   'Inscrit dans le lit du fleuve, le Parc St. Pierre est une entité indissociablement liée à la Somme dont l'eau garde la mémoire et l'identité des lieux.' Jacqueline Osty, 'The park on the Somme at Amiens' *Topos*, 10 March 1995, p.102.

3   See: publication provided by the Association pour la Protection et la Sauvegarde du Site de l'Environnment des Hortillonnages (1997).

4   *Alnus viridis, A. cordata, A. glutinosa, A. incana*; *Populus tremula, P. alba "nivea", P. canescens, P. simonii, P. balsamifera, P. trichocarpa*; *Prunus padus*; *Salix alba, S. alba 'tristis', S. caprea.*

Contributors

Stephen Bann
is Professor of Modern Cultural Studies at the University of Kent at Canterbury. His publications cover a wide range of areas, ranging from the history of museums and collections to critical appraisals of contemporary art. His latest book is *Paul Delaroche: History Painted* (1997). He has published articles and translations relating to Bernard Lassus's work since the late 1960s.

Augustin Berque
teaches cultural geography at the Ecole des Hautes Etudes en Sciences Sociales in Paris, and is director of the Centre de recherches sur le Japon contemporain. He is the author of many books on Japan, including *Le Sauvage et l'artifice* (1986), and on landscape issues such as *Les raisons du paysage* (1995) and *Médiance de milieux en paysages* (1990). Two books by Augustin Berque recently translated into English are *Japan: Cities and Social Bonds* (Yelvertoft: Pilkington Press, 1997) and *Japan: Nature, Artifice and Japanese Culture* (Yelvertoft: Pilkington Press, 1997).

Jan Birksted
born in Scandinavia and brought up in France, teaches at the UEL School of Architecture, London. He is trained in philosophy (BA), in linguistic social anthropology (MA) as well as in architecture (BA, Dip. Arch., RIBA/BG Student Prize). He is chair of the International Specialist Committee on Landscapes and Gardens of DoCoMoMo (Documentation and Conservation of the Modern Movement). He is currently researching La Fondation Maeght by Sert, and the landscapes of Louis I. Kahn.

Peter Blundell Jones (AA Dipl., MA Cantab)
was trained as an architect at the Architectural Association in London. He wrote his first book on the German architect Hans Scharoun (1893–1972), and he has remained a leading expert on this area of German architecture, producing a second book on Scharoun (Phaidon, 1995) and another on his colleague and mentor Hugo Häring (1882-1958). He was appointed Professor of Architecture at the University of Sheffield,

where he is in charge of humanities courses. Peter Blundell Jones has designed buildings of domestic scale and has participated in architectural competitions. He received the CICA Award for the 'Best periodical of the last three years' in June 1985, and was made Architectural Journalist of the Year in 1992 for articles on Louis Kahn and on Authenticity in *the Architects Journal*. A general book taking a revisionist view of the Modern Movement is in preparation.

Caroline Constant

is Associate Professor of Architecture at the University of Florida and an architect in Gainesville, Florida. A Fellow of the American Academy in Rome, she is author of *The Palladio Guide* (Princeton, 1985) and a forthcoming monograph on the architecture of Eileen Gray. Her latest book is *The Woodland Cemetery: Towards a Spiritual Landscape* (1994).

Thomas Deckker

is an architect and Unit Master at the UEL School of Architecture. In 1996 he was a guest professor at the Liechtensteinische Ingenieurschule and taught in the Open University Sarajevo Student Competition. He is guest-editing an edition of *ISSUES* on landscape and architecture. He has undertaken planning studies and projects in Brasilia, where the Magalhaes House is currently under construction.

John C. Hopkins

is a landscape architect in private practice based in London. He also teaches at the Bartlett School of Graduate Studies, University College, London. He received the Diploma in Landscape Architecture from Thames Polytechnic, London and the Master in Landscape Architecture from Louisiana State University. He is a Chartered Landscape Architect in Great Britain and a Corporate Member of the American Society of Landscape Architects. He has lived and practised landscape architecture in Great Britain, Malaysia, Australia, Hong Kong and the United States of America.

Jacques Leenhardt

is Director of Studies at the Ecole des Hautes Etudes en Sciences Sociales in Paris. He is Honorary President of the International Association of Art Critics. He is director of the CRESTET Art Centre (Vaucluse, France), where research is carried out into the relationships between art, architecture and the landscape. He is a Fellow Member of the Institute for Advanced Study at Princeton. He has published widely.

Mara Miller

Mellon Post-Doctoral Fellow in East Asian Religion and History of Art at Emory University and a Master Gardener for Colorado, is the author of *The Garden as an Art* (1993). She is currently finishing a book on the impact of prints of Chinese gardens on 18th-century English garden design, and another on sex, power, and gender in Japanese prints.

Sandra Morris

graduated from St. Hilda's College, Oxford, in Modern Languages. She is currently Registrar at the Architectural Association School of Architecture. Since obtaining the AA Graduate Diploma in Garden & Landscape Conservation in 1988, she has published 'Bishop Compton and the North American plant trade' in *Garden History* (1991 ad 1993) and was awarded the Gladys Krieble Delmas Foundation Grant to work on Venetian gardens in 1994/5. Since 1990 she has lectured on historical and contemporary landscape, and run workshops and seminars for architectural students on the contemporary landscape and urban park. She is a co-director with Peter Salter of Architecture-Paysage at La Sarrette, Aveyron, doing research on the cultural history of the village and landscape.

Dimitri Philippides

teaches at the NTU of Athens in the Department of Urban and Regional Planning in the School of Architecture. His professional activities extend from architecture to urban planning. He has written many books on Greek traditional and modern architecture and planning. He was the Series Editor of the six-volume *Elliniki Paradosiaki Architectoniki* [Greek Vernacular Architecture] (1980–88). As guest editor, he has contributed to many issues of *Architecture in Greece*, and he contributes regularly to Anti.

Agni Pikionis

is an architect whose professional activities include the design of houses, tourist complexes, and public open spaces as well as the restoration and re-use of traditional buildings. She teaches at the School of Architecture of the NTU of Athens. She has also actively encouraged the study and publication of the archives of her father, Dimitri Pikionis, with the publication of *Pikionis exhibitions texts* (1987) and his work as architect (1994) and as artist. She has curated retrospectives of the work of Dimitri Pikionis at the National Gallery in Athens (1978), Holland (1981), the Venice Biennale (1992), Finland (1993–94) and Norway (1994).

Peter Salter

graduated from the AA School of Architecture, where he taught a Design Unit. He is Professor of Architecture and Head of the UEL School of Architecture. Awarded the 1991 AJ/Bovis Royal Academy Prize for a Thai Fish Restaurant (unbuilt project), he has built a Folly for the Garden and Greenery Exposition, Osaka (1989), the Kamiichi Mountain Pavilion for the Japan Expo, Toyama (1992/3), and Inami Museum for Woodcarving (1993). He is currently working on a project for Glasgow 1999. He has exhibited in London, Dublin, New York and Tokyo, and has been a frequent contributor to the AA Files. Other publications include *Macdonald and Salter, Building Projects 1982–86*, *Themes VI: Intuition and Process* (1989) and *Three Japanese Projects* (1995).

Peter Shepheard

graduated in Architecture from the University of Liverpool in 1936. After the War, he worked in the Ministry of Town and Country Planning, especially on Patrick Abercrombie's team for the Greater London Plan and on the design of Stevenage, the first New Town. In 1948, he began private practice in architecture, planning and landscape (Shepheard Epstein and Hunter). The firm specialized in housing, schools and universities. They designed the first comprehensive school for the Greater London Council, the University of Lancaster, and the landscape for part of the Festival of Britain South Bank Exhibition. From 1959, Shepheard was a visiting professor at the University of Pennsylvania and from 1971 to 1979 was the Dean of Penn's Graduate School of Fine Arts. He resigned from Shepheard Epstein and Hunter in 1989 but continues to design and teach Landscape Architecture in the UK and USA. He was President of the Institute of Landscape Architects in 1965–7 and of the Royal Institute of British Architects in 1969–71. He was knighted in 1980.

Jan Woudstra

is a landscape architect and historian. He has recently completed a Ph.D. on modernist landscape theory and design. In private practice he has specialized in conservation projects, including work on the Privy Garden at Hampton Court, Chiswick House Grounds and Cornbury Park. He has taught at the Architectural Association and now teaches in the Department of Landscape at the University of Sheffield.

Index

Note: Page numbers in **bold** refer to illustrations.

Ackerman, James 4–5
Acropolis project 177, **194**, 195–201
  in-situ improvisation 201
  Philopappou Hill **198–9**, **200**
  walkway **196**
adventure playgrounds 69–73
after-care, gardens 35
Alphand, Jean-Charles Adolphe 83
Andersson, Sven-Ingvar 3
Army Ministry, Brasilia 92, 94
art
  collective identity 206–7
  David Jarman's garden 252
  genius loci 207
  Maeght Foundation **107**, 113–17, **114**, **116**
  public 215, 221, 222–3
Art as Experience (Dewey) 206
art history 4–5
Arte Povera, Burle Marx 90
artifice
  Burle Marx 87, 92–7
Ashihara, Yoshinobu 148, 157
Asplenium viride **30**
assemblage, David Jarman's garden 252–3
Association pour la Protection et la Sauvegarde du Site et de l'Environnement 271
associations, of plants 31
asymmetry, utilitarian style 61–3

Baensch house, Berlin-Spandau **185**, 186–7
Baljon, Lodewijk 3, 9
Banco Safra rock garden, Sao Paulo **93**
Bann, Stephen 2, 233–43, 281
Barthes, Roland 156, 157
Bauer, Walter 64
Beazley, Elisabeth 59, 61, 63
Bégon, Michel 242
Begonia 242
Bellinzona, Ticino Valley 161
  plan **162**
Bengtsson, Arvid 71, 73
Berger, Otti 181
Berlin, *Planungskollektiv* 188–9
Berque, Augustin 105, 147–57, 281
biodiversity
  maintenance of 208–9, 211, 218
  Sizewell nuclear power station 248
biological time, Japanese gardens 44
Bird, Erik L. 64
Birksted, Jan 105, 107–19, 244–60, 281
Blanc, Alan **72**, 74
Blechnum spicant **33**
Blom, Holger 64, 67, 68
Bode, Paul 191
Bodorff, Ulla 64
Boer, Wim 69
Bonnard, Pierre 108
Booth, Kenneth 67
borough engineers 36
Botanical Gardens
  Berlin-Dahlem 77–8
  Rio de Janeiro 77

285

boundaries 184, 253–5, 266
Bournemouth, cast concrete planters **65**
Brandt, G.N. 66, 67, 74
Braque, Georges 108, 111, 115, 117
Brazil
    Burle Marx 77–101
    cultural awakening 79
Brecht, Bertolt 86
breeding, plants 28, 31
British cottage garden 252
British Institute of Landscape Architects
    19
British Royal Horticultural Society, Wisley
    gardens 32
Broadway, Gloucestershire 32
Bromeliaceae 87, 96
Brookes, John 61
Brown, Capability 17, 19, 31
Buddhism 155
    Japanese gardens 44, 51, 52, 55–6,
    251, **252**
Bundesgartenschau (1955), Kassel 189,
    190
Burckhardt, Lucius 237
Burle Marx, Roberto 41, 77–102
    individual style 83
    pastel garden study **78**
    superimposed garden plans **79**, 80

Calder, Alexander 108, 111
Calthorpe, Peter 208
Camp Pendleton, landscape planning
    209–11, **210**, **211**, **212**, **213**
Campanula latifolia **34**
Canna glauca 96
Casson, Hugh 64
Castelgrande, Bellinzona, Ticino Valley
    160, **162**, 163, **164**
Centranthus ruber 247
Centre de Recherche d'Ambiance 233–4
Chadwick, George 66
Chagall, Marc 108, 111
Chambers, William 21
Charles Bridge, Prague 124
chemicals 247–8
cherry blossom, Japanese gardens 51
child areas, Mattern house, Potsdam **182**,
    183
China 38, 43, 59, 149
chrysanthemum 51
Cisneros residence, Caracas **82**, 89, 94
city planning, Manchester 211, 213–17,
    214, **216**

city-living, high density 213
Clark, Frank 64
Clark, H.F. 66
Claucium flavum 247
Clematis vitalba **16**
climbers, Scandinavian use of 63–4
collaboration
    architects and artists 111–12
    architects and landscape architects 15,
    179–92
    designer and manual workers 177,
    197, 202–3
    in-situ improvisation 201–3
collective fantasy 147–8
collective identity 206–7
colour
    David Jarman's garden 244, 251
    Parc St. Pierre, Amiens 278–9
Colvin, Brenda 67
commercialisation, plant breeding 28
Communism 140–1
communities
    art-ecology relationship 206, 221
    artist as interpreter 207
    sustainability 208
Conan, Michel 240
conflation, cottage and landscape garden
    253–4
Constant, Caroline 105, 120–46, 282
contemporary environments 231–80
context, architecture 263
contrasts, Maeght Foundation 114–15,
    117–18
Corajoud, Michel 272
corrosion, Osaka Folly 264
Costa, Lúcio 83
cottage garden, landscape garden
    conflation 253–4
Crambe maritima 246
crazy paving 184
Crinum asiaticum 94
critical landscape (*paysage critique*) 237
Crowe, Sylvia 67
Culpepper, Nicholas 251
cultural perspectives, gardens 2
culture, Brazilian traditions 87, 89
Cunha, Euclides da 79, 101
curragh, construction of 261–2, **262**
curved sofa walls, Mattern house,
    Potsdam 183–4
cyclical time, gardens 49
Cypripedium calceolus **18**
Czechoslovakia

Prague Castle 121–40
    national identity 121–6, 136

Davey, Grenville 215, 223–6, **224**, **225**
De Gaulle, Charles 108
Debord, Guy 171
Deckker, Thomas 105, 158–73, 282
decoration, Brazilian tiles 87, 89
demarcation, land and buildings 266
Dendrobium nobile 94
Denmark
    adventure playgrounds 69–71, **71**
    directional paving **66**, 69
Denver Botanic Garden, Japanese garden
    43, **45**, 49, **49**
design
    Chinese gardens influence 59
    Parc St. Pierre, Amiens 273–4
    Sert's notes **109**
    three dimensional 32, 35
*Design and Detail of the Space
    Between Buildings* (Beazley) 59
detailing, outdoor space 41, 59–76
Dewey, John 206
Digitalis purpurea **29**
directional paving, Denmark **66**, 69
DIY 248
dog rose 247
Donne, John 250–1
Dungeness
    Derek Jarman's garden 245–57
    view from the lighthouse **254**

Earth in Balance (Gore) 208
earth, structure of 32
Eckbo, Garrett 206
eclecticism, nineteenth-century 20
ecology 31–2, 205–8, 221, 248
    see also green movement
Edmundo Cavanellas' residence, Rio de
    Janeiro **88**, 97
Edo era, Japan 147
education
    landscape architecture 19, 35–6
    public 36
elder trees 255
Eliade, Mircea 49
Elizabethan age 251
England
    Derek Jarman's garden 245–57, **254**
    eighteenth century 48
    landscape 32, 253

Manchester City Centre 211, 213–17,
    214, **216**
Newcastle Drawdock project 221–6,
    222, **224**
post-World War II 15
Speke Garston redevelopment
    218–21, **220**, **221**
town and country planning 23
English Heritage 223
English landscape garden, eighteenth-
    century 19–20, 38, 46, 48
English Partnerships 217, 218
Epilobium augustifolium **26**
European Community 217
European Economic Community 108
existentialist landscape 205
Expressionist Movement 180

Fairbrother, N. 3
Festival of Britain 15, 64
Filothei playground, Greece 197, **201**
Fink, Dan 70
flood defence threshold, Newcastle
    Drawdock project 223, **224**
flood-plain, Ticino Valley 163, 165, 167
*Flore des serres et des jardins de
    l'Europe* (Van Houtte) 81
flowers
    misuse of 32
    see also plants
Foerster, Karl 180–1
folk tradition, Brazilian art 89
folklore 255
forest settlement, Russia 266
form
    Japanese 149
    serial 167, 169, 171
foxgloves **29**, 247
Frampton, Kenneth 1, 6, 7
France
    Jardin des Retours, Rochefort-sur-Mer
        233, 237, **240**, 241–3
    Maeght Foundation 105, 107–18,
        107, **112–14**, **116**
    Nîmes-Caissargues motorway rest area
        232, **236**, **238**, 239–41
    Parc St. Pierre, Amiens 269–80, **270**,
        273, **275**
French formal gardens 235, 251, 279
functionalism 19
funding
    Manchester city centre reconstruction
        217

Speke Garston redevelopment, Liverpool 218
furniture 183–4
future, definitions of 206

Galfetti, Aurelio 159, **160**
garden furniture, Stockholm Parks Department 64
Garden and Greenery Exposition (1990), Osaka 264
gardens
    after-care 35
    Chinese influence 43, 59, 149
    historical allusions 48–9
    intellectual ideas 2
    time 41, 43–56, 92–3, 100
Gardens in the modern landscape (Tunnard) 61
Gasworks Park, Seattle 1
genius loci 24, 207
Geographic Information Systems (GIS) 209
geological time, Japanese garden 44
geometry
    Burle Marx 96–7, 99–100
    Maeght Foundation 118
    marginal sites 159
    Prague Castle 137
Germany
    landscape architecture 67
    Scharoun and Mattern 179–92
Giacometti, Alberto 111, 115
Gibberd, Frederick 67
Ginkgo biloba 277, 278
GIS *see* Geographic Information Systems
Glass, Philip 55
Glaziou, Auguste François Marie 81, 83
Glemme, Erik 64, 69, **70, 72**
gold, Kinkaku-ji Temple 55–6
granite setts, Scandinavia 67
Gray World, Green Heart (Thayer) 207–8
Greece
    Acropolis project **194**, 195–201, **198–200**
    Filothei playground 197, **201**
green movement
    Mattern's anticipation of 192
    see also ecology
Gropius, Walter 19
groups, Japanese society 150, 155
Guévrékian, G. 99

Haag, Richard 1
ha-ha, English landscape garden 253–4
Haemoatoxylum braziletto 77
Hamaguchi, Eshun 154, 157
Hammerbacher, Herta 180–1
Handbook of Urban Design (Tandy) 61
Hapsburg rule, Prague Castle 121, 124, 134, 136
Havel, Václav 141
Haywood, Sheila 67
heather moorland 31
hegemony, Japanese 147–8, 156
Heidegger, Martin 110
herb garden 247
herbalism 251
Hermelin, Sven A. 61, 64
heterogeneity 235
Higashi-honganji Temple, Kyoto 44, **45**
historians 4
historical allusions
    gardens 48–9
    Prague Castle 125–9, 133–6, 139–41
history, Plečnik 122, 124–5
homogeneity, modern landscapes 206
Hopkins, John C. 205–27, 282
horizontality, Burle Marx 86–9, **88**
horned poppy 247
hortillonnages, Parc St. Pierre, Armiens 269–72, **273**, 276–7, **276**, 280
house building, gardens as afterthought 179
Hydrangia hortensis 32

Ibirapeura park, Burle Marx 85
Imada, Takatoshi 150–1, 157
improvisation, Acropolis project 201–3
incongruity, plant use 27–8
industrialisation, England 48
Inisheer community 261–2
in-situ improvisation, Acropolis project 201–3
instability, Prospect Cottage 255–6
Isle of Dogs development, Newcastle Drawdock project 221–6
Italy, Venice 263–4

Jackson, J.B. 205
Jameson, Fredric 2
Japan
    Chinese influence 149
    Osaka Folly 264–6, **265**
    society 150–5

tea ceremony 53–5
Tokyo 147–57
Japanese gardens 38, 43–56
    Chinese influence 43
    The Tale of Genji 49–51, 52–3
    time 41
Japanese Zen gardens 251, **252**
jardin à la française 235, 251, 279
jardin anglais 19–20, 46, 48
Jardin des Retours, Rochefort-sur-Mer
        233, 237, 239, **240**, 241–3
Jarman, Derek, Dungeness garden
        245–57
Jefferson, Thomas 205
Jekyll, Gertrude 20, 23, 28, 251
Jones, Peter Blundell 178–93, 281–2
Journal of Garden History 233
Judd, Donald 167, 171

Kakureta chitsujo [*The Hidden Order*]
        (Ashihara) 148–9
Kalantzopoulos, Pavlos 197
Kalman House, Ticino Valley **160**, 161
Kamiichi Mountain Pavilion 266–8, **267**
Kant, Immanuel 5
Kassel
    Baroque expansion **188**, 189–90
    Karlsaue Park 189
    Mattern **188**, 189
Kassel Theatre 179, **188**, 189, **191**
Katsura Detached Imperial Villa, Kyoto
        52–3
Kawana, Kaichi 43
Kent, William 253
kinetics, Lassus 234
Kinkaku-ji garden, Kyoto 55–6
Klein group 3–4

Laguna West sustainable community,
        California 208
Land Art 90–2
Landform Geography 261
landscape architecture
    definition 24
    traditional techniques 17, 19
landscape art, Burle Marx 78, 80
landscape painting 81
landscape planning, Camp Pendleton,
        California 209–11, **210**, **211**, **212**,
        213
Landschaftspark, Duisburg-Nord,
        Germany 1

Lassus, Bernard, garden landscapes
        233–43
The Last of England (film) 251
Latz, Anneliese and Peter 1, 268
lawns, chequerboard 97, 99
Le Corbusier 1–2, 6, 83, 107, 181
Leenhardt, Jacques 41, 77–102, 282
Les Mots et Les Choses (Foucault) 4
Lessing, Doris 47–8
light 35, 111, 256
lighting, Swedish parks and gardens 64
Lilium canadense **37**
Linnaea borealis **38**
local materials, outdoor space 60
Lombardy poplar 279
London Docklands Development
        Corporation 221
low-cost housing
    refurbishment 235, 237
    Ticino Valley 167, **168**, 169
        plan **170**
Lutyens, Edwin Landseer 20

McHarg, Ian 209
Maeght, Aimé and Marguerite 108,
        110–11
Maeght Foundation 105, 107–18
    Braque rooms **114**, 117
    entrance **112**, 113–14
    Giacometti Terrace **107**, 113, 114–15,
        117
    Miró Labyrinth 115, **116**
    plan **113**
The Makioka Sisters (Tanizaki) 52
Malraux, André 107–8
Manchester city centre, planning 211,
        213–17, **214**, **216**
Masaryk, Thomas Garrigue 121–5, 126,
        130, 136, 138, 140–1
Matisse, Henri 108
Mattern, Hermann 179–92
Mattern house
    Bornim, Potsdam 181–4, **182**
    Kassel 191, **191**
Meinig, D.W. 205
Merleau-Ponty, Maurice 110
Migge, Leberecht 180
Miller, Mara 41, 43–58, 282
minimalism, Land Art 90, 92
Ministry of Education and Health, Rio de
        Janeiro **80**, 83, 85, 87
Minoan allusions, Prague Castle 136

Miró, Joan 108, 110–12, 117
Mishima, Yukio 55
Modern Gardens (Shepheard) 2, 15–38
Modern Movement 1–2, 17, 107, 121–2
Modernism 1–2, 78–9, 83, 181
modernist housing, Sweden **62**
Monte Carasso, Ticino Valley 163, **164**,
    165, 167
    plans **166**
Montigny, Grandjean de 80
moorland 31
morals, indivisibility with art 206–7
Morawski, Stefan 53
Morris, Sandra 269–78, 283
motorways 3
    Nîmes-Caissargues rest area **232**,
    236, **238**, 239–41
mountain site, Kamiichi Pavilion 266–8,
    267
Moutsopoulos, Nikolaos 202
movement 101, 115, 234
Museum of Modern Art garden, Rio de
    Janeiro **84**, 85, 89, **92**, 99

Nakane, Chie 150, 155, 157
Narcissus cyclamineus **33**
national parks 24
native plants 27–8, 246–7
nature
    building in 261–8
    partnership with 38
    Swedish closeness to 63
    technology 208
nature reserves 24
Nazi Germany 184, 186
negative space 3
Netherlands, Danish influence 69
Newcastle Drawdock project, London
    docklands 221–6, **222**, **224**
Niemeyer, Oscar 83, 85, 87, 88, 97
Nîmes-Caissargues motorway rest area
    236, 239–41, **239**
Nininha Magalhaes Lins' summer
    residence, Rio de Janeiro 93–4
nippology 147–8, 151, 155
Norfolk 262–3, **263**
Norr Mälerstrand **72**
nuclear power station
    Dungeness 245–6, 252, 254
    Sizewell 248, 249

oak tree 31
objective time 48, 49

Odette Monteiro's residence, Rio de
    Janeiro **97**, **98**
Olivio Eames garden, Sao Paulo **96**
on-site supervision, Acropolis project 197
open spaces, Parc St. Pierre, Amiens
    277–8
Os sertoes (da Cunha) 79
Osaka Folly 264–6, **265**
Östberg, Ragnar 63
Osty, Jacqueline 272–3, 280
outdoor space, detailing and materials 41,
    59–76

painted tiles, Brazil 87, 89
Panteleakis, Periklis 202
Papageorgiou-Venetas, Alexandros
    201–2
Parc de la Villette, Paris 1
Parc St. Pierre, Amiens 269–80, **270**,
    273, **275**
    formal structure 275–8
    plan **272**
park buildings, Scandinavia 64
Parthenon 1, 107, 108
partnership, with nature 38
Pascal, Blaise 92
patterns
    Burle Marx 97, 99
    of vegetation 31–2
paving 24, 27
    Bellahøj development, Copenhagen **66**
    oya stone 264–5
    Parc St. Pierre, Amiens 273
    Prague Castle 128, 137
    random 184
    Scandinavia 67–9, **67**
    tiled 97, 99
paysage critique, Lassus 237
perception, dynamics of 100–1
perennials 181
perspective 4–5, 35
Perspective as Symbolic Form
    (Panofsky) 4
Philippides, Dimitri 194–204, 283
Philodendron 94
physicists' time, Japanese gardens 46–7
Picasso, Pablo 89, 110
Pikionis, Agni 194–204, 283
Pikionis, Dimitri 194–204
place, creation in landscape 159, 161,
    165
plane trees 277
planning

290

Camp Pendleton 209–11, **210**, **211**, **212**, **213**
  Manchester city centre 211, 213–17, **214**, **216**
  Speke Garston redevelopment, Liverpool 218–21, **220**, **221**
  town and country 15, 23, 111
planters, Scandinavian design 64–6, **65**, **72**, 74
planting, Parc St. Pierre, Amiens 278–9
planting design, Sweden 64–7
plants
  associations of 31, 32
  breeding 28, 31
  Derek Jarman's garden 246–7
  hybrids 28
  incongruity 27–8
  native 27–8
  natural species 28, 31
  new varieties 28, 31
Planungskollektiv, Scharoun 188
Platanus x hispanica 277
playgrounds
  Filothei, Greece 197, **201**
  Scandinavia 69–71, **70**, 73
Plečnik, Jože 121–40
  Slavic heritage 122–3
poetic invention, Lassus 237, 239
Poetics of Space (Bachelard) 87
politics
  ecological aims 208
  Prague Castle 121, 124–5, 135–6, 139–41
Polygonatum multiflorum **21**
pools, Burle Marx 94, 96
Populus alba 277
Populus nigra 277
portable gardens, Stockholm Parks Department 64
Portinari, Candido 87, 89
post-industrial landscapes 3, 15, 93, 187, **187**
postmodernity, Japan 147–9, 151, 156
Prague 187
Prague Castle 105, **121**, **125**, **127**, **131**
  castle courts 126–30, **128**, **129**, **135**
  Columned Hall 125 **126**
  Czechoslovakian national identity 121–2, 123–5, 136
  integration with environs 124–5
  New Bastion Garden 137–8, **137**, **138**, **139**
  Paradise Garden 123, 130–2, **131**, **132**

plan **120**
  Southern Ramparts Garden 123, 132–6, **133**, **135**, **136**
preservation, *genius loci* 24
Prospect Cottage, Dungeness 248–51, 253–6
psychoanalytical theory 4
public art 215, 221, 222–3
public consultation
  Manchester city reconstruction 215
  Newcastle Drawdock project 223
public space, Sweden 64

Ralf Camargo residence, Rio de Janeiro **91**
rammed earth construction, Osaka Folly 265
reconstruction
  Castelgrande, Bellinzona 163
  Manchester city centre 211–17
recycling 208
regeneration, Speke Garston scheme, Liverpool 218–21, **220**, **221**
rehabilitation, low-cost housing 237
relationships
  building and setting 99, 179
  ecology–community–art 206, 221
  garden and landscape 253
  house and garden 179, 181, 183–4, 186–7
  humans and nature 206
Renaissance gardens 38, 46
Rest-harrow 247
Rhododendron ponicum 32
Richards, J.M. 63–4
Rittweger, Otto 181
Robinson, William 20, 66
rock crystal 92
rock gardens 93
Romanticism 81
Room Outside (Brookes) 61
Rosa canina 247
Rothmayer, Otto 123, 133
Royal Society of Arts 223
Russia, forest settlement 266
Ruys, Mien 69

Safra Bank, Sao Paolo **81**, 85, 87
Saiho-ji Temple, Kyoto **53**
St. Dimitrios complex, Greece **194**
Salix alba 277
Salter, Peter 261–8, 283
Santos, Miguel 87

Sartre, Jean-Paul 110
scale
    conflicts of 254–5, **255**
    site/non-site 91–2
    trees 3
Scandinavia
    Modernist tradition 41, 59–76
    see also Denmark; Sweden
Scarpa, Carlo 163, 165
Scharoun, Hans 179–92
    open-mindedness 181
    spiritual standpoint 180
Schinz, Alfred 180
Schminke house, Löbau, Saxony **178**,
        180–1
school, Monte Carasso 165, **168**
schools of architecture 35–6
Scilla nutans **22**
sculptures
    Army Ministry, Brasilia **86**
    Maeght Foundation 115–17, **116**
    Newcastle Drawdock project 223–6,
        224, **225**
    see also statuary
sea kale 246
seashore vegetation 31
sedimentation, Venice 264
self-expression, art 206–7
serial form 167, 169, 171
Serra, Richard 171
Sert, Josep Lluis 107, 110–12
shape, Burle Marx 85
Shepheard, Peter 2, 15, 17–38, 61,
        283–4
shingle landscape 245–6, **257**
simplicity, Jardin des Retours, Rochefort-
        sur-Mer 242
sites
    peripheral to cities 159–73
    post-industrial 3, 15, 93, 187, **187**
    re-invention of 159–73
sites of special scientific interest (SSSI)
        247
Slavik style, Prague Castle 123–4
Smithson, Robert 91–2
Snozzi, Luigi 159, **160**
society, Japanese 150–5
The Society of the Spectacle (Debord)
        171
Somme River, Parc St. Pierre, Amiens
        269, 273–6, **276**, 277
Sørensen, C.Th. 66, 69–70
Southern Spain, gardens 38

space 3, 4–5, 105
    Burle Marx 85–7, 96–7, 99–101
    dynamic experience of 41, 101
    Giacometti 115
    Glaziou 81
    Land Art 90–1
    Maeght Foundation 113–14, 117
    materials 263
    Modern Movement 23
    night 256
    outdoor detailing 41, 59–76
    Prague Castle 130
    Sert 111
Spain, gardens 38
spatial instability 255
spatial order, Tokyo 148–9, 155–6
Speke Garston, Liverpool, redevelopment
        218–21, **220**, **221**
SSSI *see* sites of special scientific interest
statuary
    David Jarman's garden **251**
    see also sculptures
Steinitz, Carl 207, 209
Stenatophrum secundatum **88**, 97
Stockholm 36, **60**
    town hall 63
Stockholm Parks Department 20, 64, **68**,
        69, **70**
    children's playgrounds **70**
    paving 67
structuring time, Japanese gardens 43–58
Study for a Garden (Burle Marx) 79
subjective time, gardens 47–8
The Sunne Rising (John Donne) 250
sustainability 205–8
    communities 208–9
swamp cypress 278
Sweden
    building materials **60**
    buildings-landscape design 61–4
    children's playgrounds 69, 73
    modernist housing **62**
    planting design 64–7
    see also Stockholm
Swedish Association of Garden Architects
        61
Switzerland, Ticino Valley **158**, 159–71
symmetry, Renaissance gardens 38

tactile space
    Braque 115
    Lassus 241
The Tale of Genji 49–51, 52–3

Tandy, Cliff 61
Tanizaki, Jun'ichiro 52
Taut, Bruno 180
Taxodium distichum 278
tea gardens, Japanese 53–5, **53**
technology, disassociation from nature
    208
techniques, landscape architecture 17, 19
temporality
    gardens 92–3
    Japanese gardens 44, 46, 47–8, 56
Tennis Club, Bellinzona, Ticino Valley **164**,
    165
Thayer, Robert 207–9, 226
theorists 4
Theresian continuities, dissolution of 139
Thoreau, Henry David 205
thrift, Dungeness 248
Tiberghien, Gilles I. 91
Ticino valley
    map **158**
    Switzerland 159–71
tiles **66**, 87, 89, 97, 99
time
    garden structure 100
    Japanese gardens 41, 43–58
    landscape gardens 3
    perceptions of 46
    Prospect Cottage 255–6
Tivoli Gardens, Copenhagen **65**, 66
Tokyo 105, 147–57, **152–3**
    spatial order 148–9
tokyology 147–8, 151
town and country planning 15, 23, 111
    see also city planning
town planning, Rio de Janeiro 80–1, 83–5
traditional techniques, landscape
    architecture 17, 19
training, landscape architecture 19, 35–6
transition, systems of 235
transport 215
trees
    destruction by children 36
    scale 3
triadic relationship, ecology–community–art
    206, 221
Tulipa clusiana **25**
Tulipa sprengeri **25**
Tunnard, Christopher 61–3
Typhodorum lindleyanum 96

Umbilicus pendulinus **30**
United States of America (USA)

Camp Pendleton 209–11, **210–13**
Denver Botanic Garden 43, **45**, 49, **49**
Gasworks Park, Seattle 1
sustainable communities 208–9
urban growth, Ticino valley 161
urban landscapes
    planning 211, 213–17
    Ticino Valley 165–71
urban parks 3
    nineteenth century 20
    Parc St. Pierre, Amiens 269–80, **270**
urban periphery sites 159–71
urban planning *see* town planning
utilitarian style 61–3
Utopia, striving for 205–6, 209

Valerian 247
Van Houtte, Louis 81
vandalism 36
Vargem Grande fazenda 96, 100
vegetable gardens 247, 269–72, **273**,
    276–7, **276**, 280
Venice 263–4
vernacular architecture 248–9, 263
Versailles 48
verticality
    Burle Marx 86–7
    Japanese society 150
    Nîmes-Caissargues motorway rest area
    240
Victoria amazonica 94
Village Homes sustainable community,
    California 208–9
Vriesa imperialis 97

Wagner, Otto 122
walkways
    Acropolis project **196**
    garden dynamics 100–1
    Japanese gardens 52
    Jardin des Retours, Rochefort-sur-Mer
    242
    Parc St. Pierre, Amiens 275–7
    Prague Castle Southern Ramparts
    Garden 133
walls, curved 183–4
water
    Japanese gardens 44
    Parc St. Pierre, Amiens 272–4, 279
water gardens
    Army Ministry, Brasilia **86**
    Burle Marx 94
water lilies, giant 94, **95**

water lily gardens, Parc St. Pierre, Amiens 274, **274**, **278**
Watsuji, Tetsurô 155, 157
Weilacher, Udo 233
white poplar 277
white willow 277
woodland 31–2
Wornum, G. Grey 63

Woudstra, Jan 41, 59–76, 284

Yerbury, F.R. 63
Youngman, Peter 248

Zen Buddhism 55
    Japanese gardens 251, **252**
    see also Buddhism